GIDEON AND THE JUDGES.

A Study,

HISTORICAL AND PRACTICAL.

BY
REV. JOHN MARSHALL LANG, D.D.,

MINISTER OF THE BARONY PARISH, GLASGOW, AUTHOR OF "THE LAST SUPPER OF OUR LORD," "LIFE, IS IT WORTH LIVING?" ETC.

WIPF & STOCK · Eugene, Oregon

Wipf and Stock Publishers
199 W 8th Ave, Suite 3
Eugene, OR 97401

Gideon and the Judges
A Study, Historical and Practical
By Rev. John Marshall Lang, D.D.
Softcover ISBN-13: 978-1-7252-9767-8
Hardcover ISBN-13: 978-1-7252-9768-5
eBook ISBN-13: 978-1-7252-9769-2
Publication date 1/19/2021
Previously published by Anson D. F. Randolph and Company, 1890

This edition is a scanned facsimile of
the original edition published in 1890.

PREFACE.

So to reproduce the story of a far-past age as to present it with the clothing, and in the warmth, of living reality is no light task. There are special difficulties in regard to the period to which the volume now sent forth relates. Its surrounding, scenery, and characteristics are so widely different from all we can even conceive that it seems scarcely possible to get into touch with its burdens and its endeavours. In its chronicles, nations and tribes pass under view whose antecedents are sometimes lost in obscurity, and which long ago have wholly disappeared. These chronicles, moreover, are very fragmentary; in respect of dates, order of events, of all that is essential to a consecutive history, they are often apparently confused. They are compiled from records or memoranda which, giving at length narratives whose briefest form only we possess, contain many links that are now missing. Finally, the uncertainty which prevails as to many of the localities mentioned cripples the imagination in the effort to vivify the prowess of the heroes of Israel. Much indeed has been done in recent years, by explorations in Palestine, towards identifying the places of Holy Scripture; and the labours of Major Conder and those associated with him in his scientific surveys deserve the gratitude of all students of Biblical antiquities. The contention of Conder is that two-thirds of the places named in the Bible have been ascertained. It may be so; but experts on the subject have raised the doubt whether in several instances the identifications have a more substantial reason than a resemblance of sound between the ancient name and the modern. And, notwithstanding all research, there are sites—*e.g.*, the cities named in connection with

Gideon's pursuit of the kings—which cannot be fixed with precision.

But, notwithstanding these and other difficulties, the work undertaken in the following pages is both historically interesting and homiletically profitable. It is hoped that the attention of the reader will be sustained; that, whilst history is presented as history, nothing of the *dry-as-dust* will be felt to attach to the presentation, and that the persons to whom he is introduced will be recognized as men who, in their day, fought that fight of faith which he is called to fight in his day. The volume is mainly biographical; what of the national life is unfolded is associated with the typical persons whose influence and judgeship are traced. One of these persons occupies the chief place on the canvas; and without unduly "improving" the features of his career, the wealth of "instruction in righteousness" contained in his Life is indicated.

The author has availed himself of the valuable and manifold help given by Commentator, Traveller, Poet, and Historian. Commentaries are numerous; those whose exposition was entrusted to the Bishop of Bath and Wells—Lord Arthur Hervey—may be specially instanced as of great value. The "Cambridge Bible" and Principal Douglas's Handbook are useful. So are Bible Dictionaries, and other works shedding light on questions of Ethnology and Chronology. Ewald has always flashes of light, and his views, as well as those of Wellhausen, even when there is room for doubt with regard to them, are suggestive. Stanley, of course, is the delightful companion of all study. Dr. Robinson's "Researches," Canon Tristram's "Bible Places," "The Land and the Book," Major Conder's books, and his "Great Map of Western Palestine," must be consulted. Josephus and Kimchi, among Jewish writers, are entitled to be heard; and Bishop Lowth, Milton, Byron, Tennyson, have touched the story, at different points, with the hand of poetic genius.

It is a story in which the impression of wars, and social chaos, and "evil in the sight of the Lord," and the retributions of His holy government, predominates. There is much in its development, much in the character and doings of even the best of the men whom God raised up, which cannot be reconciled with the testimony of the Christian conscience. But we must recollect that the Christian conscience is an unfolding of those last days in which God has spoken in His Son. Chrysostom has remarked that one can get at the truth of an earlier time only by investigating "the period, cause, motive, difference of person, and all the attendant circumstances"; and he has added, with striking force, that the highest merit of the Old Testament Scriptures is that we now see the defects of that time; that "if they had not trained us so well that we have become susceptible of higher things, we should not now have seen their deficiency."[1]

But this treatise will have been written in vain if those who peruse it are not made sensible of contact with minds whose companionship is good, and in whose thought and action we discern the work of that Spirit of Truth Who has illumined the children of wisdom in all generations.

[1] Homily on Matthew xvii. 5, 6.

GLASGOW, *July* 1, 1890.

CONTENTS.

CHAPTER I.

THE PORTION OF HISTORY TO BE REVIEWED 1

A period apparently unattractive—But its importance is shown by three considerations: 1. It is a transitional epoch, illustrating the growth of the national character, and the education through which Israel was prepared for its future—2. It is an age marked by variety and intensity of human feeling, the interest chiefly centering in some great persons whose figures are grand, and who prove themselves men of like passions with ourselves—3. A distinct Providential purpose is to be traced—The difference between the Heroic age of Israel and this age in other peoples—The inspiration of the Judges; in what sense to be regarded?—The period an important link in the chain of history.

CHAPTER II.

THE BOOK OF JUDGES 6

The Book—When and by whom compiled?—The history not complete—Difficulty of framing a satisfactory chronology—The Judges—Differences between the Phœnician Suffes and the Hebrew Shophet—The characters of the Judges—Their function—Their tribal relations.

CHAPTER III.

THE PERIOD OF THE JUDGES 14

The social condition of Israel during the period—How best illustrated—The victory at the waters of Merom—The rest which followed only temporary—The hold which the conquered races maintained—These races—How classified—Their licentiousness.

CHAPTER IV.

ILLUSTRATIONS OF THE PERIOD 21

First Illustration : The Levite of Mount Ephraim—Three Time-Marks—The tale told in the nineteenth chapter of the Book of Judges—The gathering together of the congregation—The war with Benjamin—The terrible revenge—The compunction—The means adopted to prevent the complete extinction of the tribe—The significance of the episode. *Second Illustration:* The establishment of a schismatical centre of worship—The two parts of the history—Micah ; his mother ; the ephod and teraphim ; the Levite—The raid of the Danites ; Their capture of the Levite, Who he was, The sanctuary at Dan. *Third Illustration:* Much worth preserving—Naomi—" A mighty man of wealth "—The simplicity of Oriental life—The Spirit secretly working—A fresh current of blessing—An illustration of Israel's social condition.

CHAPTER V.

THE PROPHETESS OF THE NORTHERN TRIBES 34

The Judges who belonged to the southern tribes : Othniel, Ehud, Shamgar — The lapse into idolatry, and the new period of servitude at the death of Ehud—Jabin, king of Hazor—Harosheth — The great army of the oppressor — The two Deborahs—The second Deborah ; Who was she? A unique figure in the history of Israel—Her ally in the north—The hesitation of Barak—The trumpet-blast—The fight, and the victory—The fate of Sisera—Jael, the wife of Heber the Kenite ; her action to be condemned, but circumstances to be taken into account.

CHAPTER VI.

JEPHTHAH, THE HERO OF GILEAD 46

The history of Gideon reserved for the concluding part of the volume—Gilead : its mountains and rich pastures : its forests and cities : its place in the literature and history of the nation—The backsliding of Israel into idolatry, and the period of servitude under the children of Ammon—The revival of national life and piety—The call to Jephthah ; his character, and his surrounding in the land of Tob—Vows and human sacrifices among heathen peoples—The action taken by Jephthah ; his vow ; views concerning it ; his daughter ; the sacrifice ; his future career, short and stormy—The strife between the Ephraimites and the Gileadites—" Shibboleth."

CHAPTER VII.

SAMSON, THE HERO OF DAN 64

The territory of Dan—the Philistines : Their origin and early history—The form of their idolatry—Their national character—The period and scene of Samson's judgeship—The prophetical forecasts of Dan—The completeness of the biography as contrasted with that of other judges—The nature of the story of his life and exploits—Zorah—The appearances of the man of God to Manoah's wife and to Manoah and his wife. With regard to these appearances, three points—The Nazarite vow and the institution of the Nazarite order—Mahaneh-Dan—Timnath, and what happened in connection with it—The Rock of Etam, and what happened in connection with it—The authority afterwards conceded to Samson—Gaza and its gates—Enhakkore—The Valley of Sorek—The treachery, and what followed—Milton and his " Samson Agonistes "—The climax of the tragedy, and what it suggests.

CHAPTER VIII.

GIDEON, THE HERO OF THE CENTRAL TRIBES 81

The scene of the story, Esdraelon—The memorable events connected with it—The two Ophrahs—Abiezer, the Manassite community—The habits and ways of the farmers of Palestine—The dangers and toils illustrated—Joash, the father of Gideon, and his stalwart sons—Evidence of the hold on the popular imagination of the story of Gideon—Its appeal to us.

CHAPTER IX.

GIDEON: ISRAEL'S CRY AND GOD'S ANSWER 86

The situation of Palestine—The series of invasions—The Midianites. The ancient city Madjan: Mahomet's greeting: The Tawara: The branches comprehended under the name Midianite: Their commercial character The links connecting Israel and Midian · The corrupting influence of Midian—The Amalekites: The battle of Rephidim—The "children of the East" The fierce character of the inroads of these Bedouins—The destruction caused by the march through Palestine—The cry of the people—The man—The prophet, and his message—The man, the deliverer: His occupation: His thoughts: The lesson suggested by the view obtained of him.

CHAPTER X.

GIDEON: THE CALL AND THE RESPONSE 95

The terebinth near the house of Joash—The interest attaching to the oak or terebinth in Holy Scripture—A visitor one day—Who was this angel?—The "deep Providential meaning" of the Old Testament Theophanies—*The Call*—It particularizes—The separation and selection of the man—The crisis of his life—The progress in the call—"Learn to labour and to wait"—The call discloses the secret of the power—*Gideon's Response*—The need of inward strengthening—Likeness between Gideon and the Apostle Thomas—The *Ifs* projected by the mind, and the corresponding disciplines—The sign asked—The meal-offering—The angel's commands, and what followed—Anticipation of the Supper of the Lord—The assurance given to Gideon—Yet, there is death to the old man—The resurrection into newness of life.

CHAPTER XI.

GIDEON: THE BEGINNING OF THE ENTERPRISE 106

The change in the idea and aim of the life—The altar, Jehovah-Shalom—The sign of a transferred allegiance—"The same night," the time for action—The illustration given in the narrative of the right witness for God—Where and how it begins—Three features in the instruction given to Gideon: First, look to home: Second, build the altar in the conspicuous place; Third, offer the sacrifice as prescribed—Gideon obeys, but with fearfulness—The wrath of the villagers—The answer of Joash—The new name—The story of Jerrubbaal spreads.

CHAPTER XII.

GIDEON: THE TRUMPET-BLAST 113

The return of the Midianites—The clothing of Gideon with the Spirit of the Lord—The trumpet-blast—The response of Abi-ezer—The summons to the northern tribes—The junction of the forces—The emotion of Gideon—Weak, but not faithless—Two differences between his pleading and the reluctance of Moses—We must do justice to him—The patience of God—The craving for a sign—The signs asked intended for the confirmation of his own faith—Signs which would naturally occur to him—Two points from which to regard them—The previous sign and the two to be regarded—What these two, reversed, said to Gideon—Their effect on him—Their symbolical meaning—More than an idealization of the qualities which characterized him—The fleece a symbol of Israel; and the dry ground a symbol of the nations—Their significance for and beyond the immediate moment—A prophetical meaning—A parable of the Church of Christ—Teaching many lessons bearing on personal religion.

CHAPTER XIII.

GIDEON: TESTS AND SIFTINGS 126

"Jerubbaal, who is Gideon"—The well of Harod, where was it?—The situation of the opposing armies—"God's thoughts not our thoughts"—The main interest of the history of Israel a religious interest—The protection against "vaunting"—The proclamation enjoined by the Law—The effect of the proclamation at the spring of Jezreel—The conduct of the Israelites has its counterpart in that of many Christians—The additional command—The second test and its effect—A sign of the quality of the man—The lessons taught us.

CHAPTER XIV.

GIDEON: "THE CAKE OF BARLEY BREAD" 134

The equipment for the campaign—The necessity of immediate action—Rapid and bold movements a traditional policy of the Israelites—The command, and the offer of a sign—The nocturnal expedition—The camp of the Midianites—The dream—Its terms and its matter—The interpretation—What this betokened to Gideon—His grateful recognition of God—His return to the three hundred, and his call to arise.

CHAPTER XV.

GIDEON: TRUMPETS AND TORCHES 139

The boldness of Gideon—The reason for the restriction as to number of men—The stratagem—The instructions given to the three hundred—The march under cover of night—The quiet of the camp rudely and suddenly broken—The panic and confusion—The action of the men—The flight—Israel "cried together"—Similar stratagems, but none so completely successful—The passages of the Jordan occupied by the Ephraimites—Oreb and Zeeb—The traces of this flight in the Old Testament—The small

CONTENTS. xi

PAGE

and inadequate means, and the issue—The trumpet: its significance—The torch and the pitcher—The excellency of the power is of God.

CHAPTER XVI.

GIDEON "FAINT, YET PURSUING" 148

The one rallying cry for the time—What of Gideon and his three hundred?—The tale of their enterprise now resumed—The pursuit to the river—The escape of the kings with a remnant of the army—The pursuit into the Hauran—The power of a supreme purpose—Held up to the light of the word applied to the hero and his men, how many characters are shown to be wanting in unity and consistency—Some sketches of John Bunyan—The contrast between the spirit and the flesh illustrated —The picture of Gideon, a stimulant to perseverance and energy.

CHAPTER XVII.

GIDEON: THE PURSUIT AND CAPTURE OF THE KINGS . . 154

The flight of the kings eastward—Gideon on their track—The conduct of the Israelites to whom he appealed for help—Ephraim, and its arrogance—The tact and self-control of Gideon in his dealing with Ephraim—The opposition of the men of Succoth and Penuel of another type—Difficulty of tracing the route of the Hero—The places mentioned, Succoth, Penuel, Nobah, Jogbehah, and Karkor—How the request for bread was met at two of these places, and the threats of cruel punishment — The circuit taken by Gideon—His surprise of the host which thought itself secure—Capture of the kings—The vengeance taken on Succoth and Penuel—Gleams of moderation of spirit—The fate of Zebah and Zalmunna — The ornaments — The return to Ophrah.

CHAPTER XVIII.

GIDEON: THE JUDGESHIP—LIGHT AND SHADE 168

The national sentiment reflected in the offer of a hereditary rule— The new sense of national unity—Considerations favourable to the idea of a succession of rulers in Gideon's family—Monarchy contemplated in the Book of the Law, and the conditions prescribed there—The attitude of Samuel when the elders of Israel demanded a king—The dominating reason of his displeasure— The answer to his prayer, and what this answer implied— Gideon's feeling similar to that of Samuel—The offer of the crown a great temptation—Two kinds of ambition—Gideon's election—A grand decision; but tokens in the narrative of a royal state, and of moral deterioration—Three such tokens: First, his house with its surrounding; many wives and children. Second, the name *set* to one of his sons, Abimelech. Third, his request when he declined the hereditary rule, willingly yielded to by the men of Israel—The ephod: its symbolical significance— Why Gideon determined to make and put the ephod in Ophrah: Gratitude, Piety, Policy—The result of the act deplorable—The current of movements sometimes bears men beyond, even contrary

xii   CONTENTS.

                                                                                     PAGE

to, their original intention—Israel made to sin—The snare to Gideon and his house—Gideon's rule and its beneficial character—The close of the life, and the burial in the sepulchre of Joash.

CHAPTER XIX.

GIDEON: WHAT HAPPENED "AS SOON AS HE WAS DEAD" . 183

The character and effect of his rule—Apparently, there was no striking disturbance of harmony for some years after his decease: but the tendency to idolatry operated in apostasy to the worship of Baalberith—How Gideon had prepared for this—The craving for a visible god—The warning sounded for all times—St. Paul's expression of the teaching conveyed—Baal, and the types of Baal-worship indicated in the historical books—The parody of the true worship in the form adopted by the men of Shechem—Covenant, in what is it rooted?—The contrast between the man-god and the God-man—Mr. Maurice's entreaty—The lapse of Israel "the certain presage of slavery."

CHAPTER XX.

GIDEON: THE RECORD AS TO THE FATE OF HIS HOUSE . 183

The ingratitude of the people connected with forgetfulness of God—Significance of Abimelech's history—Shechem: its beauty and associations — Abimelech made king there — How his ambitious designs were promoted—The money given him out of the house of Berith, and the use made of it—Wealth of heathen temples illustrated—Wholesale murder—Jotham on Gerizim—Could he be heard from that altitude?—Parable and fable—His fable, and its meaning—His running away—Fulfilment of his prediction—Insurrection in Shechem—The siege and destruction of the city—The tower of Shechem: how it was burnt—Thebez, where was it?—What happened there?—The retributions of Providence illustrated in Abimelech's end—The witness of the Scriptures for righteousness—The changing and the abiding.

CHAPTER I.

THE PORTION OF HISTORY TO BE REVIEWED.

A period apparently unattractive—But its importance is shown by three considerations: 1. It is a transitional epoch, illustrating the growth of the national character, and the education through which Israel was prepared for its future—2. It is an age marked by variety and intensity of human feeling, the interest chiefly centering in some great persons whose figures are grand, and who prove themselves men of like passions with ourselves—3 A distinct Providential purpose is to be traced—The difference between the Heroic age of Israel and this age in other peoples—The inspiration of the Judges; in what sense to be regarded?—The period an important link in the chain of history.

IN the scenery of an extensive landscape there are frequently rugged tracts which do not invite the eye of the observer, but which, when explored, are found to contain features of interest and beauty. Such a tract in the history of Israel is the period which begins with the occupation of Canaan by the victorious tribes, and which extends to the days of the monarchy. To one who hastily surveys the history, this may seem the least attractive of all its spaces. The repose of the Patriarchal age has vanished. It is wanting in the variety of effect which marks the age of the Exodus and the wilderness. We no longer hear the firm tread of the irresistible armies as, with a scarcely broken onward march, they follow the standard of Joshua. And, when compared with the compact organizations of the era of the Kings, the records of the period bear the signs of social chaos and confusion. There is much, therefore, which tends to dull the attention and even repel the mind. But those who yield to the temptation to pass lightly over the narrative will miss many a glimpse of ancient things which it is profitable to study, and many a lesson for even modern times which it is profitable to learn. Three points may be emphasized as indicating its importance.

In the first place, the Epoch surveyed was transitional. And such an Epoch has a special value for those who, not satisfied with regarding results, desire to trace the processes through which results are realized. The constituents of national life are then presented as passing out of their most elementary form: we see forces and energies separated from the yesterday which concealed them, and struggling towards the to-morrow which they are to shape. The growth of character in a people corresponds to the growth of character in an individual. Sometimes, we may say, the growth is under ground—growth rather of the root and its fibres than of the stem and its branches. But the one prepares for the other; only in the measure in which the root is made firm in the soil beneath, is the upward and outward development accomplished. So it was with the people which had been called out of Egypt. The era of the Judges was that in which the Monotheism imposed in the desert was brought into contact with ancient and firmly-welded idolatries. It was the probation of Israel. The consequences, it might seem, were only disastrous. The consciousness of a higher vocation which Moses had so earnestly enforced becomes dim and torpid; for long intervals it is all but obliterated. But the subsequent history shows that, through the dreary centuries in which evil-doing alternates with spasmodic repentances, a work under the surface of events was being done; by a discipline of fire the people were being led into a wealthier place. That era taught the generations to come that the secret of all greatness lay in obedience to the Divine will; it showed what could be achieved when this obedience was the mainspring of action; it showed also the degradation which was inevitable when its restraints were thrown aside, and the ways of the heathen were followed. Milton sees in "the illustrious and sunny locks" of Samson the image of the laws under which, whilst they are kept "undiminished and unshorn," man grows into a noble strength and perfection.[1] The time of the Judges was a manifestation of the truth which the English poet thus connects with the hero of Dan. And, by this education, Israel was made ready for higher things. There is disintegration; the Israel of the earlier day, Patriarchal and Nomad, is dissolved; but

[1] "Reasons of Church Government," vol. i. p. 149.

out of this disintegration, through a sore birth-travail, came the religion which is mirrored in the Psalms, and the nationality which culminated in the reigns of David and Solomon.

In the second place, the Age which we are reviewing was marked by variety and intensity of human feeling. It was full of striking and stirring incident. Some of the sketches which have been preserved are highly dramatic. They possess a force which is characteristic of many of the narratives of Holy Scripture; by one or two delicate touches they bring out the heart of things; they set scenes and circumstances before us glowing with reality. Of some of the most distinctive features of tragedy, it is difficult to cite finer illustrations than those to be found in the Book of Judges. And their appeal to the imagination is, perhaps, all the more powerful that there is little evidence of artistic skill in their compilation. Nor is it tragedy only; the story of Ruth which, although contained in a separate book, is really a story of the Age, is an exquisite picture of rural simplicity; it is a beautiful idyll, celebrating the domestic virtues, the morals and manners, which softened the harshness of the time, and were the savour of the salt that salted the earth.

But it is in certain great persons whose exploits and whose rule are recorded that the interest chiefly centres. These great persons were "the modellers, patterns, and, in a wide sense, creators of whatsoever the general mass contrived to do or attain." They differed in genius and in all that constitutes the surrounding of a man. They did not wield the same kind of influence; and the circuits of the influence were in some instances wider, and in some narrower. But whatever the range and manner of their power were, they appear on the stage of events in figures grand and bold; in the might of a divinely inspired manhood they move before us; and as they move we recognize in them "not the kindled lamp only, but rather the natural luminary shining by the gift of heaven."[1] And it has been well remarked that "in other portions of the Hebrew annals the Divine character of the revelation is so constantly before us, or the character of the human agent reaches so nearly to the Divine, that we may, if we choose, almost forget that we are reading of men of like passions with ourselves. But, in the history of the Judges, the whole tenor of the book, especially of its concluding chapters, renders this

[1] Carlyle's "Lectures on Heroes," Lect. 1.

forgetfulness impossible. The angles and roughnesses of the sacred narrative which elsewhere we endeavour to smooth down into one uniform level, here start out from the surface too vividly to be overlooked by the most superficial observer."[1]

Yet, let it be noted, in the last place, that with all this play of humanity, often far from saintly, we cannot forget that the memoranda contained in the Sacred Book are connected with a distinct Providential purpose. The time of the Judges has been called the heroic age of the Hebrew nation; and the correspondences between it and the same age in the development of other peoples have been traced. As, for example, that there is struggle, protracted and sometimes fierce, between the race which has conquered and the races which have been dispossessed; that the condition of society is disturbed and almost anarchical; that there is a surrounding atmosphere of wonderland portent and prodigy, appearances of gods and the like; and that the element of wild and daring adventure is conspicuous—men rising above ordinary levels and waxing valiant in fight. But resemblances between the heroic age of Israel and that of Greece or other lands only suggest the differences which separate the chronicles of the one from the poetries and mythologies of the others. Whilst, in the one as in the others, there is a wonderland, the colouring of the Hebrew Scripture is comparatively sober, the reference to appearances of spiritual beings is comparatively sparing, and is never introduced except with regard to some moral end, or to the announcement and mission of a saviour of Israel. And whilst again, in the one as in the others, there is contest, stern and cruel, between the ancient inhabitants and the aggressive warriors who seize on their soil, there is a consciousness in the Israelite mind which is wholly absent from that of heathen peoples. There was something else than the mere lust of conquest in the wars of Joshua: there was the feeling of a Divine will that was being executed, of a Divine vocation that was being obeyed. Israel was the servant of the Lord. The extermination of the Amorite and Canaanite was a judicial sentence of the Most High. The cup of their iniquity was full; if the elect people were to be preserved in truth and holiness as a prophet to the whole world, and the repository of God's covenant, their removal was necessary. And Joshua, and all in whom his

[1] Stanley's "History of the Jewish Church," Lect. xiii.

mind survived, understood that the occupation of Palestine, and the subjugation of its heathen tribes, were parts of His ordination, who is wonderful in counsel and excellent in working

With regard to the Judges of Israel, pious minds have often stumbled over words asserting the inspiration of men such as Samson. But we must remember the degree and object of their inspiration. It was not to teach truth; it was not to prophesy. It was to act, and to act with a specific end in view. So far as that action and that end were concerned, they were inspired by the Spirit of God, "from whom all holy desires, all good counsels, and all just works do proceed." And they possessed the illumination of a faith which might be narrow, often confused, but which at least grasped the fact with which faith connects, "that God is, and that He is a rewarder of them who diligently seek Him." They accepted His rule; they were captains, under Him, of His host; they trusted Him; they recognized that He alone is the living and true God; their own loyalty was not perfect—sometimes very imperfect—but, under the guidance of the Spirit, they fought and laboured for the crown rights of Israel's King. And by this faith they have obtained a good report.

Thus the Book of Judges is an important link in the chain of that history which, more than any other history, appeals to the spiritual in human nature, illustrates the ways of God to men, and exhibits the working of that Divine life which is the light of men. Verily, in this book the light shines in darkness, and the darkness, ever closing on it, yet overtakes it not. And it exhibits in a most striking manner the influences which corrupt this life, the temptations to which the worshipper of the living and true God is, in every time, exposed, and the only mode of salvation alike for nation and individual. The things related happened to the chosen people "for ensamples: and they are written for our admonition, on whom the ends of the world are come." "He that hath an ear, let him hear what the Spirit saith."

CHAPTER II.

THE BOOK OF JUDGES.

The Book—When and by whom compiled?—The history not complete—Difficulty of framing a satisfactory chronology—The Judges—Differences between the Phœnician Suffes and the Hebrew Shophet—The characters of the Judges—Their function—Their tribal relations.

BEFORE studying the portraits of the more prominent Judges, let us regard the Book which is our authority, and let us take a general survey of the social and moral conditions of the period in which the Judges lived and ruled.

When and by whom the Book was compiled cannot be definitely ascertained. Internal evidence points to the time when there was a king in Israel,[1] and to the earlier days of the monarchy.[2] The

---

[1] See chap. xvii. 6; xviii. 1; xix 1; xxi. 25.

[2] The indications of the date of compilation in the book are obscure. A time as late as the Captivity is fixed on by Ewald, Davidson, De Wette, and others. And the statement in chap xviii. 30 to the effect that the sons of Jonathan were "priests to the tribe of Dan *until the day of the captivity of the land*" is held to favour this view. It seems to point to the carrying away of the tribes into Assyria, related in 2 Kings xv. 29. On the other hand, the reference in chap 1 21 to the Jebusites as dwelling in Jerusalem "unto *this* day" is regarded as pointing to a period before the capture of Jerusalem by David. Lord Arthur Hervey ("Pulpit Commentary") argues that "it would meet all the requirements of the passages in the Book of Judges (except the reference to the captivity of the ten tribes) and in the other books in which reference is made to Judges if we were to assign the compilation to the reign of Saul, the separate contents of the book being known even earlier." In "TheSp eaker's Commentary" he argues that the

Schools of the Prophets, founded by Samuel, were a kind of collegiate institution, which fostered the study of literature as well as music. And to the court of David, who was himself a man of letters, some who had probably been trained in these schools attached themselves. We read, for instance, of Gad, the king's seer, and of Nathan the prophet; and they were more than preachers declaring the word of the Eternal; they were the historians of their age; in their books "David's reign and his might, and the times that went over him, and over Israel, and over all the kingdoms of the countries were chronicled." It may have been one of these seers or prophets, one of the cultured men whom the king gathered around him, who collected the traditions or documents relative to the heroes of previous generations, and gave them the form of a historical volume. As has already been said, there is little to remind us of the artist. The chronicles are not dove-tailed each into the other, nor is a continuous narrative constructed out of them. The editor's part consisted chiefly in a retrospective and homiletical chapter towards the beginning, and in occasionally supplying explanatory or connecting statements. A complete and orderly history is not to be looked for. Some incidents or biographies

compilation "may, with most probability perhaps, be assigned to the later times of the Jewish monarchy." With regard to the allusion to the Captivity, there is a good note in "the Book of Judges" (Cambridge Series) bearing on the impossibility of supposing that the idolatrous worship of Micah could have been maintained at Dan during the reign of David, pointing out that Jeroboam's *cultus* would have been fatal to it, and reminding the reader of the other note of time in chap. xviii. 31, "All the time that the ark was in Shiloh" (see chap. iv. of this vol.). Lias, in this note, supposes the captivity to mean the Philistine domination which extended, no doubt, even as far as Dan, and says, "this opinion is confirmed by the Hebrew of 1 Sam. iv. 21, 22, where the expression, 'captivity of the land,' is replaced by 'captivity of the glory of Israel.'" The allusion to the Jebusites as dwelling in Jerusalem "unto this day" does not involve fixing a period before David's taking of Jerusalem. He did not take it until he had been king for seven years, so that the compilation at any time during these seven years is consistent with the supposition that the reference would be inaccurate after the conquest of the city. But, in point of fact, the Jebusites did continue to dwell in Jerusalem after it fell into David's hands. We read, 1 Kings ix. 20, 21, that Solomon made the Jebusites who were left bond-servants. On the whole, the date assigned is, at least, as probable as any other, and the style and language of the book agree with it. These differ from the Book of Joshua, and are at the same time "untainted with Chaldaisms or Persicisms as the later books are."

are so expanded as to be thrown out of proportion with others, and expanded, we might say, to a length that is scarcely justified by their importance. Probably the reason was that the traditions in which these incidents or biographies were embodied having more vividly impressed the popular imagination, had been more fully preserved. Thus the story of Samson bulks largely in view, although, as compared with others, the record of whose work is compressed into a few sentences, the circuit of his influence as a Judge was narrow. The compiler is less a historian than a seer; he is less occupied with events in their wider combinations and relations than with persons, in the springs and principles of their conduct, and with the evidence given by them of the sovereignty of the Divine election and equipment of instruments, the power of a living faith in God, and the struggle of this faith against the contaminations of idolatry, and the seductions of the devil, the world, and the flesh.

It is impossible to draw up a consistent chronology of the Book. More than fifty such chronologies have been suggested.[1] Some are extravagant, and objections may be taken to each of them. The difficulty of arriving at any quite satisfactory result arises chiefly from the character of the Book, and from the absence of thoroughly reliable data outside of it on which to found.

It is usual to divide the volume into three parts—the Prefatory, comprehending the first three chapters; the History, from the third chapter to the sixteenth; and the Appendix, from the seventeenth chapter to the close. Now, there are mixtures of dates throughout. Thus the account given in the second chapter of the angel coming from Gilgal to Bochim and testifying against the people, belongs to a time antecedent to the death of Joshua—the time of the parliament which he summoned at Shechem, when he solemnly adjured the people to renounce idolatry and serve the Lord.[2] Again, the story of the

[1] Keil and Delitsch Commentary.

[2] See Supplemental Note A in "Speaker's Commentary," giving eight considerations from which it appears that the events in chap. i. and in the first five verses of chap. ii. happened before Joshua's death. "The Angel's Message at ii. 1–5 is not only fixed to the lifetime of Joshua by the force of ver. 6, compared with Joshua xxiv. 28, but all the other details identify the occasion of its delivery with the assembly spoken of in Josh. xxiv. . . . When to these remarkable coincidences in the two narratives it is added

Levite, so graphically related in the nineteenth and twentieth chapters, connects certainly with the beginning of the era. It is placed by Josephus immediately after the death of Joshua.[1] It would seem, moreover, that some of the numbers mentioned are to be regarded as "round numbers" rather than the exact interpretation of fact, as when we are told of the land having rest forty or eighty years.[2] And otherwise the notices bearing on time are so brief or so vague that they cannot be too far pressed. We have before us, in a word, a series of sketches arranged, not in strict order of event, but in observance of some association of ideas or, adopting the phrase of Ewald, "without the constraint of a continuous chronology."

Nor, looking outside the Book, do we find any firm standing ground. A valuable hint is supplied in the opening verse of the sixth chapter of the First Book of Kings. There it is said that "the beginning of Solomon's temple was made in the fourth year of his reign," and "the 480th year after the children of Israel were come out of the land of Egypt." There is no occasion to challenge the correctness of the date thus specified;[3] and, going back from it, we can frame some scheme or schemes as to the duration of the age of the Judges. But there is a constant disturbance of calculations. We cannot be sure, for instance, as to the length of Joshua's retirement after the conquest of Canaan;[4] nor yet as to the space which intervened between his death and the death of the last of the elders who

that they both close with the identical words, 'and Joshua let the people go, . . . every man to his inheritance,' it is impossible to doubt that Judg. ii. 1-5 belongs to the lifetime of Joshua."

[1] "Antiquities of the Jews," book v. chap. ii.

[2] Not only so; "it is notorious that numbers are peculiarly liable to be corrupted in Hebrew manuscripts, as, *e.g.*, in the familiar example of I Sam. vi. 19; so that these numbers are very uncertain, and not to be depended upon" ("Pulpit Commentary," Introduction, p. 3).

[3] "This statement approves itself as perfectly accurate. . . . The events of the times after Moses and Joshua are often related without the constraint of a continuous chronology, and with only more general notices of time; the years of the Judges being specified when the deeds of those heroes were the principal subject (so in Judg iii 16), and single events being defined by the time of some high priest or other such general indication" (Ewald, vol. ii. pp. 140, 141).

[4] Josephus says that the assembly at which Joshua delivered his farewell charge was summoned in the twentieth year after his retirement to Shechem ("Antiquities," book v. chap. i.).

outlived him;[1] nor yet as to the number of years comprehended in the earlier portion of the Book of Samuel;[2] whilst, as has been pointed out, figures bearing on Judgeships, and on the rests and servitudes of Israel, are not to be received as exact and final. Hence the difference in the views taken — four centuries, three centuries, two centuries, one century and a half, have been named. It is sufficient, for all purposes, to assume that somewhere between B.C. 1300 and B.C. 1000[3]— perhaps through two centuries—the events related in the Book occurred, and the persons who pass before our view performed the service to which, in the providence of God, they had been called.

The Book derives its title from those whose prowess and faith it relates. The time, it has been said, makes the hero; with equal justice it may be said that the hero largely contributes to the making of the age. Whatever lustre belongs to the period of the Judges is borrowed from them. They were "the flowing life-fountains" of all that was healthy in its life and noble in its movement. They are called Judges. *Shophetim* is the Hebrew word. A parallel has been traced between the Israelite Shophet and the Phœnician Suffes, as the head of the Carthaginian state is styled in the pages of the Roman historians.[4] The parallel does not hold at all points, for the Suffes was a magistrate elected by the people, and his function was legally recognized; whereas the Shophet was one commissioned by the Invisible Ruler, whose first duty was to arouse the slumbering energy of the people, and whose power depended on the ability he possessed to deliver the people from the hand of the enemy, and restore it to the consistency of self-rule. But the title, Shophet, taken from the same root as the Carthaginian,

---

[1] "We cannot be far wrong in assigning a period of about fifty years from the entrance into Canaan to the death of the elders, or twenty years after the death of Joshua, supposing his government to have lasted thirty years " ("Speaker's Commentary").

[2] Probably the Judgeship of Eli, and possibly even that of Samuel, for twenty years coincided with the Judgeship of Samson (Keil's Commentary)

[3] Lord Arthur Hervey is led to the conclusion that the events related in the book occurred within a space of 150 years, but he admits that the chronology is a matter of uncertainty ("Speaker's Commentary," Introduction).

[4] Livy compares him to the Roman consul.

is in itself a sign of the influence which the richer culture of Phœnicia gradually exercised over Israel. It is not the natural Hebrew phrase for the position of a magistrate,[1] and it is noteworthy that the phrase Shophetim came into use in the latter part of the era, suggesting that its adoption was owing to the filtration of ideas originating in the richer literature of the conquered races into the scantier literature of the conquerors.[2]

In their selection, in the diversity of their gifts, in their personal character and history, the thirteen Judges who pass before our eye in the Book illustrate the freedom of administration and operation which is characteristic of the Spirit " who divideth to every man severally as He wills." The first of the thirteen is Othniel, the son of Kenaz; the last is Samson. And sometimes men—once a woman—are taken from circles to which we would not naturally look for leaders. The lesson, so often repeated, is enforced that God's choice of instruments does not necessarily harmonize with the principles which regulate men in their choice of instruments, " that no flesh may glory in His presence." Let us observe these Judges. They are not set before us as models of righteousness. Their faults are not concealed. They are not credited with virtues which refer to a later stage of moral development. There is no making light of the frailties of their conduct and rule. The tale is told without varnish of any kind. " We live by admiration," but the Bible never makes its great men in all things admirable. It is too Divine to fall into such an error. It takes men for what they are, and the human nature which is common to all men for what it is ; its aim is to show that there is a "something not of ourselves " which, notwithstanding the errors of the individual and the imperfect standards of the time, " makes for righteousness." And if we would realize its "profitableness for correction and instruction," we must recognize this when we read its records. To expect Christian excellence, even a consistently high level of moral excellence, in those who had scarcely emerged from the cruder

---

[1] "The peculiar Israelite name for such a dignity would rather be קָצִין " (Ewald, vol. ii. p 133, note). This is the word used in Josh. x. 24; Judg xi. 6; and it is applied to civil rulers, Isa i 10.

[2] " The name is the first trace of the influence of the Syrian usages on the fortunes of the chosen people, the first-fruits of the pagan inheritance to which the Jewish and the Christian Church has succeeded" (Stanley, "History of the Jewish Church," Lect. xiii.).

forms of civilization, and whose only oracle was the Urim and Thummim of the priesthood—(even that, as we shall see, disappears)—would be to expect an anachronism. In their day the lamp of God burned low and dim in the temple, and there was no open vision. What we are enjoined to follow is not their action in detail, but that which was the source of all things good in it; and this is uniformly described as a descent of the Spirit of God bidding them undertake issues vaster than they themselves comprehended. The response to this call of the Spirit is their faith, and "through faith they subdued kingdoms and turned to flight the armies of the aliens."

The portraits of many of these uncrowned Hebrew kings are attractive. Some of them, notably the one whom we shall specially consider, rise to the higher pinnacles of heroism, and there is a commendable self-abnegation manifest in all whose Judgeship is particularly specified. Except in one instance [1]—and he is a person outside, rather than inside, the circle of the true Shophetim—they rule without reigning. The title Melek is never given to them.[2] The best of them refused the kingly estate. We are not told of new laws made, or of new taxes imposed, by them. A rude splendour is attributed to the families of one or two who belonged to the later half of the era. But there is no evidence that this splendour was purchased by any oppression of the people. And it does not appear that the ordinary machinery of government was interfered with. In the country, or in portions of the country, they fill the place which Moses and Joshua had filled—they hear and decide on the greater causes; they give their counsel when appealed to by tribes or individuals. They wield the power because they have proved their right to be leaders and commanders of the people. They do not challenge or deny the idea of the theocracy. In the name of Jehovah they raise the banner, they revive that "shout of a king" which used to smite hostile ranks with terror, they judge of the right as between man and man. This done, their mission is ended. They are only the servants and witnesses of Jehovah, the Judge, the Lawgiver, the King of Israel.

[1] Abimelech.

[2] "That name would have ascribed to them a power which they could not claim, a power logically and necessarily co-extensive with the State itself" (Ewald, vol. ii. p. 132).

One point must be kept in view. There may have been more than thirteen Judges in the centuries briefly noticed in the Book. But it would be a mistake to suppose that the rule even of these thirteen was uniformly acknowledged by all the tribes. In point of fact, the great southern tribes of Judah and Simeon were outside the storm-circles by which the central and northern tribes were desolated, and they did not directly acknowledge the sway of the Hebrew chiefs. Judah contributed only one of these chiefs. The song of Deborah demonstrates that, in her day, the isolation of the southern limbs of the old nationality was marked, and, as the years rolled on, the isolation became more and more distinct.[1] The tribal surrounding of each Judge is intimated in the book, and this surrounding marked the chief theatre of his action. It might so happen that some parts of the land were at rest, whilst others were groaning under the heel of the oppressor. Of course a deliverance from any hostile power at any part was really a deliverance for all the tribes. And possibly the moral influence of the deliverer was so widely acknowledged that, far and near, persons submitted to his government. But the campaigns of the several captains of the Lord's host and their following were, in the main, limited to the eastern, central, western, and northern parts of Palestine. The four heroes on whose careers we shall afterwards dwell have been thus apportioned: "Deborah is the typical prophetess of the northern tribes; Gideon is the great head of the central tribes; Jephthah is the pride of the land beyond the Jordan; Samson is the ideal of joyous strength, striving at unequal odds against Philistine ascendancy in the west."[2]

[1] Chapters v. 14-18; vi. 35; xii. 8-15.
[2] Ewald, vol. ii. p. 137.

CHAPTER III.

THE PERIOD OF THE JUDGES.

The social condition of Israel during the period—How best illustrated—
The victory at the waters of Merom—The rest which followed only
temporary—The hold which the conquered races maintained—These
races—How classified—Their licentiousness.

RIGHTLY to estimate the mission and work of the Judges, we must regard the social condition of Israel at the beginning and during the continuance of their period. This condition may best be illustrated by a comprehensive survey of the tribes as their situation is unfolded in the Book, and by a glance at three pictures of manners and morals—two derived from the appendix, which occupies so large a place in the book, and the third from the exquisitely beautiful supplement which is associated with the name of Ruth.

The victory which decided the fate of Palestine was gained at the waters of Merom, in the far north, where a great army had assembled, "with horses and chariots very many," to make a last desperate stand against the invader. This conflict at the Land's End of Palestine has been compared to the final gathering of the ancient British chiefs in resistance to the Saxon conqueror at the Land's End of England.[1] The result in both cases was the same—the complete rout of the opposing force, the shattering of the confederacy of chieftain and tribe, and the subjugation of the land. And Joshua's triumph was followed up by a protracted warfare which issued in the slaughter of a vast

[1] Stanley's "History of the Jewish Church," Lect. xii.

number of kings, the capture of a vast number of cities, and finally the dispersion of the fierce mountaineers who are called Anakim. "The hills, the south country, the valley, and the plain," were swept by the hosts of Israel. Then came a rest which seemed to be perfect, when the old leader laid down the burden of rule and counsel, and pious hands buried him "in the border of his inheritance, in Timnath-Serah."[1]

We are soon reminded that the rest was only for a time. Remnants, but in considerable numbers, of the inhabitants whose territories had been stripped from them, remained in different parts of the land. Shortly after the death of Joshua, Judah and Simeon united in an effort to expel the Canaanites from the southern region. The effort, although so far successful, did not secure their extermination. There, as elsewhere, the heathen population remained an alien, and with the possibility of becoming a seriously disturbing, force.[2] So long as the original vigour of the old Hebrew stock was manifested, and an authority, uniting all the tribes, was recognized in the elders who outlived Joshua, that population formed only a servile element in the midst of Israel. But it exhibited a singular tenacity of life. In one of the tribes, Manasseh, there were no fewer than seven Phœnician cities—cities so situated as almost to separate the northern from the southern Hebrew communities.[3] And, here and there, the conquered peoples maintained their hold, "not only on the outermost skirts of their former possessions, but in the very heart of the country, as on little islands rising out of a stormy sea, whence they inspired even their conquerors with respect, recalling the fate of Italy after its subjugation by Germans when the old inhabitants here and there in favourable spots held closely together, and soon, with their array of flourishing towns, raised their head bravely against the surrounding barbarians."[4]

Who were the peoples thus left, in the words of the chronicler, "to prove Israel and to teach them war, at the least, such as before knew nothing thereof"?

---

[1] Otherwise called Timnath-heres: Judg. ii. 9.

[2] Judg. i.

[3] Judg. 1. 27: "The Canaanites would dwell in that land." One of the places in which they would dwell was the important city of "Beth-Shean (Beisan) and her towns."

[4] Ewald, "History of Israel," vol. ii. pp. 98, 99.

They are variously classified. But some of the names given seem to indicate, not so much distinct races, as tribes occupying certain geographical positions in the land, and representing a mixture of races. For example, "the Perizzites" is a generic phrase for those who occupied the open country and tilled the ground. " The Hivites" were villagers, having sheep and cattle. "The Amorites" were the highlanders. "The Philistines" were the inhabitants of the southern sea-board. "Moabites" and "Ammonites" formed a dreaded environment.[1] Phœnician in origin, and in the form of their idolatry, these races, for the most part, were. The country was known as Canaan, the home of Canaanitish or Phœnician peoples.[2] And these peoples, let it be remembered, possessed a culture vastly superior to that of the Hebrews. The one dark blot was a licentiousness so vile, so leprous, as to make even their existence incompatible with the preservation of Israel in moral purity and truth. It had enfeebled them; it had rendered their conquest an easier task for the sons of Israel. They were worshippers of Baal and the Ashtaroth, the male and female divinities of Phœnicia. And the Asherah (or "groves," as the Authorized Version translates), in which the rites of this idolatry were conducted, were scenes of unblushing sensuality. The neighbourhood of a population

---

[1] The peoples of Canaan are grouped in different ways in the historical books of the Old Testament. In Gen. xiii. 7, it is said, "the Canaanite and Perizzite dwelled then in the land." Josh. vii. 9 speaks of "the Canaanites and all the inhabitants of the land." In Josh. v. the distinction is drawn between "all the kings of the Amorites which were on the side of Jordan westward, and all the kings of the Canaanites which were by the sea." Six peoples are specified in Deut. xx. 17, and Josh. ix. 1, as occupying the hills and the valleys and the coasts of the great sea over against Lebanon, viz., "the Hittite, the Amorite, the Canaanite, the Perizzite, the Hivite, and the Jebusite." These races may have dispossessed still older races. The shadow of a race of giants called the Rephaim is traceable in the earliest of the sacred Scriptures. The Anakim, whom the children of Israel so much dreaded, were probably descended from it. "Whether," says Mr. Oliphant, "these tribes were preceded by a still older autochthonous population, namely, the Anakim, Hivites, and so forth, is a question which has so far been beyond the reach of scientific research" ("Haifa," p. 110). The Fellaheen of Palestine are supposed by many to be descendants of the ancient tribes. For an account of these peasants see "Abraham," by Rev. W. J. Deane, M A., pp. 40, 41.

[2] The language of Phœnicia was closely related to the Hebrew.

THE PERIOD OF THE JUDGES.

thus corrupted was an ever active cause of evil.[1] Patriotic, as well as religious, interests demanded a complete separation. This Joshua had emphatically proclaimed, warning all against contamination through inter-marriage and mixture of race. The congregation of Jehovah must dwell apart, must wage war to the knife, if the old shout of a king was to be heard in its hosts

Too soon did the probation verify the complaint of prophet and poet, that "Israel was a stubborn and rebellious generation that set not the heart aright, and whose spirit was not stedfast with God."[2] "Out of sight, out of mind," says Matthew Henry; "and here begins all the wickedness that is in the world."[3] When the mighty works of Jehovah in the Exodus from Egypt and the journeyings through the wilderness became only a tradition of the past, "the people forgat the Lord their God, and served Baalim and the Asherah." And as their leader had foreseen, the apostasy was chiefly promoted by the taking of the daughters of the heathen to be their wives, and the giving of the daughters of Israel to the sons of Canaan.

Two influences—in the case of Israel inseparably connected—might have prevented this apostasy : the one, the political condition, and the other, the national worship. But, during the era of the Judges, these influences were so weak as to be unable to stem the tide of "evil in the sight of the Lord."

Theoretically, the government was a theocracy. Jehovah was the King. All power came directly from Him. His throne was the mercy-seat above the ark. He sat between the cherubim. The priests were His ministers, keeping knowledge, interpreting the oracle, declaring His law. He was both the Shepherd of Israel, and the Stone of all the social fabric.[4] Rulers were only His hand. He had led His people like a flock by the hand of Moses and Aaron. Moses was not a king. He was not even the law-giver. The law came by him. He was the servant of Jehovah, the exponent of the will of the Invisible Supreme. Joshua claimed only the same subordination. He, too, was the servant. When the land was conquered, he disbanded the army, and he himself retired into private life. The only Rock of Israel was the living and true God.

---

[1] "Thus they are ordered to hate, not only impiety, but the persons of the impious lest their friendship should be an occasion of going astray" (Chrysostom on 1 Cor. xiii.).   [2] Psa. lxxviii. 8.
[3] Commentary on Judg. iii.   [4] Gen. xlix. 24.

But the consciousness of this had become pale and feeble. The signs of the desert were no longer seen; no longer were there the pillar of cloud by day and the pillar of fire by night. Except at rare intervals, the Tabernacle was all but forsaken. "Of the rock that begat him, Jeshurun was unmindful."[1]

The executive of the state, as fixed in the third month after the Exodus from Egypt,[2] had, more or less, fallen into abeyance during the time of the Judges. There are indications of the old executive in the annals of the time.[3] But, owing to the comparative isolation of the tribes from each other, and the pressure of several co-operating causes, its outline became gradually less distinct and its operation more uncertain. Apparently, the congregation always had its elders. In the assembly which discussed the terrible plight of Benjamin, they are recognized as the counsellors of the people.[4] But the basis on which their authority rested—whether that of popular election or that of a tacitly accepted hereditary position—it is impossible to determine. Nor is there any evidence of power exercised by these elders, in their official capacity, in ordinary circumstances. We infer from the strains of Deborah's song that the tribes were headed by chieftains — "governors," "nobles," "princes,"[5] so they are designated—who exercised a kind of patriarchal or feudal authority. So that, practically it would seem, the nation was divided into a number of petty sovereignties, or of communes presided over by head-men, hereditary or elected. The sense of a common bond was not wholly lost; it existed as a potential force of action. But there was no steady and supreme authority which all acknowledged to be the national over-man, with strength sufficient to control what was rude, to check the capricious violence of ambition, and to harmonize the various elements of the social life. Again and again, the chronicler, contrasting these days with his own, writes, "There was no king in Israel;" and quaintly adds, "Every man did what was right in his own eyes."[6]

A confused and disturbed action was inevitable, when the centre of the state was inadequate to the supply of the needed

---

[1] Deut. xxxii. 18.   [2] Exod. x.
[3] *E.g.*, Judg. vii. 15: "My thousand is the meanest in Israel." So also, Josh. xxiv. 1: "The Elders of Israel, their heads, their judges, and their officers."   [4] Judg. xxi. 16.   [5] Judg. v.
[6] Judg. xvii. 6; xviii. 1; xix. 1; xxi. 25.

strength and inspiration. That centre was the tabernacle, or tent of meeting, with its priesthood, and its sacrifices and observances. Where was its seat?

The first of the sacred places of Israel was Bethel, now Beitin.[1] There, on his way to Padan-Aram, he, whose name the nation bore, beheld the mystic ladder, and there, after his return to the land of his fathers, he erected the altar, and changed the name of the spot from Luz to Bethel, the House of God. And proofs of the veneration in which this place was held are to be found in the records before us.[2] But, in the days of Joshua, Bethel was not free from the taint of Canaanite idolatry.[3] A temporary resting-place for the ark was found in the camp at Gilgal, in the Jordan valley. But Gilgal was in a corner of the land;[4] and, after victory had crowned the warfare of Israel, a solemn convocation was held at a place called Shiloh,[5] there to set up the tent of meeting.

There is no doubt as to the site of Shiloh, "a desolate hill on which only two buildings remain, and even these, although modern, and doubtless Christian churches, more than half ruined;"[6] "a place so utterly featureless, that, had it not been for the preservation of the name (Seilun), and the extreme precision with which its situation is described, the spot could never have been identified."[7] But a careful examination of the undulating ground has disclosed many traces of an ancient

[1] Beitin is a place of uninviting aspect. "The miserable fields are fenced in with stone walls; the hovels are rudely built of stone; the hill to the east is of hard rock, with only a few scattered fig-gardens. The ancient sepulchres are cut in a low cliff, and a great reservoir south of the village is excavated in rock. The place seems, as it were, turned to stone" (Major Conder, "Tent Work," p. 52).

[2] At Bethel the children of Israel asked counsel of God before going to battle against the children of Benjamin (chap. xx. 18). The word rendered House of God in the A. V. is Bethel.

[3] It was conquered by the house of Joseph (chap. i. 22–26).

[4] In Josh. ii. 1 the article is prefixed, The Gilgal. The word signifies *rolling*, with a reference, as the occasion of the name, to the rolling off of the reproach of Egypt from the people through the administration of the rite of circumcision. The name was given, apparently, to more than one of the encampments of Israel. The Gilgal, which was the site of the first camp, and of the tabernacle, was about five miles distant from Jordan, and two from Jericho. [5] Josh. xviii. 1.

[6] Thomson, "The Land and the Book," Central Palestine, p. 104.

[7] Stanley, "Sinai and Palestine," chap. v.

city, and, with the wide plains all around, there was ample scope for the tents of Israel's thousands when they went up to worship Jehovah. The situation was central, and its seclusion was favourable to the repose which befits the worship of the great King. There was reared the tent—" a structure of low stone walls with a tent drawn over the top;" there were the altar, the oracle, and the mercy-seat, until, in Eli's priesthood, the tragic Ichabod was pronounced, and "the Lord refused the tabernacle of Joseph and chose not the tribe of Ephraim."

But, although Shiloh was the sanctuary, and the Lamp of God was kept ever burning beneath its roof, the Book of Judges shows, both in what it states and in what it omits, that the requirements of the Hebrew ritual were loosely observed, some probably not observed at all. No mention is made in the Book of the festivals, at which all the males were held bound to appear before Jehovah. We do read of a yearly dance of the daughters of Shiloh, which had a semi-religious character; but the dance was no part of the religious code, and the circle in which it was observed was narrow. In the whole history of the time of the Judges, the high priest is only once referred to,[1] and the worship of the Tabernacle is not spoken of except in connection with the Benjamite catastrophe. Very soon, indeed, a schismatical worship was set up in the northern part of the country.[2] And we read of even Ephraimite villages which had fallen into the idolatry of Canaan.[3]

Thus the bond of unity was gradually loosened, and heathen practices gained a foothold in homes and hearts. No doubt, the centrifugal tendency was promoted, not only by mixture with the aboriginal tribes, but also by the dangers attending the journey to Shiloh in days when the highways, infested by robbers, were unoccupied, and travellers walked through bypaths.[4] The disjointed condition of society, with all the consequences of such a condition, are strikingly exhibited in the narratives alluded to in the beginning of this chapter. Two of these shed a lurid light on the political situation; the third, relieving the gloom of the delineation, shows how much in the manners and spirit of the people was worth preserving and attuning to finer issues.

[1] Judg. xx. 27, 28.   [2] Judg. xviii. 30.   [3] Judg. vi.
[4] Judg. v. 6.

CHAPTER IV.

ILLUSTRATIONS OF THE PERIOD.

First Illustration: The Levite of Mount Ephraim—Three Time-Marks—The tale told in the nineteenth chapter of the Book of Judges—The gathering together of the congregation—The war with Benjamin—The terrible revenge—The compunction—The means adopted to prevent the complete extinction of the tribe—The significance of the episode. *Second Illustration:* The establishment of a schismatical centre of worship—The two parts of the history—Micah; his mother; the ephod and teraphim; the Levite—The raid of the Danites; Their capture of the Levite; Who he was; The sanctuary at Dan.

WITH regard to the first of the narratives alluded to, we can distinguish three time-marks in the Book of the Judges. One of the three is the reference made to Phinehas, the son of Eleazar, the son of Aaron. "He stood before the ark in those days."[1] This Phinehas was priest in the time of Joshua, and his priesthood could not have extended for long after the death of Joshua, certainly not for long after the death of the elders who survived Joshua. The other two marks are found in two clauses of the history. "The congregation," it is said, "was gathered together as one man, *from Dan even to Beersheba*."[2] Now, this phrase does not occur in the account of previous convocations: it could have been used only after the events belonging to the second of our narratives—the migration of the Danites and their capture of Laish or Leshem in the far north, henceforth called Dan. But the clause which immediately follows "*with the land of Gilead*," suggests that this convocation, and, by inference, that migration, was in the earlier portion of the era. For "the land of Gilead" being east of the Jordan was held to be outside the geographical Israelite territory, and its people became gradually alienated from the other children of Israel. Their inclusion in "the assembly of the people of God" is a witness for the day when

[1] Judg. xx. 28. [2] Chap. xx. 1.

the feeling which had prompted the erection of the great altar by Jordan, not for burnt-offering or sacrifice, but as a witness between the two tribes and a half and their compatriots"[1]—the feeling of fraternal unity—was still fresh and strong. We are warranted, therefore, in connecting the tale now to be told with the commencement of the epoch of the Judges.

The tale is this. A wife of the second rank[2] had proved faithless to her husband, "a certain Levite sojourning on the side of Mount Ephraim." In dread of her husband's wrath "she went away to her father's house in Bethlehem-Judah, and was there four whole months." The Levite, moved by kindly feeling towards her, set forth to bring her again. They met, and the wife, rejoicing in the affection for which she had not dared to hope, brought him to her father's house. The most genial hospitality is shown to him; and for four days he is the guest of "the father of the damsel." On the evening of the fifth day the Levite begins his return. The shades of night fall on him and his wife as they come to Jebus; but they will not turn aside to the city of the stranger. And they press forward to Gibeah—a city of Benjamin—four miles distant from Jebus. No home in Gibeah opens to them; and they are preparing to encamp in the mound or square of the city when a stranger, a poor workman, but a fellow-tribesman, seeing them, insists on being their host, and takes them to his house. Then follows the story of a terrible wickedness, of brutal men wishing to indulge unnatural lust, and to whose importunities, with the view of saving them from horrible bestiality, the wife is sacrificed. The Levite carries home the dead body of the outraged woman, and divides the body, "together with her bones," into twelve pieces, which he sends into all the coasts of Israel. "And," in the quaint words of the chronicle, "it was so, that all who saw it said, There was no such deed done or seen from the day that the children of Israel came up out of the land of Egypt unto this day: consider of it, take advice, and speak your minds."[3]

This was the occasion of the gathering together of the congregation as one man. Never did fiery cross more rapidly convene an assembly of excited warriors. The stain of the wickedness which the Levite is summoned to relate is felt to

[1] Josh. xxii. 10, 29.
[2] Judg. xix. 1. In Hebrew, "a woman or a wife, a concubine"—a wife of inferior station.
[3] Judg. xix. 30.

lie on the whole congregation: and, quick as lightning, fierce and stern, is the action taken. Benjamin is summoned to surrender the men of Belial in Gibeah who had disgraced the name of Israel. And, on the refusal to do so, war is declared. Sanguinary is the fight; fearful is the bloodshed. Israel, at first defeated, finally, by a successful ambush, overcomes: Gibeah is given to the flames, and, with the exception of six hundred men who had fled to the rock Rimmon and lived there for four months, the tribe of Benjamin is exterminated.[1]

It was a terrible vengeance; and, when the bloody work is done, there comes a bitter compunction. Before Shiloh's mercy-seat the people stand from morning until evening, "weeping sore and saying, O Lord God of Israel, why is this come to pass in Israel that there should be to-day one tribe lacking in Israel?" To repair the breach, another iniquity is perpetrated. When the muster is taken it is apparent that one town, nestling in a valley of Gilead, had furnished no contingent for the army; and to this town twelve thousand men are sent with the command to smite its inhabitants with the edge of the sword, sparing only the unmarried women. These, numbering four hundred, are brought to Shiloh, and given to the surviving remnant of Benjamin. The closing chapter of the book describes the *ruse* by which the Benjamites, not thus mated, were provided with wives. A solemn vow had been taken that no Israelite would give his daughter to a son of Benjamin. But the Benjamites are encouraged to rush into the scene of the dance at Shiloh, and, abstracting the maidens dancing there, hasten to their mountain fastnesses,[2] the elders undertaking to make peace with the fathers and brethren of the maidens.[3]

Thus the tribe was saved from complete extinction. Gradu-

---

[1] Judg. xx.

[2] "Our road," says Mr. Oliphant, "lay through a fertile plain called the Meadow of the Feast, possibly in connection with the yearly feast which used to be held by the Jews in old times at Shiloh, from which historical site we were not far distant. It is a comfort now and then to come upon a Biblical site about the identity of which there is not the slightest doubt, and such is the case with Seilun, the modern name for Shiloh. It stands in an extremely retired valley. It was probably in this meadow, while the maidens were dancing at the festival in honour of the ark, that the remnant of the Benjamites concealed themselves among the vineyards on the hill sides and carried off two hundred maidens" ("Haifa," p. 231).

[3] Judg. xxi.

ally the broken-down cities were rebuilt, and boys and girls again played in their streets.

This tragic episode is, in many respects, an index to the internal condition of the time of the Judges It presents both the kindly lights and the dark shadows of its social life. The kindly lights, in the picture of the Levite setting forth on his journey, with the servant and the two asses ; in the hospitalities extended by the father of the wife whom he had forgiven ; in the declinature to lodge in the city of aliens to the commonwealth of Israel ; in the friendliness of the poor workman who, himself a stranger, knew the heart of a stranger ; and, finally, in the simplicity of the yearly merry-making of the daughters of Shiloh. But the dark shadows also, in the chief features of the narrative. For it reminds us of the rudeness, degenerating too often into unbridled licentiousness, which prevailed, and whose prevalence proved how far the law given by Moses was in advance of the people, and how even the worst traits of the Canaanite surrounding had written their mark in the characters of many. It reminds us also of the inferior position occupied by woman. That position may have been more elevated in Israel than in heathen communities, but we observe the evidences of a degrading subserviency of woman to the passions of men. The wife of lower degree—the concubine—is recognized in Levitical circles. And, to protect the man whom he had taken into his house, the Ephraimite host does not hesitate to offer his daughter to the vile lust of the men of Gibeah ; whilst, to protect both his host and himself, the traveller thrusts his concubine out of the house and leaves her to the mercy of the band of ruffians until the dawning of the day.

Otherwise the story is suggestive. For instance, when, in answer to the question, " Whither goest thou ?" the Levite replies, " I am now going to the house of the Lord,"[1] we are, incidentally, told of a regularly maintained worship in Shiloh, and of courses of priests and Levites discharging their functions according to order. However it may have been neglected by the people, the worship of the Lord we may infer was duly maintained, Phinehas or his successors standing before the ark. The latter part of the story not only confirms this, but indicates the hold which the Hebrew worship still kept over the congregation. In great emergencies it sought after God. It asked

[1] Judg. xix. 18.

counsel of Him, either through Urim and Thummim or by lot. As Dean Stanley points out, the action taken and the subsequent repentance reflect the spirit conspicuous in Phinehas on a previous memorable occasion, and was probably, therefore, largely influenced by him as the priest whose lips kept knowledge.[1] When the thousands of Israel are smitten down, the congregation comes to Shiloh, and sits before Jehovah, and offers burnt-offerings and peace-offerings. And, once more, as proving the reverence felt for the sacred symbols, the ark is removed from Shiloh, first to Mizpah in Benjamin and then to Bethel, that it might be in the neighbourhood of the army, and the priest, standing before it, might announce the holy oracle. All this reminds us that, notwithstanding the failure to keep many parts of the law, and the growing tendency to lapse from the holiness enjoined by the covenant, the tabernacle and the ark were still, and ever, a potential force in the life and destinies of Israel.

And it is interesting to observe the rapid blaze of indignation in every part of the country when the ghastly appeal to it was sent by the Levite. The response to the appeal is an evidence of ill-balanced and excessive zeal. With its vows and curses, with its violent heat and awful retribution, it was the sign of a community which wanted the judicial temper, even in regard to vengeance, which the regular administration of law tends to promote. But, both in the sudden flaming up of the wrath, and in the remorse after the wrath had spent itself, we are reminded of one wide distinction between Israel and the tribes by whom they were encompassed. In Israel, beneath all the chaos of years, when "every man did what was right in his own eyes," there was the underlying sense of an eternally right and true, and of the duty of the nation, as such, to maintain the righteousness on which social well-being rests. The twelve tribes were, in this matter at least, the one people of Him whose name is Holy. It was, in respect of this consciousness, and of the capability of a higher education which it ensured, that Israel, even in its darkest hours, was the salt of the earth—the foremost of the divinely-appointed agencies in the elevation and sanctification of mankind.

A second illustration of morals and manners, introducing us to events which have an important political bearing, is supplied

[1] "History of the Jewish Church," Lect. xiii.

by the history of a schismatical centre of worship in the north of Palestine. The time of this history is fixed by the previous narrative, for Dan, as we have seen, was the recognized northern boundary of the land of Israel when the congregation gathered together as one man; and this assembly was held during the priesthood of Phinehas, who stood before the ark in the days of Joshua. It will otherwise appear that Josephus is probably accurate when he assigns the story of the seventeenth and eighteenth chapters of the Book of Judges to a date very shortly after the death of Joshua.

The history divides into two parts.

First, we are taken to the hill-country of Ephraim. In one of its great homes we see a widowed mother and her son. The mother had been left, at her husband's decease, with ample means, a considerable portion of which [1] somehow disappeared And, in the hearing of her son, she appeals to Him to whom all hearts are open to bring to light the plunderer of this wealth. Moved by the adjuration, the son confesses that he had yielded to the whisper of avarice, and abstracted the money. For this confession she blesses him, and intimates that, for his sake, she had intended to devote the stolen shekels to the Lord. It is a striking evidence of the confusion of thought which prevailed even in days when the memory of Joshua and his protestations was fresh, that she could think of honour to Jehovah in a course of action which transgressed His most solemn commands, and set at nought the emphatic warnings of His servants. For her purpose was, with these shekels "to make a graven image and a molten image." And this purpose is carried out, although, from the chronicle, it seems that only a fifth of the sum mentioned was appropriated to the superstitious worship.[2] A house of God is reared in the very region in which Shiloh was situated. The metal is fused into the image of a calf, beside which, as the more important feature, there is also a graven image. We read, too, of an ephod—an important part of priestly garment, and of teraphim—small

---

[1] Eleven hundred shekels of silver, amounting to between £130 and £150.

[2] Judg. xvii. 4. "His mother took two hundred shekels of silver and gave them to the founder, who made thereof a molten image and a graven image." Perhaps the other nine hundred shekels were devoted to other objects connected with the worship.

images which were treasured as household gods, the custom of having which is noted even by prophets of later periods.[1] One feature, to complete the worship, is wanting. There is no priest. Micah is bold enough to set apart one of his sons as the family priest. But he does so with a misgiving which, by and by, is relieved.

For it happens that a Levite, dissatisfied, for some reason, with his position, leaves the city of his residence, Bethlehem in Judah. The law of his God is not hidden in his heart, and he sets out in search of a place. The house of Micah was on the route of travellers, and he claims its shelter and hospitality. His consecration having been ascertained, the young man is easily persuaded to become a father and a priest to the Ephraimite family, at a hire of a few shekels per annum, and a suit of apparel and his living. A worthless mercenary we judge him to have been, without loyalty to either God or man. "Want of maintenance, no less than conscience, draws him on to the danger of idolatrous patronage. When need meets with unconscionableness, all conditions are easily swallowed, of unlawful entrances, of wicked executions."[2] The superstitious feed on semblances of things. He who scruples not to break Divine law is satisfied with this simulacrum of a priesthood. Having the service of a Levite, Micah exclaims, "Now I know that the Lord will do me good."

The confidence is rudely broken by the second series of events related. In the account of the settlement of the tribes, it is said that the inheritance assigned to Dan was "too little"; and the narrative of its extension, which is told at length in the Book of Judges, is, in a few sentences, anticipated.[3] Circumscribed as the territory originally was, it was still further contracted by the successful opposition of the Amorites, who would not suffer the tribesmen to come down into the valley. The desire to find elbow-room, to move from mountainous regions to fairer and wider lands, prompts the descendants of Dan to send five men of valour in search of pastures new. *En route*, they come to the Mount Ephraim sanctuary. They hear the voice of a priest engaged in acts of worship—a grateful sound to the stalwart Israelites—inviting them within, and offering them the opportunity of asking counsel. They are

---

[1] Hosea iii. 4.   [2] Bishop Hall's "Contemplations," book x.
[3] Josh. xix. 47.

encouraged to proceed on their way. They accomplish their mission. They return and report that they had found a country very different from their barren highlands, wide and roomy, and with "no want of anything that is in the earth," a country whose only inhabitants were a Phœnician colony, "dwelling careless and secure," without an efficient magistracy, and "having no business," with more powerful peoples outside their border. And six hundred men, stirred by the report, leave Zorah and Eshtaol to go and enter into possession of the land. They are guided to Micah's house. They hail the mercenary Levite. And he accepts their call to be their priest, and to steal the sacred things of his master. And bearing him and them away, they move northward to the city at the base of Mount Hermon, known as Leshem or Laish; they smite it with the edge of the sword; they seize the fertile territory, and, settling in it, they erect a sanctuary over which the Levite presides [1]

This Levite is no other than Jonathan the son of Gershom. In subsequent times the children of Israel were ashamed to mention the lineage of the idolatrous priest. But there can be little doubt that the rendering in the Authorized Version, "the son of Manasseh," should be "the son of Moses." Gershom was the son of Moses, not Manasseh; and, although Jonathan may not have been the grandson of the Lawgiver, in direct lineal succession, he certainly belonged to the family of which the Lawgiver's son was the head.[2] It is sad indeed to reflect that the descendant of Moses was the man through whom a priesthood and a ritual were originated, which marked a revolt from Divine ordinance, and prepared for the days of "Jeroboam who made Israel to sin."

For we are told that a tribal priestly caste remained in the family of this Jonathan "until the captivity of the land." What this phrase denotes is not obvious; but the view to

[1] Judges xviii.

[2] "In the Hebrew text, the name here rendered Manasseh is written M^{n}SH. Without the little n suspended over the line it reads Moses whose son was Gershom (Exod. ii. 22), whose son or descendant Jonathan clearly was. The Masorites, probably grieved that a descendant of Moses should have been implicated in idolatrous worship, adopted this expedient for disguising the fact without absolutely falsifying the text " ("Speaker's Commentary," p. 209).

ILLUSTRATIONS OF THE PERIOD. 29

which the majority of commentators incline is that it refers to the ascendancy of the Philistines in the time of Samuel, when the ark of Jehovah was taken, and the "Ichabod, Ichabod" was sounded. The concluding sentence of the narrative suggests this, intimating, as it does, that the mongrel worship of Dan continued "all the time that the house of God was in Shiloh."[1] Now Shiloh ceased to be the place whither "the tribes went up" after the capture of the covenant-symbol by the armies of the uncircumcised. Reckoning to this capture as the end of the Danite schism, we give it a limit of at least a hundred years. It typified and it accentuated that departure from the truth of Israelite government, worship and manners, which the chronicler traces in the sentence, "Every man did that which was right in his own eyes."

The impression left on the mind by the two previous narratives is that which is naturally caused by records of unrest and anarchy. But, lest it might be supposed that all nobility and grace had vanished from the life of Israel, a short book, expressly connected with "the days when the Judges judged," exhibits a series of pictures which show how much piety and simplicity of manners adorned even those rude days, how much was worth preserving because it had the possibility of higher things. The sketches whose centre is Bethlehem of Judah, with its cornfields and its farms, are no doubt the sign of similar scenes and ways in other parts of the land, and they remind us that, even under the most unfavourable conditions, virtue and truth can flourish, that the real growth of a nation is not to be measured by events detailed in histories, but by the types of character fostered in its homes, and the faith and the gentleness which inspire its people.

The Book receives its name from the fair Moabitish woman whose romance it tells. During a protracted famine, an Israelite called Elimelech, his wife Naomi, and his two sons, Mahlon and Chilion, resolve to cross the line of blue mountains on which they had often gazed from the uplands of Bethlehem. "And they came into the country of Moab and continued there." Elimelech died. His two sons married maidens of Moab, Orpah and Ruth. And for ten years, all lived happily. But the sons also died, and died without issue.

[1] See note, p. 7.

The craving of Naomi for her native land was increased by the loss of all dearest to her; and on hearing of the prosperity which had again visited it, she resolved to return. Her daughters-in-law accompanied her on the way. One of the two, yielding to Naomi's request, bade her farewell, but the other refused, in words that have become classic. "Intreat me not to leave thee, and to return from following after thee: for whither thou goest I will go; and where thou lodgest, I will lodge: thy people shall be my people, and thy God my God: where thou diest will I die, and there will I be buried: the Lord do so to me, and more also, if ought but death part thee and me."[1] We are chiefly interested in the unfolding of the tale from the time when all the city of Bethlehem was moved about the arrival of the two women "in the beginning of barley harvest."

The Book of Judges is full of "mighty men of valour," their wars and heir victories. The strain of the Book throughout is martial. This fragment of biography introduces us to "a mighty man of wealth," advanced in years, with broad acres and many dependants, esteemed by all for his integrity and piety. Most graphic is the outline presented of rural ways and manners. The salutation, master to men, men to master, still maintained in the East, especially at harvest time, breathes a spirit which strikingly contrasts with the attitude of employer and employed in our Western world. Quaint and touching is the account of the gleaning, of the kindness shown to the poor, in accordance with the provisions of law. The burly, high-minded, man of wealth, in the frankness of his bearing and the ordering of his household, is a splendid type of the Israelite indeed. No more charming sketch can be found in literature than the sketch of his farm at the period of the barley harvest.[2]

He becomes the husband of Ruth, and in this wise. Boaz is the kinsman of the deceased husband of Naomi. No doubt she had often spoken to the Moabitess of her rich relation. And it is a sign of the simplicity of Oriental life that Ruth begs to be allowed "to go to the field, and glean ears of corn after him in whose sight she shall find grace." Her "hap"[3]— perhaps there was a method as to the "hap"—is to light on a part of the field belonging to Boaz. Coming from Bethlehem

[1] Ruth i. 16-17.   [2] See Ruth, chap. 2.   [3] Ruth ii.

ILLUSTRATIONS OF THE PERIOD. 31

and walking through the fields, he observes her, inquires concerning her, is at once attracted by her. He tells her to keep to his reapers, whom he had charged to be courteous and attentive, whom he still further charged, "to let fall also some handfuls of purpose for her, and leave them that she may glean them." And thus, to the end of both barley and wheat harvests, Ruth gleans, with the hearty good-will of all and the special favour of the owner of the field. When the harvest is concluded, what next? Naomi hits on a plan which again gives a glimpse into curious customs, and which lays on Boaz the rights and duties of the kinsman.[1] How the plan succeeded, how the kinsman's part was claimed and discharged, the Book relates. And it concludes with a brief narration of the redemption of Elimelech's estate, and the marriage of Ruth. As we read the words of the biographer, we seem to see the people of the village, headed by their elders, deponing that they had witnessed the plucking off of the shoe by the next of kin, and the giving of it to Boaz, in token that the kinsman's place was transferred to him: and then we seem to hear the benediction, in which all join, on the union of the Bethlehemite with the daughter of Moab. Months pass, and a little son is the crown of the union: and now the women surround Naomi, and congratulate her on the child who is to be the restorer of her life and the nourisher of her old age—the son of the daughter-in-law who had been better to her than ten sons. The babe whom Naomi lays in her bosom and nurses is called Obed, and Obed was the father of Jesse, and Jesse was the father of David.[2]

The treatise thus briefly outlined has been the subject of many expositions and homilies wherein, to quote the title of a volume of discourses, "the wonders of Providence, the riches of grace, the privileges of believers, and the contrition of sinners are judiciously and faithfully exemplified and improved."[3] And undoubtedly Ruth is the portrait of a life in which, though outside the pale of the Covenant, God's Spirit was secretly working, reminding us of the sovereignty of His will and the freedom of His gifts, of the truth afterwards conveyed to the Apostle of the Circumcision that "on the Gentiles also is

[1] Ruth, chap. 3.　　　　　　　　[2] Ruth, chap. 4.
[3] "Discourses on Ruth, and other important Subjects," by John Macgowan, published in 1711

poured out the gift of the Holy Ghost." We recognize in her a trustful and affectionate nature attracted by the piety of the Israelite mother-in-law to the God of Israel, under whose wing, as Boaz discerned, she had learned to repose.[1] The way in which she is led, the recompense provided for her, with all the accessories of the story, suggest the reflection of an expositor: "Who would not forsake the shadow of all the trees in the world to be covered under such wings."[2]

Additional interest is given to the narrative by the links in genealogy which it supplies. It indicates a striking feature in the family tree of the dynasty which for five centuries reigned in Judah, and whence—as concerning the flesh—Christ came. Hitherto association with Moab had only been a curse to Israel. Through the gentle daughter of Moab, introduced into the congregation as the wife of Boaz, there came a fresh current of blessing—a hint of the more catholic conception of the Kingdom of God, which was to be realized in David's greater son—"a light to lighten the Gentiles," as well as "the glory of God's people Israel." The babe born of Ruth was named Obed, "the servant"—one who would serve as the kinsman, restoring Naomi's life, and nourishing her old age. In direct succession from this Obed, after many generations, came the Child who is called Wonderful, the Obed of the Eternal Love, whose mission was, not to be ministered to, but to minister and give His life a ransom for many—the true kinsman of all the times, in whom the life of a sorrow and sin-stricken humanity is restored, and the old age of the world is supported and renewed.

But to trace the manifold significance, and to point the many-sided moral of the story of Ruth is foreign to the purpose contemplated in this chapter. The story is here presented as an illustration of Israel's social condition in the days when the Judges judged. And, regarded in this special connection, it relieves the gloom left by the chronicles of these days, full as they are of depressions and servitudes, of apostasies from Covenant standing with all the bitter fruits of such apostasies, of evil in the sight of Jehovah, and of a confusion which degenerates into violence and lawlessness. It

[1] Ruth ii. 12.

[2] "The Reward of Religion delivered in Sundrie Lectures upon the Booke of Ruth, &c.," by Edward Topsell; published in 1613.

bids us remember that, even in the darkest hours of the national history, there was a remnant according to the election of grace, that many hearts were faithful to the best traditions of the race, and refused to bow the knee to Baal. It shows us the soil whence sprang the noble faith which inspired the heroes who rallied the thousands of Israel around their standards. It proves that the salt had not wholly lost its savour, that, here and there at least, in dwellings and hearts of pious villagers, there was nourished the spirit of the mind which made the judgeship of Samuel memorable, and which found its sweetest and highest expression in the Psalms of David. And thus, amid the storms and struggles at which we are called to glance, we are invited to wait patiently for God, sure that "He has not cast away His people whom He foreknew."

CHAPTER V.

THE PROPHETESS OF THE NORTHERN TRIBES.

The Judges who belonged to the southern tribes : Othniel, Ehud, Shamgar—The lapse into idolatry, and the new period of servitude at the death of Ehud—Jabin, king of Hazor—Harosheth—The great army of the oppressor—The two Deborahs—The second Deborah ; Who was she? A unique figure in the history of Israel—Her ally in the north—The hesitation of Barak—The trumpet-blast—The fight, and the victory—The fate of Sisera—Jael, the wife of Heber the Kenite ; her action to be condemned ; but circumstances to be taken into account.

HAVING indicated the more prominent features of the social and political life of Israel in the time " when the Judges judged," let us now regard some of those Judges by whose faith the darkness of that time was lightened, and the land which had no king was, notwithstanding, blessed with decades of rest and peace.

In the beginning of the Book we find brief notices of three deliverers, belonging to the southern tribes, whom Jehovah raised up.

The first of these earliest heroes connects the history of the period with the mighty men of the wilderness and the long rest. Of such mighty men, no figure is more outstanding than that of Caleb, the son of Jephunneh—the gallant comrade of Joshua, who had shared with him and others the dangers of " spying out the land," who, when the courage of the people failed because of the report of the spies, stood like a rock,[1] and who, almost alone of those who had taken part in the exodus, participated in the glories of the settlement in Palestine. Caleb is distinguished as the Kenizzite,[2] a race, if not identical with, at least akin to the Kenites : and his place in the armies of Israel illustrates the saying that "a mixed multitude" went with the Israelites out of Egypt.[3] He had a younger brother

[1] Numb. xiii. 30, and xiv. 6–24. [2] Joshua xiv. 6. [3] Exod. xii. 38.

THE PROPHETESS OF THE NORTHERN TRIBES. 35

who bore a distinctly tribal name, Kenaz ; and in Othniel, the son of this Kenaz, the virtues of the elder brother were manifested. It was Othniel who, by his daring, won the hand of Caleb's daughter, and, through Caleb's daughter, obtained not only a dry south land, but also the special blessing of a territory with upper springs and nether springs.[1] His descendants took root in the land ; in the era of the monarchy they are ranked among the aristocracy of Judah.

There came a dark and cloudy day when "the anger of Jehovah was hot against Israel, and He sold them into the hand of Chushan Rishathaim."[2] It is impossible to identify this potentate with any of those whose names are recorded on Assyrian inscriptions. The title given him in ancient books is "Chushan the wicked, king of Syria in Euphrates."[3] From the country between the Tigris and the Euphrates—that known as Mesopotamia[4]—he led his hosts against the sons of Jacob, and, for eight years, his yoke was heavy on their neck. Then rose up Othniel, in the might of a sacred inspiration, and under his leadership the foreign usurpation was repelled. And the land returned to a rest which, says the historian, was unbroken during forty years.[5]

His death was followed by a grievous lapse into idolatry ; and this lapse, weakening the sense of unity and destroying the courage of the people, exposed them to a second invasion. Eglon, king of the hostile and banned people of Moab, called to his aid the children of Ammon (on a later occasion to figure in our history), and the children of Amalek, of evil memory. The united army "smote Israel, and possessed the city of palm-trees." For eighteen years the lusty, haughty Eglon dominated over the tribes. Israel was brought very low ; and in the time of its humiliation it turned to Jehovah ; and again, in answer to its pleading, He sent a saviour. The saviour was a Benjamite. One peculiarity of the Benjamites was the number of left-handed men :[6] this Benjamite, Ehud, the hero of Gera, was a left-handed man. "What a strange choice doth God make of an executioner," exclaims Bishop Hall, "a man wanting of his right hand. Who would not have thought both hands too

[1] Joshua xv. 16-19.   [2] Judg. iii. 8.
[3] The Targum, and the Syriac and Arabic versions.
[4] "Syria of the two Rivers " is the translation of the Hebrew word.
[5] Judg. iii. 11.   [6] Judg. xxi. 16.

little for such a work, or if either might have been spared, how much rather the left! It is the ordinary way of the Almighty to make choice of the unlikeliest means."[1]

Josephus describes Ehud as a young man.[2] Dean Stanley takes the account of him in the Book of Judges to imply that he had acquired a fame for prophetic power in the country.[3] Be this as it may, it appears that he was entrusted with tribute money due to King Eglon. Before discharging his mission, he provides himself with a two-edged sword or dagger, which he conceals under his white garment. The tribute having been presented, he returns with his attendants as far as Gilgal, close to which were "quarries,"[4] rather, scooped-out places in which images were kept. There he dismisses them, and thence retraces his way to the royal residence. Representing that he had a secret errand to the king, the officers of the Court show him to the royal presence and leave him. The king is seated in a kiosk, so constructed as to admit every cooling breeze, and there he receives him with the respect due to a prophet. When the two are alone, the left hand—the hand whose use would disarm suspicion—grasps the hilt of the dagger, draws it forth, and thrusts it into the corpulent body of the king. He himself escapes through the entrance reserved for persons having a private audience, and, locking the door of the kiosk, speeds to the mountains of Ephraim. It is the opportunity of the enslaved people. The hardy Ephraimites, responding to his call, descend from their fastnesses, seize the fords of Jordan, and when the alarmed Moabites rush to the fords in flight to their purple hills, they suffer not a man to pass. That day, thousands of warriors fall beneath the hand of Israel. And another long rest-period is ushered in.[5]

A third deliverance, but local in its range, is recorded. Apparently, its occasion was a partial disturbance of the tranquillity enjoyed under Ehud's judgeship. The troublers of Israel were the Philistines (of whom more again). One Shamgar, the son of Anath, is the hero of their repulsion. The feature

---

[1] "Bishop Hall's Contemplations," Book ix.
[2] "Antiquities of the Jews," Book v. chap. iv.
[3] "History of the Jewish Church," Lect. xiv.
[4] The Hebrew word is Pesilim. *Cf.* Deut. vii 25; Isa. **xxi.** 9; Jer. viii. 19; where it is translated "graven images." Only in this passage is it rendered "quarries." [5] Judg. iii. 12-29.

of his prowess which is noticed is the instrument he used
An ox-goad, it is called. But the ox-goad was "a really formidable weapon, sometimes ten feet long."[1] It is noted that
six hundred Philistines felt the deadly effect of this weapon as
wielded by the stalwart son of Anath.[2] The incident reminds
us of the battles of the Scottish Covenant, in which farming
implements, scythes, and long poles with iron blades affixed to
them, were used by the farmers and peasants who formed the
main body of the army of the Covenanters.

"The children of Israel again did evil in the sight of the
Lord, when Ehud was dead."[3] With the removal of the strong
hand from the helm of the state, the drift towards social chaos
and idolatry reappeared. And another period of servitude
began ; the new oppressor being "Jabin, king of Canaan, that
reigned in Hazor." In the account of the great battle at
Merom, in the Book of Joshua,[4] we read of *a* Jabin who reigned
in *a* Hazor, and who was the head of a powerful confederacy,
with chariots very many. This Jabin, we are informed, was
killed with all the inhabitants of the city, and the city itself was
burnt with fire. The mention of the same city, with a king of
the same name, at the head of a great army which possessed
nine hundred chariots, in the Book of Judges, has suggested
that the narratives in the two books are two versions of the
same event. But there are features in the two versions which
cannot be harmonized ; and we must conclude, therefore, that
the kingdom so terribly shaken by Joshua and his warriors had
been reorganized, that the burnt city had been rebuilt, that
Jabin, meaning "the intelligent," was, like "Pharaoh" in Egypt,
the hereditary name of the king, and that, as is customary with
heathen and savage tribes, nursing the purpose of revenge, the
weakness of Israel was hailed as the opportunity of carrying
the purpose into effect. The new Hazor occupied the site of
the old, near Lake Merom. It was the seat of Jabin's Court,
although the head-quarters of his army were further south. At
Harosheth, in the great plain of Esdraelon, were gathered hosts,
numerous as the sand that is on the sea-shore, and including
various nationalities comprehended under the word, "the Gentiles or the nations."[5]

[1] Dr. Porter's "Giant Cities of Bashan," p. 201.   [2] Judg. iii. 31.
[3] Judg. iv. 1.   [4] Josh. xi. 1-14.
[5] "The name 'Harosheth' signifies workmanship—cutting and carving,

These hosts, with their array of horses and chariots, dismayed the luckless Israelites, ill-provided, as they were, with even spears and shields;[1] and, for twenty years, Sisera, the commander-in-chief of Jabin's army, oppressed them with force. The oppression, it would seem, was felt almost entirely in the northern and central parts of the country. And it is in connection with this Canaanite tyranny that we are introduced to one of the most picturesque and spirit-stirring episodes in the history of Israel.

On the borderland between Benjamin and Ephraim there was a narrow ravine, at whose southern extremity was the city of Ramah, afterwards associated with Samuel, the last of the Judges. This ravine, "a deep, hot valley,"[2] was connected with an event in the history of Jacob, which, although purely domestic, was never forgotten by his descendants. There was buried Deborah, the faithful nurse of Rebekah, and the oak under which her remains were laid was called Allon-Bachuth,[3] "the oak of weeping." In that same valley, centuries afterwards, a second Deborah held her courts of appeal, and spoke to the people in the name of Jehovah. The terebinth and the palm trees have a prominent place in the history and poetry of Israel. A wide-spreading terebinth overshadowed the burial-place of Deborah the nurse; the branches of a graceful palm waved over the oracle of Deborah the prophetess. "She dwelt under the palm tree, between Ramah and Bethel, in Mount Ephraim, and the children of Israel came up to her for judgment."[4]

Who was she? The only feature of a personal nature recorded is that she was "the wife of Lapidoth."[5] Hebrew names are always significant. Her name means "the Bee," her husband's, "Lamps or Torches." Hence the tradition that she was not literally the wife of one Lapidoth, but that she

whether in stone or wood (Exod. xxxi. 5)—and hence might be applied to the place where such works are carried on. It has been conjectured that this being a great timber district, rich in cedars and fir-trees, and near great Zidon, Jabin kept a large number of oppressed Israelites at work in hewing wood and preparing it at Harosheth for transport to Zidon; and that these woodcutters, armed with axes and hatchets, formed the soldiers of Barak's army" ("Speaker's Commentary," note on Judg. iv. 2).

[1] Deborah, in her song, asks—"Was there a spear or shield seen among forty thousand in Israel?" (chap. v. 8).
[2] Canon Tristram, "Bible Places," p. 116.   [3] Gen. xxxv. 8.
[4] Judg. iv. 5.   [5] Judg. iv. 4.

was the woman of lamps, of light as well as learning, of fiery spirit and courage, and that her husband was really the Barak —signifying "lightning"—whom she called from the north. To accept this tradition would do violence to the narrative, but it gives a hint which need not be lost sight of—the hint that it is the junction of the Bee and the Torch, industry and illumination, patience consecrated and irradiated by Divine genius, which marks the truth of the God-inspired, God-announcing light.

She was a prophetess. To another woman in early Israelite history this lofty title is attached. That woman was Miriam, the sister of Moses.[1] But Miriam did not judge or rule. On one occasion she is joined with Aaron in revolt against Moses, and was punished for this prominence by being smitten with leprosy.[2] And although, after the passage through the Red Sea, Miriam led the daughters of Israel in singing the Triumphal Hymn, the hymn was not the product of her mind, it was the Song of Moses. To Deborah, therefore, who herself sat in the seat of Moses, and whose song was the outburst of her own enthusiasm, belongs the higher place. Similarly, she is distinguished from other women who, in Holy Scripture, are represented as partakers of prophetic gifts.[3] She is a unique figure in the annals of the chosen people. With one exception,[4] she is the only female ruler mentioned in these annals.[5] Her hymn is a splendid expression of thought and feeling stirred into intensest energy, and conveyed in purest rhythmic form. "As long as I have the image of Deborah before my eyes," writes Coleridge, "and while I throw myself back into the age, country, and circumstances of this Hebrew Boadicea, in the yet not tamed chaos of the spiritual creation; as long as

[1] Exod. xv. 20. [2] Numb. xii.
[3] For example, Huldah (2 Kings xxii. 14), Noadiah (Neh. vi. 14), Anna (St. Luke ii 36), the daughters of Philip the Evangelist (Acts xxi. 9).
[4] Athaliah, the mother of Ahaziah (2 Kings xi. 3).
[5] "She is the magnificent impersonation of the free spirit of the Jewish people and of Jewish life. On the arms of the Roman Empire, Judea is represented as a woman seated under a palm tree, captive and weeping. It is the contrast of that figure which will best place before us the character and call of Deborah. It is the same Judean palm under whose shadow she sits, but not with downcast eyes, and folded hands, and extinguished hopes; with all the fire of faith and energy, eager for the battle, confident of the victory." (Stanley's "Lectures on the Jewish Church," Lect. xiv.).

I contemplate the impassioned, high-souled, heroic woman in all the prominence and individuality of will and character, I feel as if I were among the first ferments of the great affections, the proplastic waves of the microcosmic chaos, swelling up against and yet towards the outspread wings of the dove that lies brooding on the troubled waters." [1]

Other judges won their reputation, and gained their supremacy over the people, by exploits issuing in national deliverances. The reputation of Deborah was won by the force of her character, by the quickness of her discernment of the right in causes submitted to her judgment, and by a faculty of sight into the future. Her fame spread in the declining period of Ehud's sway; after his death she arose "a mother in Israel." And her oracle under the palm tree superseded the Urim and Thummim of the priest in Shiloh. No doubt, the oppression of Jabin was, for long, a heavy burden on her prophetic soul. She pondered and prayed, and with the industry of the Bee she planned and prepared, in readiness for the moment to be indicated by Him before whose presence even the stony mountains of Sinai had melted.

Her ally was a northern chieftain, to whom the hardy highlanders of Palestine turned as their leader. He lived at Kadesh or Kades, amongst the hills of Naphtali,[2] in close vicinity to Hazor. His name was Barak or Barca ("lightning"), "a mighty man of valour," but without the intrepidity which a Divine impulse swaying the mind imparts, capable of great things when aroused, but cautious even to the degree of irresolution, and needing the support of a will swifter in its flash and prompter in its action. Two circumstances may have increased his timidity. The one, the knowledge which, from his position, he possessed, of the vast resources of the enemy, and the tremendous odds against which any uprising of Israel must contend. And the other, the isolation of his tribe from the stronger tribes. For the army of Sisera, which occupied the plain of Esdraelon, virtually cut off all intercourse between Naphtali and the parts of the country south of

---

[1] "Confessions of an Inquiring Spirit," p. 34.

[2] Now, a village called Kadez, fully four miles to the west of Lake Huleh, the ancient Merom, on the heights above the basin of the Jordan. Canon Tristram ("Bible Places") describes it as full of interesting ruins.

the plain. Thus, the gleam of "the lightning" was for long faint and intermittent; the sword of the Lord lay for long within the scabbard of the son of Abinoam. He, too, waited for the sign which invited movement and gave the pledge of victory.

The sign came in the message sent by the prophetess to the effect that, at length, the word of Jehovah burned like a fire in her bones. "Hath not Jehovah, God of Israel, commanded, saying, Go, and draw unto Mount Tabor, and take with thee ten thousand men of the children of Naphtali, and the children of Zebulon, and I will draw unto thee to the river Kishon, Sisera, the captain of Jabin's army, with his chariots and his multitude, and I will deliver him into thine hand."[1]

An instruction so authoritative and specific must be obeyed. Still Barak hesitated. The enterprise seemed so hazardous, almost hopeless, that he and his warriors demanded some visible token of the Divine will and presence. At other crises, the ark of Jehovah was brought unto the host; at this crisis, the prophetess herself must give the inspiration. "If thou wilt go with me," replies Barak, "then I will go; but if thou wilt not, then I will not go."[2] She, who is the weaker vessel, has the stronger faith, and she yields to the demand; but she intimates that as Moses, by his backwardness when called to stand before Pharaoh, lost a fulness of strength and blessing, the chieftain of Naphtali, by his slowness to believe, had lost the complete advantage which would have accrued to him. "The journey thou takest shall not be for thine honour, for the Lord shall sell Sisera into the hands of a woman."[3]

And now, over hill and dale, sounds the trumpet-blast. Far and near, the summons to arms is sent. In the ode of victory we are told of the result. Governors of Israel, riding on white asses,[4] hasten to the captain's standard. Naphtali and Zebulon give their bravest for the enterprise. From Ephraim comes a detachment of patriotic volunteers. Benjamin sends its contingent. From Jordan's banks Manassite leaders head willing companies. Issachar, too, is represented by its princes. But the brunt of the fight, and the heat and burden of the day, fall to the two northern tribes. From many quarters there is no

---

[1] Judg. iv. 6, 7.   [2] Judg. iv. 8.   [3] Judg iv. 9.
[4] White, with a red tinge. "White-dappled," Stanley, following Ewald's version, renders the phrase. Such she-asses were rare and costly.

response. Judah is absent. Gilead abides beyond Jordan, Dan remains in his ships. Asher continues on the seashore. True to the traditional character, Reuben, unstable as water, does not act; though he discerns the necessities of the struggle, he abides "among the sheep-folds."[1] The want of national unity, of an indomitable national spirit, is made only too apparent in that supreme hour. It is the resolution of Naphtali and Zebulon that saves the nation. "They jeoparded their lives to the death."

Ten thousand men took the field; and, according to the plan of the campaign, moved stealthily through the mountain defiles towards the valley of Jezreel. Sisera, informed of the insurrection by the Kenites, marched, with horses and chariots, to the centre of this valley. From the curious conical hill of Tabor, which rises abruptly out of the centre, Barak saw the mighty host. "Up," cries Deborah, "this is the day. Is not Jehovah gone out before thee?"[2] It was a day of storm and flood. The Kishon, swollen and rapid, overflowed its banks, and the land was soft and boggy. Down from the heights poured the sons of Israel, the old shout of a king again ringing forth. They rushed through the plain and charged the enemy. The very "stars from their courses" seemed to fight for them. A tremendous thunderstorm broke over the plain, and huge hailstones were driven against the faces of the Canaanites, blinding and confusing them.[3] With ever increasing vigour, the Israelites shouted and charged. And, before their fierce onset, the ranks of the foe were parted; in the heavy clay the cavalry were impeded and the chariots were ineffectual. "The ancient torrent, the torrent Kishon swept them away"; and "then did the horsehoofs stamp by reason

---

[1] "By the water-courses of Reuben
There were great resolves of heart,
Why satest thou among the sheepfolds
To hear the piping for the flocks?
At the water-courses of Reuben
There were great searchings of heart."
Judg. v. 15, 16 (Revised Version).

[2] Judg. iv. 14.

[3] Josephus writes: "There came down from heaven a great storm, with a vast quantity of rain and hail, and the wind blew the rain in the face of the Canaanites and so darkened their eyes that their arrows and slings were of no advantage to them" ("Antiquities," chap. v.).

THE PROPHETESS OF THE NORTHERN TRIBES. 43

of the prancing, the prancing of their strong ones." The infantry turned and fled, and the rout was complete.[1] Sisera himself, leaving his chariot, fled on foot. The victorious Israelites gave hot chase—Barak pursuing even to the headquarters of Sisera. And so terrible was the slaughter that it seemed as if not a man was left.[2]

What of the Canaanitish general? Barak sought him, but he had escaped: and the story of the escape and of his end is one of the most picturesque and tragic incidents of the time when the Judges judged. A branch of the Kenites who accompanied Israel to Palestine and settled at the south, had migrated northward and planted itself as a Bedawin community in the valley of Jezreel.[3] It was in friendly relations with Jabin and his army; and to the tent of Heber, the chief, Sisera fled. Now comes the part of the drama in which the prediction that the full honours of the victory would be taken from Barak is fulfilled. It is the part which dims the lustre of the day. Studying the historian's narrative and the Song of Deborah, we see the flying warrior approaching the tent of Jael. Desperation leads him thither; for, as being the wife's home, it affords him a shelter more secure than that of her lord. None might enter the harem for purposes of violence. Jael goes out to meet him, and invites him to enter without fear. We are told of the care with which she covers him with her rug. He is faint and thirsty, and he asks water. She brings him cream[4] in "a lordly dish." Having partaken of her hospitality, he is safe to rest. And she bids him do so, herself consenting to stand as sentinel over him. Profound is the sleep of the weary

---

[1] The description of the battle and the victory in Deborah's song is "full of poetic fire and vivid dramatic effect—its striking characters thrown into high relief by the stroke or two of genius" (The Bishop of Bath and Wells, "Pulpit Commentary").

[2] Dean Stanley ("History of the Jewish Church," Lect. xiv.) traces the resemblances between this battle and the battle of Cressy, and the battle of Crimesus in Sicily, in which the Carthaginians were defeated by Timoleon.

[3] "Heber the Kenite had severed himself from the Kenites, and pitched his tent unto the plain of Zaanaim, rather 'unto the terebinth in Zaanaim,' which is by Kadesh" (Judg. iv. 11).

[4] Or butter, or curds. Josephus ("Antiquities," chap. v.) says, "She gave him sour milk, of which he drank so unnecessarily that he fell asleep."

man. We can imagine her gazing on him for a few moments—a struggle waging in her own heart between the sense of the rights of hospitality, and the impulse which seized her to avenge the wrongs of Israel. The impulse prevails ; and, taking the peg by which the tent is fastened to the ground, she puts "her hand to the nail and her right hand to the workmen's hammer, and with the hammer she smites Sisera, she smites through his head, piercing and striking through his temples, until at her feet he bows and falls down dead.[1] No more—thus the song plaintively proceeds—shall mother, looking through the lattice, greet her valiant son. She will ask why his chariot wheels tarry? and her ladies will answer—she herself will join them in saying, Surely he and his comrades are dividing the spoil, bringing back with them Hebrew maidens, and needle-work of divers colours. But soon, soon, all will know that the tarrying hero is dead. " So," concludes the song, " let all Thine enemies perish, O Lord ; but let them that love Him be as the sun when he goeth forth in his might."[2]

The Hebrew prophetess exclaims, "Blessed above women shall Jael, the wife of Heber the Kenite be, above women in the tent." The exclamation we cannot echo. Even from the Bedawin point of view, the conduct of the chieftainess is a violation of social custom in its most sacred place, "the *dakheel* or protection which is never sought in vain, and which, when once granted, is never dishonoured."[3] Nay, she had given him "the lordly dish,"[4] which was the pledge of peace and safety, and the pledge had been falsified. From a higher point of view, the conduct can only be condemned. But we must recollect whose the action is we are reviewing. It is that of a passionate Arab woman, whose conscience had not even the education of a Hebrew. Travellers have found that women, more eager in nature and more easily swayed by personal feeling than men, will more readily trample on tribal usage and accepted conventionalities.[5] And, in the case of Jael, there is a special feature to be taken into account. Her people were in

---

[1] Judg. v. 26, 27.   [2] Judg. v. 28-31.
[3] Kitto's " Daily Bible Illustrations," vol. ii. p. 353.
[4] "Among these people to give a person drink is to give a pledge of protection, even with life, against all danger and wrong " (Kitto, *ib.*).
[5] Lange, in his Commentary, cites Burckhardt as having had personal experience of this in his wanderings.

league with Jabin, she herself was in sympathy with Israel. And in this sympathy she reflected the ancient alliance of her race. The Kenite had become almost a part of the Hebrew nation. All her instincts, therefore, attracted her to the oppressed. She may or may not have been personally a believer in Israel's God. The probability is that she was. And, at all events, her election, as between Canaan and Israel, was decided. To her, Sisera was the ruthless tyrant, the violator of Hebrew homes, the man who had lifted himself proudly against Jehovah. And swiftly, sternly, she executed what she believed to be a righteous vengeance. She did it in a wrong way, but a high moral sentiment did not belong to her time or race. We can appreciate her courage, her intrepidity, and the faith which was its mainspring, even though we reprobate the means which she took to accomplish her end. And, whilst we censure her, let us take heed that a like courage, a like intrepidity, and a still higher faith, are the characteristics of our warfare as good soldiers of Jesus Christ

CHAPTER VI.

JEPHTHAH, THE HERO OF GILEAD.

The history of Gideon reserved for the concluding part of the volume—Gilead: its mountains and rich pastures: its forests and cities: its place in the literature and history of the nation—The backsliding of Israel into idolatry, and the period of servitude under the children of Ammon—The revival of national life and piety—The call to Jephthah, his character, and his surrounding in the land of Tob—Vows and human sacrifices among heathen peoples—The action taken by Jephthah; his vow; views concerning it; his daughter; the sacrifice; his future career, short and stormy—The strife between the Ephraimites and the Gileadites—"Shibboleth."

THE history of Gideon and his family follows that of Deborah and Barak. But, since the intention of this volume is to dwell at greater length on it than on any of the narratives in the Book of Judges, its consideration is reserved for the concluding part. The object aimed at is not so much to give the events of the period in orderly sequence as to present the portraits of the outstanding heroes of the period, recording their struggles and achievements when they waxed valiant in fight and subdued kingdoms. We overlook, then, for the present, the interval between the victory which has been traced, and the time of the Judge who was called to lead Israel in its effort to shake off the yoke of the Ammonites. The scene shifts to the eastern side of Jordan, to the region between the Sea of Chinnereth, afterwards known as the Sea of Galilee, and the Dead Sea, and vaguely designated Gilead.

The complaint of Deborah, in her review of the tribes and their response to the call of Barak, was that "Gilead abode beyond Jordan." Under the word Gilead were specially included Gad and the half tribe of Manasseh, to whom, in the distribution of the inheritance of Israel, the mountainous part of that country was assigned. The rich pasture land, "up to the point where it melts into the steppes of the wilderness,"

JEPHTHAH, THE HERO OF GILEAD.

remained in the possession of the sons of Ammon. From a small headland on its southern boundary, Moses surveyed that land of promise which he was not allowed to enter. The outlook north and west and south was magnificent; but no part of it equalled the view of Gilead.[1] Its whole extent northward to the Lake of Chinnereth could not, from any one point, be seen; but the portion visible was so fair that, in the words of Dean Stanley, "the wonder—it may be said, the thankfulness—is that the Israelites exchanged it for Palestine itself, inferior, as it might naturally have seemed to them, in every point except for the high purposes to which their permanent settlement on the eastern side of the Jordan would, humanly speaking, have wholly unfitted them."[2]

The land is now barren and solitary, the camping-ground of Bedawin; scarcely a hamlet, scarcely even a tree, breaking the monotony of the scene. But in the olden time it had forests; its plains and elevated plateaus were studded with villages, and the ruins which the traveller visits prove that for many centuries it was the dwelling-place of a large population, and the centre of a troubled but busy life. It has no mean place in the history and literature of the Chosen People. The most striking of the prophets—Elijah—was "of the inhabitants of Gilead,"[3] and his appearance and ways reflect the wild and rugged character of its inhabitants. Towards the oak-clad mountains near the Jabbok David fled when Absalom stole from him the hearts of the people; and among the most loyal of his friends were Barzillai the Gileadite and Rabbah of the children of Ammon.[4] One of the most tender and touching of Israel's songs is that of an exile in Gilead, familiar with the gazelle bounding from peak to peak, and panting in the summer heat, or when chased by the hunter, for the water-streams; an exile crying from some little hill, some Mizar, to God his Rock—the eye wandering to the distant Hermon, the ear hearing the roar of the rushing stream—and, with this strange environment, remembering God, and bidding the soul cast down within him be of good hope.[5]

---

[1] "The Lord showed him all the land of Gilead unto Dan and all Naphtali, and the land of Ephraim and Manasseh, and all the land of Judah unto the utmost sea, and the south, and the plain of the Valley of Jericho, the city of palm-trees, unto Zoar" (Deut. xxxiv. 1–3).
[2] "Sinai and Palestine," chap. viii.
[3] 1 Kings xvii. 1.
[4] 2 Sam. xvii. 27.
[5] Psa. xlii.

48 GIDEON AND THE JUDGES OF ISRAEL.

To one of the historical associations of Gilead our attention is now directed.

The tale of grievous backslidings into idolatry is one with which the reader of the history of Israel during the time of the Judges is only too familiar. But a specially heinous lapse occurred after the death of that Jair whose thirty sons possessed thirty cities in Gilead.[1] To adopt the language of St. Paul, since the Israelites "did not like to retain God in their knowledge, He gave them over to a reprobate mind."[2] The historian tells us that they paid homage to all the deities around—"to the Baalim and Ashtaroth, to the gods of Syria and the gods of Sidon, and the gods of Moab, and the gods of the children of Ammon, and the gods of the Philistines, and forsook the Lord and served Him not."[3] And, as the inevitable consequence of this evil-doing in the sight of Jehovah, they became the prey of the idolaters to whose worship they conformed. For eighteen years the tribes on the other side of the Jordan were oppressed by the Ammonites, moving on them from the east, and the Philistines, moving on them from the west, and preventing all intercourse between them and their brethren on the western side of the river.[4] At the end of these eighteen years, a further aggressive raid was organized by the Ammonites on the southern tribes of Judah and Benjamin, and the central tribe of Ephraim.[5] And, thus menaced, Israel awoke from its ignoble lethargy; "it was sore distressed"; and as, in times before and after, in its affliction there was originated the cry, "Come and let us return to the Lord, for He hath torn and He will heal us: He hath smitten, and He will bind us up."[6] Shiloh, which had been all but neglected for long years, was again visited by the princes and elders of the congregation; before the mercy-seat they prostrated themselves, beseeching the direction of the sacred oracle. That oracle had only, in the first instance, words of doom—"Go and cry unto the gods which ye have chosen. Let them deliver you in the time of your tribulation." But the goodness which expressed itself in the cry for help did not prove as the morning cloud or the early

---

[1] "The sixty or the thirty towns of Jair, the ancient chief of the tribe of Manasseh, were not called cities, but Bedouin villages or tents" (Stanley's "Sinai and Palestine," chap. viii).
[2] Rom. i. 28.   [3] Judg. x. 6.   [4] Judg. x. 7, 8.
[5] Judg x. 9.   [6] Hos. vi. 1.

JEPHTHAH, THE HERO OF GILEAD. 49

dew. The repentant congregation submitted to the judgment of Jehovah, put away the idols which had been harboured in its homes, and entered anew into covenant with its King. And in the quaint phraseology of the Chronicle, "the soul of Jehovah was shortened for the misery of Israel."[1]

The revived faith was the spring of a new determination. It was indeed a perilous time. Nothing less than the extinction of the independence of Israel and the wiping out of its name and traditions were threatened as the result of this Ammonite invasion. The hour for action had come—it was then or never. But who should, who could, lead the thousands of the people? A man of promptitude, of daring, of ready and various resource, was called for; where was this man to be found?

In a remote district called Tob, there lived a notorious freebooter, at the head of a company of "vain fellows," reckless, light-hearted, who would not conform to the ordinary conditions of life imposed by society. *Tob*—signifying "Good"—was a part of Syria, probably a fertile part, and capable of sustaining a large population. In the wars of David, we read of twelve thousand warriors who issued from its villages.[2] There, this freebooter with his merry men levied *black-mail* on the peaceful Syrians, or made foraging raids on the Ammonites, and their exploits were talked of when son of Israel spoke to son of Israel. In the emergency which had occurred, the thoughts of many travelled to the Syrian plains. There was no time for further delay. The dreaded Ammonites had been mobilised; they were encamped in Gilead; the children of Israel, gathered together in Mizpah, were threatened with extermination unless the captain was immediately found; and there seemed only one hope—this freebooter of Tob.

Who was he? and what had been his environment? Little of his personal history is related. His name was Jephthah or Jiphthah. He was the son of one who is spoken of as Gilead, and whom we may suppose to have been the prince or leading man of the country, and therefore by name identified with

---

[1] Judg. x. 11-16 (Revised Version).
[2] 2 Sam. x. 6-8. The country is there called Ish-Tob. "Tob is again mentioned in all probability in 1 Macc. v. 13; 2 Macc. xii. 17, and the *Thauba* of Ptolemy agrees in situation as well as in name with Tob, but no identification with any existing place has been hitherto effected" (Lord A. Hervey, "Pulpit Commentary, Judges," p. 119).

it.[1] But Jephthah had the bar-sinister across his escutcheon. His mother was a "stranger," or "another woman," an Aramean harlot; and this child of shame was cast out by those born in wedlock. Therefore, he had fled to his mother's country—to the land of Tob previously mentioned.[2] He had married, but his quiver had not been filled with children. An only daughter—his "*yehid*"[3]—was the apple of his eye, the joy of his home. A man he was, we may say, cast in a heroic mould, yet wanting in many of the finer and higher elements of heroism. Too much must not be expected from him. He had led a rough, lawless life—a life in which his two best friends were the sharp tongue and the sharp sword.[4] But we can discern glimpses of other qualities; caution, shrewdness, and tact, appear in his conduct, at least in the earlier period of his national leadership. He will not take the command until he has extracted a confession of the wrong which had been done to him, and a pledge of unfaltering devotion.[5] After assuming the command, he enters into negotiations with the oppressors. Before the arbitrament of the sword is invoked, the arts of peace are exhausted. The protocols exchanged between him and the king of the children of Ammon are interesting, not only as a confirmation of the previous records of the history of Israel, but as an exhibition of diplomacy which reflects credit on both parties. It is only when his appeal fails that Jephthah protests, "The Lord the Judge be judge this day between the children of Israel and the children of Ammon."[6]

To form a right estimate of the action of Jephthah so far as that is brought before us, we must recall his surrounding, with its manifold influence on his thought and character.

---

[1] "*Gilead begat Jephthah.*" It has been supposed that Gilead denotes merely the country; but this is inadmissible. The name refers to a person, although, in view of chap. x. 3, the words might imply no more than that Gilead was an ancestor of Jephthah. [2] Judg. xi. 1-3.

[3] Chap. xi. 34. Isaac also is called Abraham's "*yehid.*"

[4] "How much more intelligible does Jephthah become when we remember that he was raised up, not from the regular settlements of Judah and Ephraim, but from the half-civilized region of the Eastern tribes; in the wildness of his freebooting life, in the rashness and ignorance of his vow, in the savage vengeance which he exacted from the insolence of Ephraim—a Bedouin chief rather than an Israelitish judge" ("Sinai and Palestine," chap. viii.). [5] Judg. xi. 6-10. [6] Judg. xi. 12-28.

JEPHTHAH, THE HERO OF GILEAD.   51

The time in which he lived was, as we have seen, one of grievous apostasy from the covenant and the law of God. The sons and daughters of Israel "ran greedily" after the idolatries of the heathen peoples by whom they were encompassed. From the circumstances of birth and upbringing, the influence of these idolatries on Jephthah could not but be marked. The blood of "the strange woman," the heathen harlot, coursed in his veins. Separated, while still a young man, from his father's family, banished to a district in Syria, he was brought within the circle of Syrian and Ammonite superstitions; and these were mixed with a dim and confused knowledge of Jehovah, and a faith in Him as the national God of Israel. Probably, he was not fully instructed in the Mosaic system; he may have heard of, but he could not have been personally acquainted with, the worship of Shiloh, and its priesthood and its oracle. Whatever religion the fugitive to Tob—the head of a company of "vain fellows"—possessed must have been dominated by heathen notions and practices, many of them dark and cruel.

Of two such practices we are reminded in the narrative. Vows—special voluntary obligations tendered to the unseen Powers, on account of which special favours were expected—were common to all Oriental tribes. Their use among the descendants of Abraham is evidenced in the Holy Scriptures, for example, in that vow of Jacob on his way to the Hauran of which Bethel was the standing memorial,[1] and in the vow of Hannah at a later period.[2] The Law of Moses recognized the custom. It sanctioned the Nazarite vow of separation, and prescribed a ceremonial regarding it.[3] It ordained, as a general rule, that when a vow is vowed to the Lord, the devotee should not be slack to pay it, that what had once gone from the lips should be performed as a freewill offering, according to the terms of the vow.[4] The vow was a bond over the soul, and was not to be broken, except in cases which were distinctly defined.[5] In some cases commutation was allowed. Persons, houses, cattle, possessions, dedicated under some impulse to the sanctuary might, according to estimations that were fixed, be redeemed.[6] In re-

---
[1] Gen. xxviii. 19-22.   [2] 1 Sam. i. 10-11.   [3] Numb. vi.
[4] Numb. xxx. 2; Deut. xxiii. 21-22.
[5] *E.g.*, vows of women when disallowed by father or husband (Numb. xxx).
[6] Lev. xxvii. 2-25.

gard even to these, however, it was ordained that all that was given up to Jehovah "under a ban,"—a field which had gone out in the Jubilee, a creature, man or beast, which was doomed to destruction—could not be redeemed; it was inalienably consecrated.[1]

Vows were thus a part of the Israelite Economy, as well as of the heathen. But in the worships of Phœnicia, Syria, and Ammon, they were connected with another and ghastly observance—with human sacrifices. The offering of children to propitiate deities was an importation from Chaldea, which spread through Phœnician and other idolatries.[2] Captives and criminals were presented as burnt offerings. Sometimes, with a view to signal triumphs, or, to avert the wrath of the gods, or, as an act of peculiarly meritorious piety, a life—the best the worshipper could present—was vowed. With the varieties of this kind of devotion, the Hebrew was familiar. Apparently, the command to offer up his son Isaac did not seem to Abraham one utterly alien and repugnant to the thought of God. The giving of children to be passed through the fire to Moloch[3] was a temptation so great that most positive prohibitions and threatenings bearing on it were inserted in the Mosaic system.[4] At a later period, we find the prophets protesting against the prevalence of "this abomination," causing Judah to sin.[5] No doubt, in the time of Jephthah, the submission to the gods of Syria and Zidon and Ammon had infected the mind of the Israelite with the taint of this worst and most hideous way of heathenism. Jephthah himself had received it from his heathen surrounding in the land of Tob, and the effect of this reception appears when he takes the command of the armies of Israel.

Behold, then, this lawless, superstitious son of the strange

[1] Lev. xxvii. 28–29 "The word rendered 'devoted thing' is '*chèrem*,' as in ver 21. The primary meaning is something cut off or shut up. Its specific meaning in the Law is, that which is cut off from common use, and given up in some sense to Jehovah without the right of recall or commutation" ("Speaker's Commentary, Leviticus").

[2] "Porphyry quoted by Eusebius ('Præp. Evang.' iv. 16) says: 'The Phœnicians, in all great emergencies of war or famine or drought, used to designate by vote one of their nearest and dearest as a sacrifice to Saturn, and their descendants, the Carthaginians, sacrificed their finest children to the same god'" ("Speaker's Commentary, Judges").

[3] A notable instance of this is found in 2 Kings iii. 27.

[4] Lev. xviii. 21; xx. 2.   [5] Jer. xxxii. 34–35; Amos v. 26.

woman welcomed as head over all the inhabitants of Gilead. The elders of the people pledge their faith to him whom, a few years before, they had banished; the people confirm their election; and at Mizpah, the watch-tower of the tribes, the words of the covenant between them and their captain are solemnly repeated before Jehovah.[1] The negotiations with "the king of the children of Ammon," already alluded to, follow. And, when these negotiations fail, and the judgment of the Eternal is appealed to, the campaign begins.[2] "The Spirit of the Lord," says the historian, "came upon Jephthah" —in this sentence embodying the conviction of every pious Israelite, that the heroes who delivered his nation from the enemy were filled with a supernatural strength, fitting them for the work given them to do. The new leader traversed Gilead and Manasseh, summoning their thousands to arms, and, returning with those who obeyed the summons—to Mizpah, he organized his force, and "passed over" to the territory in which the children of Ammon awaited the attack.[3]

It was a critical hour. He led men whom a long period of servitude had demoralized, and who were ill-provided with implements of war; and it was consistent with his education and temper that, at such a time, and with such material, when brought face to face with a great host flushed with the sense of the power exercised for many years over the prostrate Hebrews, he should fortify his resolution by propitiating Jehovah with a solemn vow. A vow terribly, fatally rash— one that clouded the day, and blighted the fruits, of victory. Lifting his hand to the heavens, he swore, "If Thou wilt indeed deliver the children of Ammon into mine hand, then it shall be that whatsoever cometh forth of the doors of my house to meet me, when I return in peace from the children of Ammon, shall be the Lord's, and I will offer it up for a burnt offering."[4]

Assuring himself thus of the Divine favour, he led his army to the fight. No details of that bloody war are given; we are told merely that he smote the heathens from Aroer, close to Jordan, to Minnith, sacking twenty cities, and sweeping the region as far as a place which cannot now be identified, but then called Abel-Cheramim[5]—the meadow of the vineyards—

[1] Judg. xi. 6–11.   [2] Judg. xi. 12–27.   [3] Judg. xi. 28, 29.
[4] Judg. xi. 30–31.   [5] Judg. xi. 32–33.

"with a very great slaughter." The triumph was complete; "the children of Ammon were subdued before the children of Israel."

And now comes the tragic part of the story. Radiant were the countenances of the Israelites as, with the proud consciousness that they and their fellows were again free men, they approached the famous watch-tower; radiant all—their bold captain alone excepted. We can imagine the shadow on his countenance caused by the recollection of the awful vow. Who, what would issue from the doors of his house to meet him? The portion of the narrative relating to this anxiety must be specially regarded; in it culminates the interest which attaches to the career of Jephthah.

The incident so graphically presented has been a stumbling-block to many. They have been unable to reconcile it, when interpreted according to its more obvious meaning, with the inspiration ascribed to the head over Gilead, and they have felt that its inhumanity, as thus interpreted, is a dark and foul stain on the religion of Israel. We can dismiss the one part of this objection, by observing that it proceeds on an exaggerated view of the phrase, "The Spirit of the Lord came upon Jephthah." For certainly this is not to be held as implying that he was endowed with a high and extraordinary illumination or holiness; it is to be held as implying only that he was fitted with the courage and wisdom essential to a successful campaign. And the second part of the objection has been sufficiently answered by the sketch of the heinous backsliding of Israel, in consequence of which its thought and life had been tainted by heathenish practices—of which human sacrifice was one—and more particularly of the influence of these practices on Jephthah, who had spent so many years in the midst of heathenism, and as the chief of a band of Syrian outlaws.

Those who would soften the harshness of the view generally taken suggest some ingenious explanations of the vow. It is to be feared that these explanations are more ingenious than ingenuous. It has been urged, for instance, that there is no need to suppose that Jephthah contemplated more than the offering of an animal—*that* which should come out of the doors of his house. But it is difficult to conceive that the presentation of one of his herd of cattle would be the matter of so solemn an obligation, and assuredly it is a stretch of language—quite con-

JEPHTHAH, THE HERO OF GILEAD. 55

trary to Scripture use—to suppose that he would speak of a bullock as issuing from his dwelling "to meet him." It is urged again, that the vow may be so read as to include in it two acts: "that which cometh forth from the doors of the house to meet me shall be devoted to the Lord, *and* I will offer *Him* a burnt offering."[1] The one clause expresses what would be done to the person—slave or member of the household—who would issue from the house: that person, if a male, would be devoted to Jehovah as a priest, if a female, would be devoted as a virgin; and the second clause pledges that besides this a burnt offering would be offered. This rendering is wholly inadmissible. It is, to begin with, a misreading of the text. The last clause may be translated: "*Or* I will offer it;"[2] but it cannot be translated, "And I will offer Him, that is, the Lord, a burnt offering." And in the next place the significance given to the phrase, "Shall be the Lord's," or "shall be devoted to the Lord," is evolved out of the consciousness of the critic; it is one which we cannot imagine to have been in the mind of him who vowed.[3] An honest exegesis must accept the view which Lord Arthur Hervey has briefly stated, "If the words 'shall surely be the Lord's' had stood alone, Jephthah's vow might have been understood like Hannah's; but these which follow preclude any other meaning than that Jephthah contemplated a human sacrifice."[4] His word is general—a slave, one of his household, but a human being, the first who came to meet him.[5]

That first person is his daughter—his only child. Following

[1] This rendering was proposed by an American divine, Dr. Randolph, towards the end of the eighteenth century, and has since been zealously advocated by Bishop South, Dr. Hewlett, and others. Bishop South speaks of it as having "perfectly cleared up a difficulty which, for two thousand years, has puzzled all the translators and expositors."

[2] So in the margin of the Authorized Version of the Bible.

[3] The hypothesis of Jephthah's daughter having been devoted as a nun is described by Dean Stanley as "contrary to the plain meaning of the text, contrary to the highest authorities of the Church, contrary to all the usages of the Old Dispensation" ("Lectures on the Jewish Church," Lect. xvi.).

[4] "Speaker's Commentary, Judges."

[5] Jephthah's vow and the manner in which it was fulfilled have been the occasion of "dissertations without number and endless discussions among the learned." It was not until the twelfth Christian century that the reference to a human sacrifice and the death of the daughter were questioned.

the precedent of Miriam,[1] the sister of Moses, she put herself at the head of her maidens, to receive him "with timbrels and with dances." They strike the timbrel, they execute the dance, perhaps to the music of the exalted strain of Moses, "The Lord is my strength and song, and He is become my salvation: He is my God: and I will prepare Him an habitation; my father's God, and I will exalt Him. The Lord is a Man of War: the Lord is His name." Joyous and light in step she approaches him. "But why, father, the cloud, dark as night itself, which spreads over thy countenance? Why, father, the sadness, the averted face, the downcast eye, the tear that flows down thy cheek, on this day of gladness and deliverance?" So the hero's *Yehid*, his only one, his darling, asks. And the answer is returned in the robe rent and the exceeding bitter cry, "Alas, my daughter! thou hast brought me very low, and thou art one of them that trouble me; for I have opened my mouth unto the Lord, and I cannot go back."[2]

Why this agony? Persons who give the milder interpretation of the vow which has been noticed understand that its cause was the thought of the lifelong seclusion of the daughter—involving separation even from him and his home—and of her entire consecration to God. They urge that her request to be let alone two months that she may go up and down on the mountains is explained by herself in the words, "And bewail my virginity, I and my fellows." To a Hebrew woman childlessness was the saddest of conditions; and, in the time of reprieve asked for, they see the natural working of a submissive but a stricken heart. These two months to pour out its sorrow, unchecked and unhindered, and school the unwilling mind into acceptance of the fate—it is for this that she pleads. And, at the close of this period, she returns, and is solemnly and deliberately dedicated to the service of Jehovah. This we are invited to regard as her sacrifice, for the rehearsing and celebration of which the daughters of Israel were wont to assemble four days in each year.

The obvious significance of the historian's language, and the consensus of opinion with reference to it, from Josephus to the

Rabbi David Kimchi was the first to challenge the traditional view. Principal Douglas, in his Handbook for Bible Classes, argues in favour of a lifelong surrender of the daughter to Jehovah's service (pp. 63–66).

[1] Exod. xv. 20.   [2] Judg. xi. 34, 35.

present time, prevent, as has been said, the acceptance of this rendering. It is to an actual human sacrifice that we are pointed;[1] and all that is written as to daughter and sire harmonizes with this view. If the daughter was doomed to perpetual virginity, there seems no special reason for asking a two months' space to bewail it. But, on the supposition that her life must go for her father's victory, there is a touching pathos in the opportunity for lamentation craved. It was the bitterness of the fate, that no child would think of her as mother, and no son would continue the name and fame of her father. Tennyson has, with exquisite tenderness, interpreted the feeling—

> "My God, my Land, my Father—these did move
> Me from my bliss of life that nature gave,
> Lowered softly with a threefold cord of love,
> Down to a silent grave.
>
> And I went mourning, 'No fair Hebrew boy
> Shall smile away my maiden blame among
> The Hebrew mothers'; emptied of all joy,
> Leaving the dance and song."[2]

The time of mourning ended, there is the execution of the awful vow. We blame Jephthah for the rashness betrayed in the opening of his mouth to the Lord. His promise was forbidden by law; as the Jewish historian declares, "It was neither conformable to the law, nor acceptable to God;"[3] and the rash vow might have been redeemed.[4] But he was a more than half heathen man; he had been a rough "soldier of a brutalized age." And, condemning his oath and his act,[5] we must at the same time remember his antecedents, and his ignorance. "No Levite or other sage arises to give a direction to his conscientious resolve, for it is evident that his contemporaries, also trained to barbarism, considered the precious sacrifice to be appointed by a higher necessity to fall for the

[1] "We see no alternative but to conclude, although we would gladly avail ourselves of any fair ground of escape from that conclusion, that he offered her up in sacrifice" (Kitto, "Daily Bible Illustrations").

[2] "A Dream of Fair Women." [3] "Antiquities" bk. v. chap. 7.

[4] Lev. xxvii. 1-8. Jephthah's daughter was not devoted under a ban or curse, as in Lev. xxvii. 28.

[5] "Jephthah's vow, taken in the sense in which that transaction is commonly understood, was not binding; because the performance, in that contingency, became unlawful" (Paley's "Moral Philosophy," chap. v.).

sins of the fatherland. And when such a belief pervades even the best, the courage which shrinks not from acting or suffering in obedience to it, must be accounted greatness of soul."[1]

Very sad, most tragic indeed is the end. There is a fine reticence in the words of the sacred book. They remind us of the veiled words as to Judas Iscariot—"He went to his own place." A curtain is drawn, as it were, between the mind and the awfulness of the catastrophe. "She returned unto her father, who did with her according to his vow which he had vowed."[2] This is all—as if, in the language of Dean Stanley, the writer averted his eyes from the end.

The story is one which touches the emotion, which appeals to the imagination, of the reader. Other narratives bearing features of resemblance to it are found in Greek mythology.[3] Goethe has woven one of these narratives into a drama of singular force and beauty. Diana was offended with the god-like Agamemnon, and to propitiate the irate goddess, he vowed to offer to her the most beautiful creature born in his household during the year. This was his daughter, Iphigenia. The payment of the vow was delayed from year to year, but the day came when the king was reminded that it must no longer be deferred. Behold, on the altar of sacrifice on which the fair young life was to be laid, a hind in her stead. Diana had carried her off to Tauris—

> "Which had before, each stranger's heart appall'd,
> For till her coming none e'er trod the realm
> But fell according to an ancient rite
> A bloody victim at Diana's shrine."[4]

There she was consecrated as virgin-priestess in the shrine, and there she remained until Orestes, her brother, discovered her

---

[1] Ewald's "History of Israel," vol. ii.

[2] "Let not the reader, however, take up the absurd fancy of the painters that this deed was perpetrated by the high-priest at the altar of God. The high-priest would have known his duty better" (Kitto's "Bible Illustrations").

[3] As, in the "Iliad," Idomeneus of Crete vowed to sacrifice whatever should first meet him in Crete. The first person who met him was his own son. He kept his vow, but was punished with a plague and was banished by the people. See also "The Antigone of Sophocles."

[4] Goethe's "Iphigenia in Tauris," Act 1, Scene 2.

and bore her back to Attica. Between this legend and the Hebrew tale, there are parallels of feeling. But the Hebrew tale is one of incomparably loftier and purer tone. We see the conflict in the heart of Jephthah's daughter—the bitter grief, the clinging to life, the wail over the cutting off of her days in youth and maidenhood, and yet the heroic submission, the sweet and willing response to her father's will, the piety, mistaken but therefore all the more to be noted, which blended with patriotism in her resolve—"My father, if thou hast opened thy mouth unto the Lord, do to me according to that which has proceeded out of thy mouth; forasmuch as the Lord hath taken vengeance for thee of thine enemies, even of the children of Ammon."[1] It is this willing self-devotion which lights up the transaction—ghastly as it is—with a beauty which suggests the day of Christ. It is not "a slaughter of an unwilling victim as when Gaul and Greek were buried alive in the Roman forum." We realize the sacrifice on the part of both the offerer and the offered; the terrible self-immolation—because the immolation of his heart—of Jephthah, as he does to her according to the vow; the lovely self-surrender of the daughter as she yields, not in wrath, not in the wildness of despair, but as one bound by "the threefold cord of love—my God, my Land, my Father." Another poet than Tennyson has painted the scene in his glowing verse—

I.

"Since our country's our God—oh, my sire!
Demand that thy daughter expire;
Since the triumph was bought by thy vow,
Strike the bosom that's bared for thee now!

II.

And the voice of my mourning is o'er,
And the mountains behold me no more:
If the hand that I love lay me low,
There cannot be pain in the blow!

III.

And of this, oh, my father! be sure—
That the blood of thy child is as pure
As the blessing I beg ere it flow,
And the last thought that soothes me below

[1] Judg. xi. 36.

IV.

Though the virgins of Salem lament,
Be the judge and the hero content!
I have won the great battle for thee,
And my father and country are free.

V.

When this blood of thy giving hath gush'd,
When the voice that thou lovest is hush'd,
Let my memory still be thy pride,
And forget not I smiled as I died."[1]

Jephthath judged Israel for only six years. It is not too much to suppose that his life was both embittered and shortened by the tragedy which made his home in Mizpah desolate. One event of the later years is related—an event which forms a sad, but suggestive, sequel to the deliverance which had been wrought in Israel.

Ephraim, the central tribe, had acquired a position in Israel which encouraged an overbearing spirit; and this spirit was manifested in an offensive attitude towards Jephthah. "There is scarcely any one," says La Rochefoucauld, "who does not show ingratitude for great obligations." The most black and ungenerous ingratitude was shown by the men of Ephraim. They had taken no part in the strife with the children of Ammon; and, after the armies of the valiant captain had been successful, they assemble *en masse*, and move northward,[2] demanding, "Wherefore passedst thou over to fight against the children of Ammon, and didst not call us to go with thee? we will burn thine house upon thee with fire." Poor Jephthah—heart-broken, his house silent, the light of his hearth extinguished by worse than fire!—this fills up the measure of his sorrow. He had not deserved a reproach and a threat such as those by which he was assailed. His answer, although sharp in tone, is marked by dignity. He had given the haughty Ephraimites the opportunity of helping in the war. They had declined it, leaving him and his people to do battle alone with the enemy. "Wherefore then," he rejoins, "are ye

---

[1] Lord Byron's "Hebrew Melodies."

[2] The word rendered "Northward" in chapter xii. 1, may also be rendered "to Zaphon," a city mentioned (Josh. xiii. 27) along with Succoth. Apparently the object of the movement was to cross the Jordan at the fords of Succoth.

JEPHTHAH, THE HERO OF GILEAD.

come against me this day to fight against me?"[1] But remonstrance is in vain, and, for the most miserable of causes, there ensues a fierce and bloody contention. The statement of the historian is that "there fell forty-two thousand Ephraimites at the passages of Jordan."[2] The melancholy story justifies two remarks of the Wise Man. He says that "a brother offended is harder to be won than a strong city, and their contentions are as the bars of a castle;"[3] and again he says that "the beginning of strife is as when one letteth out water."[4]

Of all wars, the most terrible are civil wars. For "to be wroth with one we love doth work like madness in the brain." It is a fearful madness that is set before us in the few sentences which record the battle between the men of Gilead and the men of Ephraim—

> "Each spake words of high disdain
> And insult to his heart's best brother."[5]

The infuriating taunt is one at whose interpretation we can only guess. "The men of Gilead smote Ephraim because they said, Ye Gileadites are fugitives of Ephraim among the Ephraimites and among the Manassites." Apparently, the sneer conveyed was that the army of Jephthah was composed of fugitives of Ephraim and Manasseh. The words bore the insult to the brother; and the hand at once grasped the sword. The question has been put, Where were the priests? They might have prevented the catastrophe. They might have prevented the vow of Jephthah, and this last recorded action of his reign. Where were they indeed during all the stormy time between the death of Phinehas and the days of Eli? Certainly the Urim and Thummim has no visibility in connection with the hot and senseless controversy of the exasperated peoples of Gad and Ephraim.

---

[1] Judg. xii. 2, 3.
[2] Judg. xii. 6. "It is possible that the war between Jephthah and the Ephraimites may have lasted a considerable time, though only the single incident of the slaughter at the fords of Jordan is mentioned, so that the large number of forty-two thousand men may be less improbable than it seems at first sight. There is, however, always some doubt as to the correctness of numbers" (Lord A. Hervey in "Pulpit Commentary").
[3] Prov. xviii. 19.   [4] Prov. xvii. 14.   [5] Coleridge's "Christabel."

"The Gileadites took the passage of Jordan before the Ephraimites; and it was so that when those Ephraimites who were escaped, said, Let me go over, that the men of Gilead said unto him, Art thou an Ephraimite? If he said nay, then said they unto him, Say now Shibboleth; and he said Sibboleth, for he could not frame to pronounce it right. Then they took him and slew him at the passages of Jordan."[1] In this incident we recognize a suggestion which Christendom has not been slow to appropriate.

The word Shibboleth has a twofold meaning. It means either an *ear of* corn or a *stream*. It may possibly have been the name of a stream at or near the passages of Jordan. There is another Hebrew term *Sibboleth*, signifying *a burden;* and the curious feature is that the Ephraimite was unable to distinguish in pronunciation between the two terms. He did not frame to pronounce the *sh* right. Linguistic differences analogous to that which at once tested the man of Ephraim are not uncommon. The Northumbrian is known by his burr. Dialectic variations between different parts of the same country are most marked. Few Englishmen can pronounce in Scotch fashion the *ch*, as in the name Auchtermuchty. *Sh* is entirely wanting in some languages. And its introduction into the country beyond Jordan, whilst it was unknown on the western side is "an evidence of the sound having passed into the Hebrew from the east of Jordan, possibly from the Arabians with whom the sound is common: at least, if we suppose the Ephraimitic pronunciation to be that of the nine and a half tribes. The *sh* may have been as impossible for an Ephraimite to pronounce as *th* is to a Frenchman."[2]

We speak of the Shibboleths of sects and parties. Have not many controversies which separate Christian from Christian, making them "like cliffs which have been rent asunder, a dreary sea flowing between," originated in verbal strifes gendering a heat as unreasonable, but as intense, as that which reddened the fords of the Jordan with the best blood of Israel? Are there not differences, often passing into separations, referable to circumstances and associations which have given a determination to modes of thought and speech analogous to that betrayed in the pronunciations of Ephraim and Gilead? Are not the unions of Christians too frequently

[1] Judg. xii. 6.   [2] "Speaker's Commentary, Judges."

exclusive of all who cannot give the accent or inflection which they give to some dogma, who cannot frame to pronounce some test-word right? The Shibboleth men have seized the passages and cast out the Sibboleth men during all the centuries. " Hold what we hold, speak as we speak ; or, Anathema"—thus the spirit of intolerance and persecution has thundered in the past; and the mutters of the thunder may still be heard. Would that Christians more fully realized the Apostle's saying, " God hath given us the spirit of power and of love and of a sound mind ; " and better obeyed the Apostle's precept, " Follow after charity."

CHAPTER VII.

SAMSON, THE HERO OF DAN.

The territory of Dan—the Philistines: Their origin and early history—The form of their idolatry—Their national character—The period and scene of Samson's judgeship—The prophetical forecasts of Dan—The completeness of the biography as contrasted with that of other judges—The nature of the story of his life and exploits—Zorah—The appearances of the man of God to Manoah's wife and to Manoah and his wife. With regard to these appearances, three points—The Nazarite vow and the institution of the Nazarite order—Mahaneh-Dan—Timnath, and what happened in connection with it—The Rock of Etam, and what happened in connection with it—The authority afterwards conceded to Samson—Gaza and its gates—Enhakkore—The Valley of Sorek—The treachery, and what followed—Milton and his "Samson Agonistes"—The climax of the tragedy, and what it suggests.

FOLLOWING the stream of the history of Israel, we pass from the far north, from Mizpah, and the green forests of Gilead, and the fords of the Jordan, to the territory occupied by the southern tribes, and the maritime plain which was distinguished as the Shephelah, or Low Country. The children of Dan were settled between this Shephelah and the wilderness of Judah. Their land—bounded in the rear by barren hills, and contracted in front by the Philistine principalities, which intercepted the communication with the sea—was so circumscribed that, as we have seen, an extensive migration northward was rendered necessary. And their situation, inconvenient at best, was rendered perilous by the hostility of the Philistines who owned the rich cornfields and the pasturage of the sea-board. It is to the struggle against this hostility of the remarkable man, in whose prowess the tribe of Dan emerges from obscurity, that our attention is now directed.

Who were the Philistines? It is a curious fact that the

whole area conquered and inhabited by Israel received its name from the narrow strip which belonged to them. Palestine is the land of the Philistines. The explanation, probably, is that, being the people located near the shore of the Mediterranean, the Greeks formed their acquaintance, and called the unknown interior by their name. They were aliens to the Holy Commonwealth. Their origin and their early history cannot be made clear. They were "strangers," or "wanderers." In the genealogy of the sons of Noah they are set before us as a Hamitic race, and as issuing from an Egyptian stock. From Mizraim, which is undoubtedly Egypt, several peoples or tribes are represented as springing; and among them we read, "Casluhim (out of whom came Philistim) and Caphtorim." We need not discuss who the Casluhim and the Caphtorim were. It is to be observed that the Prophetical Books of the Old Testament associate the Philistines with Caphtor rather than Casluhim. Jeremiah calls them "a remnant of the isle of Caphtor."[1] It has been conjectured that this isle or maritime region was Cappadocia;[2] again, that it was Cyprus;[3] and again that it was Crete;[4] the last of these conjectures being strengthened by the designation of Cherethites given in the Old Testament to the Philistines.[5] Another meaning has, however, been found for the term: Caphtor is said to be identical with Capht-ur, the Great Capt. Egypt is probably Ar-Capt, or the coast of Capt; and the Capht-ur might be the northern delta of Egypt.[6]

Be this as it may, the Philistines were not Phœnician. They were not akin to the Hebrews. Possibly, the warlike race which confronted the Israelites was a composite race. The identification of Caphtor with the Egyptian delta gives plausibility to the conjecture that from the Philistines sprang the Shepherd Dynasty who conquered Lower Egypt about the time of Abraham. When the Hyksos were expelled, a large company of refugees may have fled into the rich pastural and corn-growing territory of the Avim and settled there, intermarrying with the Avim.[7]

[1] Amos ix. 7; Jeremiah xlvii. 4.   [2] The Targums and old versions.
[3] Michaelis and Rosenmuller.   [4] Calmet and others.
[5] 1 Sam. xxx. 11. David's body-guard was composed of the Cherethites and Pelethites (2 Sam. xxiii. 23. Ewald thinks that the Pelethites were Philistines.   [6] "Speaker's Commentary," Genesis, p. 91.
[7] Deut. ii. 23.

Certainly, the nation which oppressed Israel with its five satrapies and five cities, its gigantic men, and its great hosts, was immensely more numerous and formidable than the tribe, with its Abimelech, or Royal Father, and its chief captain, Phichol, which entered into leagues with Abraham, the wandering sheikh, as with a prince of importance and power.[1]

The idolatrous Philistines had some features in common with Phœnicia. But their idolatry was in many respects different. Their chief idols were a fish-god (Dagon) and a fish-goddess (Derceto), whose temples were in Ashdod, Ascalon, and Gaza, and a god of flies (Baalzebub), whose temple was in Ekron. There were priesthoods, and there were oracles. The idols were solemnly borne with their armies. In their honour great festivals were held. To the Israelites the Philistines were "the uncircumcised"; and, if an Egyptian origin is ascribed to them, this proves that their separation from Mizraim, where circumcision was practised, must have been at an early date. Though Hamitic, their language was largely Semitic; at all events, we can infer that the Hebrews could converse with them. They were a dull people, fierce in war, but wanting in enterprise. Although owners of the coast of the Mediterranean, they were not, like the Phœnicians, given to commerce. They were content with their low country, and their walled cities, and their raids into Israelite territory. At the time when our narrative opens they were the masters of the south—of Simeon, Dan, and Judah.

The precise time with which the biography of Samson connects we cannot determine. His judgeship may not have been immediately in succession to those mentioned in the chapter next before that which takes us to Zorah. It may have been during the later years of Elon's ascendancy in North Palestine, and of Abdon's in Ephraim. His exploits and influence were limited to the south of Palestine. It was there that "he began to deliver Israel."

Two forecasts of Dan occur in the early books of Scripture. Jacob, blessing his sons, predicted that Dan would "judge his people as one of the tribes of Israel, and that he would be as a serpent by the way, an adder in the path that biteth the horse's heels, so that his rider shall fall backward;"[2] and Moses, regarding the future of the tribes from his experience of their

[1] Gen. xxi. 22.   [2] Gen. xlix. 16, 17.

SAMSON, THE HERO OF DAN.

character, declared that Dan was "a lion's whelp, whose leap would be from Bashan."[1] We saw the fulfilment of this latter prediction in the fierce raid of the Danites on Laish, "the city which dwelt secure," and their seizure, by force of arms, of a northern territory. In the sketch of Samson's career we find the accomplishment of the old patriarch's picture; through Samson, the tribe becomes, for a brief space, a judge of the people. In him, too, is realized the quick, venomous bite, as of the rattlesnake, which makes the rider and his horse fall backward.

The sovereignty of God is manifest in the selection of His instruments. This Samson—this Israelite Hercules—is not the person whom pious minds would have chosen as the hero to fill the largest place in the Book of Judges. Of its twenty-one chapters, four are devoted to the record of his freaks and exploits. For all that marks permanent results he is far below the level of Gideon and Barak and Jephthah. But he is the only judge whose biography is given from the birth to the death. In the Old Testament there are only two persons whose birth is solemnly announced beforehand. Isaac, the son of Abraham, is the one; he is the other; and in his case there is an extraordinary circumstantiality in the announcement. The narrative throughout is remarkable for explicitness of detail. His quirks and quips, his irony, his grim laughter, as well as his feats of strength, are duly recorded; and, as has been observed, "there is no deliverer of whom are reported so many weaknesses or so many miracles."[2] The story is strange and fantastic—one over which we smile and sigh, one of boisterous mirth and tearful sorrow—such wit and such folly, such force and such feebleness, comedy so grotesque and tragedy so awful! As the tale proceeds, the moral interest is overshadowed by the mere prowess of the athlete; and perhaps it is to the admiration excited in the popular mind by athletic fame that we owe the preservation of so many of the traditions concerning him. With regard to his work as judge, the sacred historian tersely expresses the truth—"He began to deliver Israel." With him came a new hopefulness to the oppressed Israelites. There is something grand, after all, in the attitude he assumed. No trumpet-blast summoned the thousands of the tribes to his banner. He stood

[1] Deut. xxxiii. 22. [2] Bishop Hall's "Contemplations."

alone. Nothing daunted him; his brawny arm could rend the lion like a kid, or slay hundreds with the jawbone of an ass. He ventured fearlessly, rashly, into all kinds of perilous situations; and, except where women betrayed him, came unscathed through all. His name was "the Sunny;"[1] and a kind of wild, free sunniness of nature distinguished him in all the struggle. "In a state of universal depression," it has been remarked, "all must depend on the indomitable strength which is aroused in individuals."[2] He was the man to arouse that strength. He turned the laugh against the Philistines. He showed the Philistine up in his stolidity, his blind idolatry, the cowardice behind all the bullying. He bade his brethren be of good cheer. He himself, unaided, proved what could be done by individuals. And thus far he not only judged, but "began to deliver Israel."

The more sad, therefore, is the catastrophe to which the life-story hastens. The deliverer from the Philistines is himself manacled by the Philistines. He who saved others himself perished. He who feared not the face of man "gives up his fort of silence to a woman." He can carry the gates of a city away; the gates of the citadel of his own soul are carried away, and he himself is made a captive by Satan. God's Nazarite is the devil's slave. And thus he who began never completed his work. The column was broken in the middle. The story ends with a comma and a dash, blistered over by a tear. For the light is turned into darkness; and how great is the darkness!

We are introduced by the sacred historian to a worthy couple in a city on the borderland between Dan and Judah. It was then called Zorah; it is now known as Surah—one of a cluster of sacred sites around Beit-Jibrîn, the ancient Eleutheropolis—a mountain village with a rocky and rugged surrounding.[3] There lived Manoah, whom Josephus describes as a man of extraordinary virtue and the principal man of the place, but with one weakness—an extraordinary jealousy of his beautiful wife, shown when she told him of the visit

---

[1] Samson (Heb., Shimshon). Josephus says the "name signifies one that is strong.' It may be derived from *Shemesh* (the sun), or from Shamam (to lay waste). [2] Ewald's "History," vol. ii. p. 399.
[3] See" Land and Book," Southern Palestine, chap. viii.

SAMSON, THE HERO OF DAN.

of the angel.[1] The scriptural statement, free from all such glosses, presents to us a simple, God-fearing man, an Israelite indeed, and his spouse, whom God had not blessed with children. To her, one day—so runs the narrative—appeared an angel of the Lord. In dress and manner he resembled a prophet; but his countenance was very terrible—

> "In his face
> Terror and sweetness laboured for the place.
> Sometimes his sun-bright eyes would shine so fierce
> As if their pointed beams would even pierce
> The soul, and strike the amaz'd beholder dead:
> Sometimes their glory would disperse and spread
> From easy flame, and like the star that stood
> O'er Bethlehem, promise and portend some good;
> Mix't was his bright aspect, as if his breath
> Had equal errands both of life and death:
> Glory and mildness seemed to contend
> In his fair eyes."[2]

She did not venture to ask whence or who he was. But he gave her the astounding news that she would yet know the pains and joys of motherhood, and he prescribed the Nazarite vow for the child to be born. Manoah did not doubt or deny the vision; he only asked that the tidings borne by his wife should be supplemented by fuller information as to the upbringing of the promised son. The prayer, "Let the man of God whom Thou didst send come again," is answered; and the interview granted, with the words spoken and the things done, is related at length. It was closed by an act of sacrifice—a burnt-offering and a meal-offering laid on a rock—and He who had said that His name is Wonderful did wondrously. Passing out of sight, enwrapped by the consuming fire, Manoah and his wife fell on their faces to the ground. And, connected with this prostration, there is a sagacity, even a nimbleness of wit, in the reply of the wife to her husband's exclamation, "We shall surely die, because we have seen God," which reminds

---

[1] The angel is represented by Josephus as "a young man beautiful and tall. . . . The wife showed so great admiration of the beauty and tallness that her husband was astonished and out of himself for jealousy" ("Antiquities," book v. chap. 8).

[2] Quarles, "History of Samson," quoted by Kitto in "Daily Bible Readings,"

us of qualities afterwards illustrated in the son. "If the Lord were pleased to kill us," she answered, "He would not have received a burnt-offering and a meal-offering at our hands. Neither would He have shewed us all these things, nor would, as at this time, have told us such things as these."[1]

It is asserted that "the angel of the Lord did no more appear to Manoah and his wife." To many, the one appearance recorded is "a stumbling-stone and rock of offence." Of course, in the view of all who put the miraculous aside, it is nothing else than a piece of legendary lore. But some who allow to miracle a place in God's government of the universe, and who accept it in connection with Biblical narrative, are puzzled over this particular theophany, related with exceptional copiousness of detail. Does the manner of Samson's life, or does the importance of Samson's mission warrant it? Now, with regard to this, three points may be urged. First, the lessons of the life are immeasurably intensified by the evidence of the greatness to which it was destined. Samson was not a man whose force should have been spent in mere feats, wild and irregular. It is the contrast between the development of the career and the truth of the consecration which lies in the background, that elicits at once our sorrow and our indignation. The mark for the prize of his calling had been foreshadowed in the most striking possible form even before his birth; and we grieve and protest when we see him failing to reach the mark and obtain the prize. The more extraordinary is his designation to a lofty place, the more pathetic and instructive is the record of the fall. Farther, there are peculiarities in his career which imply specially providential circumstances. He is born after all expectation of a son had ceased. He is laid under the Nazarite vow from the moment of birth. That vow was sometimes taken for periods longer or shorter; but seldom indeed was it perpetual — one which comprehended the person, babe and man. He is not the sort of person in whom the austerities of the Nazarite might have been expected: they were contrary to the whole bent of his nature. And, as has been remarked, "whilst he keeps his vow of abstinence from intoxication, he is all the weaker and bolder with regard to the love of woman, as if he would here make up for the want of freedom elsewhere."[2] That a creature such as he—"the most frolicsome, irregular,

[1] Judg. xiii. 2-22.   [2] Ewald's "History,' vol. ii.

uncultivated, that the nation ever produced "—should have been bound by the most strict consecration, should, moreover, have been consciously dependent for his giant-strength on this consecration, requires to be accounted for; and the story of the man of God, whose countenance was terrible, and whose name was Wonderful, with his charge to both father and mother, is all that we have to account for it. Finally, though the work of Samson was left incomplete, it was, in itself, one which needed the support of an extraordinary vocation. Admit his marvellous physical strength, we have yet to recollect the single-handedness of his struggle. From beginning to end he felt that he was God's champion against the Philistines. Even in his marriage he sought an occasion against the enemy of Jehovah's people. Through all his rollicking, n all his amours, he had still a certain witness in himself to a Divine mission. Is not this explained when we remember that, in earliest years, the secret of his birth and devotion was instilled into the mind by his pious parents? That was surely the finger always pointing him onward, the source from which all that was heroic in his nature was fed. And, alike among Israelites and Philistines, the mystery of his birth would find currency, enhancing his deeds in the view of his compatriots, and adding to the terror of his foes.

We conclude, therefore, that there is nothing wanton or arbitrary in the "bit of glory" which marks the opening chapter of Samson's biography. To eliminate it is to injure the narrative and deprive it of its deeper colouring and significance. Indeed, as Dean Stanley has pointed out, it has a significance even beyond the limits of the hero's life. It was as the first-fruits of an institution which was a noticeable feature of the Jewish Church—an institution which included in its order Samuel, and Elijah, and John the Baptist, and James, the first Bishop of Jerusalem—" it was as the first-fruits of this institution, no less than as his country's champion, that the birth of Samson is ushered in with a solemnity of inauguration which, whether we adopt the more coarse and literal representation of Josephus or the more shadowy and refined representation of the sacred narrative, seems to announce the coming of a greater event than that which is comprised in the merely warlike career of the conqueror of the Philistines."[1]

[1] "History of the Jewish Church," Lect. x.

So, then, according to the instructions of the heavenly preceptor, the child of Manoah is dedicated as a Nazarite to God.[1] And Samson, the consecrated boy, grew; his bright eye, his quick, ready speech, his flowing locks, his mighty strength, were the signs of the blessing of Jehovah. As in the case of another child—"the holiest among the mighty, the mightiest among the holy"—the youth of Israel's future champion is passed over without relation of deed or exploit. The sanctities of the home-life were the covering of the Hebrew boy.

The impulses which swayed his career first (to use the Scripture phrase) *smote* him at a place under the shadow of the hills of Judah, called Mahaneh-Dan.[2] A place of some historical interest, since there—hence the name—the Danites had pitched their tents when they set out on the journey to Laish.[3] A place of family interest, since there Manoah owned a burying-ground. By and by kinsmen of the tribe will bear the remains of the once mighty Samson from the Philistine town to that sequestered spot between Zorah and Eshtaol.[4]

The purpose and the opportunity are important factors in the making of the great man. The purpose has taken shape, it is moving him at times; where, what, how, is the opportunity?

In strange and unexpected form it comes. Against the wish of his parents, Samson is bent on marriage with a daughter of the Philistines. Her residence was a village nestling in the cleft of a hill lined with vineyards and olives, and looking down on a valley waving with corn. The wayward son will not be thwarted, and, as is the way in the East, the marriage was arranged by the parents. A higher hand was guiding events; a reference even in Samson's mind indicated that "it was of the Lord," that, through the wedding, occasion against the dominant Philistines would be found.[5] It was found in a train of consequences from one incident.

For some reason unexplained, he had left, for a short time, the company of his father and mother, when they and he went down to Timnath[6] for the betrothal. On the rugged heights

---

[1] The character of the vow and the stringency of the obligation are set forth in Numbers vi. The word means "separated." How much importance was attached to the vow is evident from the space devoted to it in the Mishna, and from the lamentation in the Book of the Lamentations of Jeremiah, chap. iv. 7.   [2] Judg. xiii. 25.   [3] Judg. xviii. 12.
[4] Judg. xvi. 31.   [5] Judg. xiv. 1-4.   [6] Now Tibnah.

above the village a lion roared against him, ready to spring.[1] It was young and fierce. He had no weapon in his hand, but he received the brute with his brawny arm and rent it as he would have rent a kid. After so doing he rejoined his party, and said nothing of the struggle. "The greatest performers," remarks Bishop Hall, "make the least noise." A short time afterwards, when, the period of betrothal having ended, he returned to claim his wife, he went aside from the path to the scene of his feat : and lo ! the skin and skeleton of the lion— the flesh all picked away by vultures and insects—and within, a swarm of bees and combs of honey ![2] A curious place for bees, but "they establish themselves in situations little thought of by us." So be it they can make their honey, rock and tree, roof of house and rough hill-side, equally serve their purpose. And he takes of the honey, and goes on eating, and gives to his father and mother without telling them whence it came. "It is a weak neglect," comments the quaint English bishop, "not to take the honey because we hate the lion. It is honey still, though in a dead lion."

But the fancy of the Israelite bridegroom was set a-playing by the curious honey-making. And, as riddles were in vogue, he gave a riddle to his wedding companions which referred to his discovery. "Out of the eater came forth meat, and out of the strong came forth sweetness." The stipulation was that, if they discovered the riddle within the seven days of the feast he would give them thirty under-garments of linen and thirty over-garments ; if, on the other hand, they failed to discover it, they would give the same to him. Day followed day and the riddle remained unsolved. The secret was extracted by the coaxing of the Philistine wife. And Samson's pledge was redeemed by a raid on Ashkelon, and the slaughter of thirty of

[1] The lion was a full-grown cub. The lion is not now found in Palestine, but the references to it in the Old Testament show that it was not uncommon. In 2 Kings xvii. 25, 26. we are told that when the province of Samaria was thinly populated, in consequence of the deportation of its people, the lions so increased that they slew the men whom the King of Assyria placed in the cities.

[2] "In the East, vultures and insects, particularly numerous swarms of ants, which abound in vineyards, will, in an astonishingly short time, clean completely out all the soft parts of any carcass, leaving the skeleton entire, covered by its integuments ; for the flesh having been picked out, the skin would not be rent or destroyed" (Kitto, "Daily Bible Readings").

its men, from whose bodies the raiment was stripped.[1] Then began the deadly strife and the mutual hatred. Blood had been shed, and an implacable anger had been kindled.

Thenceforth proceeds the apparently unequal contest—Samson against the Philistine world. The theatre of the contest is limited to the territory of Dan and the Low Country inhabited by the Philistines. Once only the interest is transferred to the neighbouring tribe of Judah. And in this wise.

The vineyards and olives, the shocks of corn and the uncut corn, of the rich land around and below Timnath, had been burnt, as the result of a freak of Samson, by which he had resolved " to do his enemies a displeasure."[2] He had tied three hundred jackals together, tail to tail, and put a firebrand between the tails, and so let them go into the fields. The poor creatures, running in fright and agony, bore the devastating fire with them. In revenge the Philistines burnt his wife and her father. And he retaliated by smiting them, "hip and thigh," with a great slaughter; and then he fled to a rock or a cleft in the range of limestone hills belonging to Judah. The cleft was named Etam.

The man so long wanted had apparently been trapped. The Philistines "spread themselves in Lehi," and demanded the surrender of the fugitive; and to their demand the men of Judah pusillanimously consented. Milton represents Samson as complaining of this conduct in words which express the feeling awakened by the narrative :—

> " What more oft in nations grown corrupt,
> And by their vices brought to servitude,
> Than to love bondage more than liberty,
> Bondage with ease than strenuous liberty;
> And to despise or envy or suspect
> Whom God hath of His special favour raised,
> As their deliverer. If he aught begin,
> How frequent to desert him, and at last
> To heap ingratitude on worthiest deeds." [3]

Three thousand are sent to the rock to apprehend the one man! A striking illustration of the fear which his prowess had inspired—one, too, which bids thought onward to the day when the chief priests and scribes of the people of Judah sent a great multitude with swords and staves to arrest the One, the Deliverer,

---

[1] Judg. xiv. 5-19.   [2] Judg. xv. 1-6.   [3] "Samson Agonistes."

from worse than Philistine bondage, who had trodden the winepress alone![1] There is a touch of generous feeling which contrasts with their selfishness in the entreaty of Samson, that the three thousand would not fall on him. If God helped him, it was better that his hand should be against the common foe, and be stained with his blood, than be turned against his own brethren, and guiltiness for their blood lie on his soul. If no help came to him it was better that he should so die as that his life might be a ransom for his oppressed compatriots. The entreaty agreed to, he is bound with new cords and taken from the rock. We hear the roar of the Philistines—more terrible even than the roar of the young lion of Timnath—the shout to Dagon, when they beheld him manacled, their captive, their prey. They, too, are ready to spring. And he is as ready to receive the attack as on the former day. Filled with an extraordinary strength, "the cords that were on his arms became as flax that is burnt with fire, and his bands loosed from off his hands." Any kind of instrument is sufficient for energy thus supernaturally fed. The jawbone of an ass which had lately died is lying on the ground. He snatches it; with it he rushes on the assembled host. And seized with a panic caused by his shout, his rush, and the tokens of his awful force, they fly before him, leaving a thousand stalwart warriors dead on the field.[2]

And what of the conqueror? First, there is a gleam of his irrepressible vivacity, as, throwing away the jawbone, he indulges in a witticism on the defeat of the Philistines—

> With the jawbone of an ass heaps upon heaps,
> With the jawbone of an ass have I slain a thousand men.

"It is an elegant play upon the words — a paronomasia founded on the identity of the Hebrew word for an ass and for a heap, whereby the Philistines are represented as falling as tamely as asses."[3] And next, the exultation of spirit manifest in this pæan of victory is succeeded by a deep depression, the reaction after a terrible strain aggravated by a fierce thirst. The urgent need sends him to the God of salvation, and the desire of his heart is fulfilled in the perception of a jet of living water springing out of a cavity in the cliffs. The fountain thus opened to his view was the sign of truth which the strong man in his

---

[1] Matt. xxvi. 47.   [2] Judg. xv. 6-17.   [3] Kitto's "Bible Readings."

strength was apt to forget. It reminded him of his dependence on the Eternal. It bade him recognize whose the might and the victory are. It taught him the place and power of prayer. Ah! well had it been for him if he had from that moment realized the secret of En-hakkore—the fountain of the one who calls on God.[1]

It is immediately after the events thus related that the words are inserted, "He judged Israel in the days of the Philistines twenty years." We may infer from this notice that the effect of the exploit at Lehi was such that the Philistine power, though still dominant, was held in check, that relief from the pressure hitherto felt was realized, and that a measure of authority was conceded to Samson.

But, at length, exploit and rule come to an end—one most tragic, and yet in the last moments lit with a glory akin to martyrdom. The cause of the end was miserable. "If," remarks Matthew Henry, "we sleep in the lap of our lusts, we shall certainly awake in the hands of the Philistines." If we did not know to what criminal follies, to what wretched infatuations, sensuality will lead even men wise as Solomon and strong as Samson, we might say that the rashness of our hero in exposing himself to the most perilous situations is inexplicable. He seems to have remained in the quiet of the lion *couchant* for some years. But the wild beast in him at last broke forth. We see him in very foolhardiness tempting God by entering Gaza. He might have walked through its streets, as perhaps he had previously done, and the terror of his presence secured freedom from molestation. But "he who had strangled a lion could not strangle his own loves." He spent the night in the Philistine town, and the citizens laid wait for him, saying, " In the morning, when it is day, we shall kill him." Once more he was delivered out of his distresses. He arose at midnight, and pulled away the gates of the town, and carried them to a range of hills betwixt Gaza and Hebron.[2] Again the laugh was turned against the stupid Philistines. But though extricated from the meshes of the net in which he had involved himself

---

[1] Judges xv. 18, 19. In the A. V., the sentence is, "God clave an hollow place that was in the jaw, and there came water thereout." It should be "the hollow place that was in Lehi" In the time of Jerome there was a spring near Eleutheropolis which was called Samson's Spring.

[2] Judg xvi. 1-6

at Gaza, another net, also woven by his own reckless sensuality, was fatal. The story of Delilah, either Philistine maiden or Hebrew maiden, is one of the most graphic in the pages of the Old Testament.[1]

It is not necessary to suppose that the acts of treachery related, between the fourth and the twentieth verses of the sixteenth chapter of the book, occurred in immediate succession to each other. The narrative is very brief, and these acts may have been repeated at intervals, longer or shorter. With all his folly, Samson could scarcely have been so awfully duped as to have given away his manhood day after day, within a week or so, to the wiles of the woman by whose charms he had been enslaved. Possibly many visits to the valley of Sorek are comprehended in the chapter which reports the bribing of Delilah by the lords of the Philistines[2] to get from her lover the secret of his strength, the cunning which she brought to her task, and the success which ultimately she realized, when, "his soul vexed unto death, he told her all." Pitiful, woful, is the tale that is told : " She made him sleep on her knees, and she called for a man, and she caused him to shave off the seven locks of his head ; and she began to afflict him, and his strength went from him. And she said, The Philistines be upon thee, Samson. And he awoke out of his sleep, and said, I will go out as at other times before and shake myself. And he wist not that the Lord was departed from him."[3]

Alas ! there is no jaw-bone now. His bitter enemies take him and bind him, not with new cords, but " with fetters of brass." He who had borne away the gates of Gaza is borne through the replaced gates to prison. The first time after the narrative of Joseph in which we read of a prison-house is at the close of the free-hearted, open-air-loving, Samson's life. His lusts had made him their slave ; he is made the slave of the Philistines, and sent to grind ignobly, as the slave of the lowest

[1] Josephus calls her a Philistine, but there are good reasons to doubt this. "It is a question whether Samson, with all his weakness, would have reposed such implicit confidence in her if she had been one of his enemies. Nor, one would think, would the immense bribe mentioned in ver. 5 have been required" (Lias, "Book of Judges ").

[2] "We will give thee, every one of us, eleven hundred pieces of silver." This amounted to £135, and this sum multiplied five times was equal to £675. It may have been even more, as the shekel is sometimes rendered at three shillings.   [3] Judg. xvi. 19, 20.

order was obliged to do. His eyes had been the first offenders, they are the first sufferers—though, as it has quaintly been observed, " he was more blind when he saw licentiously than now that he sees not." " Howbeit," it is added, "the hair of his head began to grow again as when he was shaven"[1] Separated from his carnal indulgence, the Nazarite strength and the sense of the Nazarite vow gradually returned.

It is at this period that he is introduced to us in Milton's magnificent drama, " Samson Agonistes." To John Milton, with his fine intellectual and moral perceptions, there was a special charm in the story of Samson. It contained, in his view, an inexhaustible wealth of suggestion. In early years he saw, in the hero rejoicing in his strength, the picture of a noble and righteous nation, of the ideal England.[2] At a later period it spoke to him of the monarchy in its true greatness, but of the low estate into which it had fallen through the flatteries of prelates, and of the arousing sense of majesty, involving, however, loss such as that foreshadowed in the great Danite's end. The Nazarite vow spoke to him of that discipline in the precepts and practice of temperance and sobriety through which royalty grows up to a noble strength. "The illustrious and sunny locks" were the symbol of good laws. When royalty keeps them " undiminished and unshorn," the jawbone of an ass, even "the word of the meanest officer," will put thousands to confusion. Delilah and her flatteries are the forecast of prelacy and its flatteries by which "the tresses are shaved off," and royalty is delivered to "evil counsels which put out the far-sighted eyes" and make it "grind in the sinister house of evil ends," until, recalling the former days, it nourish again "the golden beams of law and right, and thunder with ruin on the heads of evil counsellors, but not without great affliction to himself."[3]

But in "Samson Agonistes" the whole strength of the poetical Samson of England is put forth. The conception of the hero is loftier, it may be, than the facts of the Biblical history warrant. But it is not the less interesting, and the remark passed by Coleridge on Chantrey's bust of Wordsworth, "It is more like Wordsworth than Wordsworth himself is," may be

[1] Judg xvi. 21, 22.
[2] Speech in behalf of liberty of unlicensed printing.
[3] "Reasons of Church Government."

applied to it. The poet has drawn forth the hero's "character from its lurking-place, and brought out the central principle in which all his faculties and feelings unite."

He is introduced to us on the last day of his life. It is a festival day, and he has been allowed to leave his prison and go forth where he can feel "the breath of heaven fresh-blowing, pure and sweet with day-spring born." And he lies on the grassy bank, "carelessly diffused, with languished head unpropped, as one past hope," mourning "the impotence of mind in body strong," mourning above all the loss of sight:

> "O dark, dark, dark, amid the blaze of noon,
> Irrecoverably dark, total eclipse
> Without all hope of day.'

Thus his countrymen who come to comfort him; thus old Manoah "with locks white as down"; thus his wife, his traitress, "sailing like a stately ship, with all her bravery on and tackle trim, sails filled, and streamers waving"; thus the giant Harapha of Gath; thus the officer sent by the lords of the Philistines, to require his presence that he may make sport to the people, find "that heroic, that renowned, irresistible Samson." Throughout, the tragedy is sustained as only Milton could sustain it. It is stately and solemn with those glances into hidden things which are characteristic of him whose orbs were sightless, but whose inner eye beheld the spiritual universe of God. Ever and again in the replies of Samson to the chorus of Danites, in his soliloquy, in his conversation with Manoah, there flash forth the rays of a faith which is still "the substance of things hoped for, the evidence of things not seen," the sense of an inspiration which he has denied but which has not denied him, the concern for interests never more fully outlined than when, blind and lonely, he is ready to die. His is the anguish of "the soul that suffers not the eye to harbour sleep or thought to rest." But it is anguish not because he must "grind in the prison-house," but because he has been untrue to the higher vision, because he has not only soiled and lost his manhood by "foul effeminacy," not only "profaned the mystery of God given him under pledge of vow," but, in doing so, has advanced "the praises of Dagon high among the heathen round." There is a grand protestation in his answer to Manoah, when, on being reminded that the bitterest reproach which could have befallen him and his father's house was the magnifying of the false fish-god, and the blaspheming of the only living and true God, he acknowledges and confesses:

> "I to God have brought
> Dishonour, obloquy, and oped the mouths
> Of idolists and atheists; have brought scandal
> To Israel, diffidence of God, and doubt
> In feeble hearts, propense enough before
> To waver, or fall off, and join with idols;
> Which is my chief affliction, shame, and sorrow."

Ah! verily, the career of the mighty man of valour is the commentary on the saying put into his lips:

> "What is strength without a double share
> Of wisdom? Vast, unwieldly, burthensome,
> Proudly secure, yet liable to fall
> By weakest subtleties, not made to rule
> But to subserve where wisdom bears command."[1]

We look to the end, to the moment when the climax of the tragedy is reached—when the destroyer is himself destroyed, "self-killed, not willingly, but tangled in the fold of dire necessity." In that moment the result is greater than the aggregate of the past years—"the dead which he slew at his death were more than they whom he slew in his life,"[2] and "Samson quit himself like Samson, and heroically finished a life heroic." But, as we see him tugging and shaking the two massy pillars "till down they came and drew the whole roof after them"; as we hear the burst of thunder when the scene of Dagon's sacrifice falls and crushes the idolaters, but crushes also the man of faith "with them immixt"; as we thus contemplate the awful *finis* of a career which the Most High had claimed from infancy, we are reminded of the instruction of eternal truth, "Let not the wise man glory in his wisdom, neither let the mighty man glory in his might, let not the rich man glory in his riches: but let him that glorieth glory in this, that he understandeth and knoweth Me."[3]

---

[1] See "Samson Agonistes."
[2] Judg. xvi. 27-30.
[3] Jer. ix. 23, 24.

CHAPTER VIII.

GIDEON, THE HERO OF THE CENTRAL TRIBES.

The scene of the story, Esdraelon—The memorable events connected with it—The two Ophrahs—Abiezer, the Manassite community—The habits and ways of the farmers of Palestine—The dangers and toils illustrated—Joash, the father of Gideon, and his stalwart sons—Evidence of the hold on the popular imagination of the story of Gideon—Its appeal to us.

NORTH of the old Roman province of Samaria, there is a plain to which the name Esdraelon—the Greek form of the word Jezreel—has been given. Travellers and geographers differ as to the extent of this plain. It is sometimes limited to a tract of country distinguished in olden times as the Valley of Jezreel. It is sometimes regarded as inclusive of the whole territory from Carmel to the Jordan. As thus extended it embraces the Valley of Megiddo, and the pass or vale—unhealthy now as centuries ago—through which flows "one of the shortest rivers in the world"—"that ancient river, the river Kishon." The branches into which the plain divides are marked by three conspicuous mountains, Jebel-el-Duhy, or Little Hermon; Gilboa, famous in Israelite history; and Tabor, the traditional scene of the Transfiguration.[1] From any of its elevated platforms one of the most striking of landscapes is beheld. To the eye accustomed to the magnificent distances of many parts of the Western Hemisphere it may scarcely seem entitled to be called a great plain. But it is great as measured by the distances of Palestine, and the variety of its scenery and the wealth of its historical associations invest it with peculiar interest. The soil is for the most part fertile; indeed, if the coast washed by the Bay of Acre is comprehended in it, it must be reckoned the

[1] "The Land and the Book," Central Palestine, p. 211.

most productive grain-growing portion of the Holy Land. "Almost every acre," says Mr. Oliphant, "is at this moment in the highest state of cultivation. It looks to-day like a huge green lake of waving wheat, with its village-crowned mounds rising from it like islands."[1] A distinguished American traveller, speaking of a view of which Esdraelon is a leading feature, pronounces it the finest that he ever saw in any part of the world.

On this broad plain were transacted many of the most memorable events, were fought many of the most memorable battles, in the history of Israel. True, it has no place in the chronicles of David's victories. Nor were any of the wars of the Conquest waged on its fields. These latter, with only one exception, were waged in the south; the one exception was the decisive battle in the far north—at Merom, "the uppermost lake of the Jordan." But in the stormy times which the Book of Judges records, the valleys of Jezreel and Megiddo were often reddened by human blood. Deborah, for example, sings of the kings who came and fought by the waters of Megiddo, of the armies that were swept away by Kishon.[2] And the story to be told in the following pages begins at the Valley of Jezreel. In the later annals of Israel, some of their darkest pages are associated with Esdraelon. It was near Mount Gilboa that the men of Israel "fell down slain before the Philistines," and that the sun of Saul's royal house set in darkness.[3] It was at Megiddo that Pharaoh-Necho vanquished the hosts which had been wantonly led against him, and that the archers fatally wounded the good King Josiah, for whom "all Judah and Jerusalem, Jeremiah and all the singing men and women, lamented."[3] And so it was that to the Jew who, in days subsequent to the heroic ages of his nation, retraced the national history, the Valley of Megiddo suggested another picture than that of peaceful husbandry—the picture to which the seer of Patmos gives a deep prophetic colouring when he selects "the

---

[1] See "Haifa," pp. 42, 59, 60. "The whole plain of Esdraelon, as well as part of the hills behind, is now all owned by one rich firm of Syrian bankers, who draw an annual income of about $200,000 a year from it. They own practically about 5,000 human beings as well who form the population of thirty villages which are in their hands."

[2] Judg. v. 19-21. [3] 1 Sam. xxxi.

[4] 2 Kings xxiii 29, 30 ; 2 Chron. xxxv. 20-25.

GIDEON, THE HERO OF THE CENTRAL TRIBES. 83

place called in the Hebrew tongue Armageddon," *i.e.*, **the mountain of Megiddo, as the theatre of "the battle of the great day of God Almighty."** [1]

Gideon, with whose biography and achievements we are now concerned, was a native of the plain of Esdraelon. His birthplace is called Ophrah.[2] Two villages bearing this name are mentioned in the Old Testament. There was an Ophrah, belonging to the tribe of Benjamin, now known as El Taiybeh —a group of hamlets " perched aloft on a dark conical hill, like the villages of the Apennines."[3] But the Ophrah in which the future deliverer of Israel was born, nestled on slopes south of the town of Jezreel, and connecting with Mount Gilboa. No trace of it remains; except for its connection with Gideon, it would have been wholly undistinguished and unknown. There, some time between the twelfth and the tenth century before Christ, resided a small clan or family, descended from Manasseh, the first-born of Joseph. Esdraelon was the inheritance of Issachar, but Manasseh had, in it and in Asher, many towns and much territory—"three countries"[4] is the phrase employed in the Book of Joshua; and thus Abiezer, *i.e.*, the sons of Jeezer, occupied Ophrah. One of these sons—perhaps we might say their head-man – was Joash, the father of Gideon.

" When the land had rest," the little community lived simply and peacefully. Manners have hitherto been stereotyped in the East. From the ways of the farming-class which may be observed to-day, we can vivify the conception of the habits of the day of Joash. We can imagine the departure in the morning—the cattle gathered together in preparation for the teams to be formed, the old men who should " abide by the stuff" aiding in arrangements for the younger who should till the land or reap the harvest, the women preparing the food to be taken and all the requisites for camping over night; and then the setting forward—oxen lowing, the children of the homes accompanying the party for a short way, and the men, with the servants, in twos and threes, guiding the cattle; and all provided with weapons of defence as well as with implements of husbandry. Even in times of comparative quiet, there is

---

[1] Rev. xvi. 14-16.   [2] Judg. vi. 11.
[3] Stanley, "Sinai and Palestine," p. 216. In later times, it was called Ephraim, and to it our Lord retired after the raising of Lazarus.
[4] Josh. xvii. 11.

more or less of risk, for the Bedouin hover about the edge of the cultivated districts, and the farmer is never safe from their marauding. Of this risk in the distant past, a graphic picture is supplied in the Book of Job. The messenger is represented in this book as hastening to the Sheikh with the tidings, "The oxen were ploughing and the asses feeding beside them, and the Sabeans fell upon them and took them away, yea, they have slain the servants with the edge of the sword, and I only am escaped alone to tell thee." Of other dangers, other messengers speak—the lightning, or fire of God falling from heaven and burning the sheep and servants, and the desolating simoom or great wind from the wilderness smiting the four corners of the hut, in whose overthrow the young men are slain.[1] Very intelligible indeed to the sons of Israel was the description in the Psalter of bands of agriculturists "going on their way weeping, bearing forth the seed." And very responsive was their heart to the promise of "the return with joy, bringing the sheaves with them."[2]

In the toils and the dangers of husbandry, Joash and his family spent their days. The narrative in Judges suggests that Joash was a man of quick and fertile wit, of mental resource, and of that strength of will which secures the deference of others. The people of the village looked up to him as their chief. He possessed that which, to a Hebrew parent, was the greatest of earthly blessings—he had stalwart sons, renowned for noble presences and beaming countenances, faces "like the faces of a king."[3] Conspicuous among them was the first-born —Gideon.

His biography, as the hero raised up and divinely endowed to meet a great national emergency, is presented at some length, and with striking beauty, in the Old Testament historical books; and the references to it in the prophecies of Isaiah—to "the day of Midian," "the slaughter of Midian at the rock of Oreb"[4]—show that, for long centuries, the story of his exploits kept the popular imagination in thrall. Nor is this to be wondered at. Even to us, far separated from the period to which it is immediately related, it appeals at many points. To begin with, it is an illustration of the highest kind of manliness. There is nothing overdrawn in the portrait. The man is set

[1] Job i. 13-19.
[3] Judg. viii. 18.
[2] Psa. cxxvi. 5, 6.
[4] Isa. ix. 4; x. 26.

before us as he actually was, in the rugged simplicity of peasant life with its homely ways and homely folk, in the pith and the weakness of his character, in his faults as well as his virtues. But in all we can discern a swiftness of glance, a promptitude in counsel and action, a reverence of spirit, a self-repression, a gentleness toning and tempering a giant's strength, a loyalty of purpose which disdained all by-ends and by-ways, a faculty of inspiring and organizing enthusiasm—in a word, the qualities which mark the foremost type of the truly great man. And these qualities found their suitable aliment and exercise in a service which stamps him as both patriot and hero. We see him burdened with the sense of his country's degradation, burning with the desire to break the oppressor's rod, heading the hosts which obey his trumpet-blasts, restoring peace to the distracted tribes, and refusing the crown which the grateful thousands of Israel pressed on him. He is not unworthy of a place among the champions, the liberators, the protectors, whom history has immortalized. Narrow as the theatre of his action was, in that narrow sphere he manifested the genius, he won the trophies, of a genuine leader and commander of peoples. More still—and this is the chief title to our regard—his life and daring form one of the most interesting pages in the records of faith. He is something else than a mere emancipator from foreign tyranny : he is a witness for the true God and the kingdom of heaven. He is the antagonist of Baal, no less than the deliverer from Midian. We are invited to behold in him, and in his call and equipment, an evidence of the work of Divine grace, in its selection of individuals for ministry and blessing, and of the manner in which the chords of the human heart vibrate to the touch of this grace, and are tuned by it to finer issues. To the devout mind this is the chief glory of the career of Gideon. The mighty acts of the warrior may be much, the mighty acts of Jehovah are more—those acts through which even the worm can thresh the mountains and beat the hills as chaff. It is a tale not of military prowess only, but, as the author of the Epistle to the Hebrews reminds us, of the faith which "subdues kingdoms, works righteousness, obtains promises, stops the mouths of lions, quenches the power of fire, escapes the edge of the sword, from weakness makes strong, waxes mighty in war, turns to flight the armies of aliens."[1]

[1] Heb. xi. 33, 34.

CHAPTER IX.

GIDEON: ISRAEL'S CRY AND GOD'S ANSWER.

The situation of Palestine—The series of invasions—The Midianites: The ancient city Madjan: Mahomet's greeting: The Tawara: The branches comprehended under the name Midianite: Their commercial character: The links connecting Israel and Midian: The corrupting influence of Midian—The Amalekites The battle of Rephidim—The "children of the East" The fierce character of the inroads of these Bedouins—The destruction caused by the march through Palestine—The cry of the people—The man—The prophet, and his message—The man, the deliverer: His occupation: His thoughts: The lesson suggested by the view obtained of him.

"PALESTINE," says Dean Stanley, "is an island in the midst of pirates. The Bedouin tribes are the Corsairs of the wilderness; the plains which run into the mountains are the creeks into which they naturally penetrate."[1] When Gideon was a young man, the plain of Esdraelon was the scene of an invasion, or rather a series of invasions, which extended over seven years, the result of which was that "no sustenance was left for Israel, neither sheep, nor ox, nor ass." It was this gigantic inroad which called forth the energy of the son of Joash.

The desolating hordes were composed of "Midianites, Amalekites, and the children of the East," the predominating power being that of the Midianites. Let us observe this confederacy.

On the eastern coast of the gulph of Elam, there was a city called Madjan. Not long ago, its ruins were shown to the traveller. The name and the ruins, it is supposed, connect with that Midian whose hand prevailed against Israel. In the time of Mahomet, the neighbourhood of the old city was occupied by a people one of whose chieftains the Prophet received

[1] "Sinai and Palestine," p. 136.

GIDEON: ISRAEL'S CRY AND GOD'S ANSWER. 87

with the greeting, "Welcome to the brother-in-law of Moses." And, at this day, the adjacent country is the territory of the Tawara, the most civilized of the Semitic tribes, and the lineal descendants of the ancient Midianites. In the very far past—a far past even when "there was no king in Israel"—it would seem that there were several branches or families comprehended under that name. One branch, aboriginal and idolatrous, was represented by the shepherds, introduced to us in the history of Moses as coming to drive away the black-veiled daughters of Reul-Jethro, who were filling the troughs to water their father's flock.[1] From some hints given in old chronicles, we conjecture that there was a second branch to which, perhaps, Reul-Jethro belonged—the Kenites, a moiety of which formed friendly relations with Israel, and divided the wilderness of Judah, "which lieth in the south of Arad,"[2] with the Amalekites. A third branch was the Semitic race, descended from Abraham by his second wife Keturah. One of the six sons of this marriage was Midian, who, like the other five sons, was sent away from Isaac, the heir of the promise, "eastward, to the east country," that is Arabia.[3] The posterity of Midian and his five sons spread rapidly in a westward direction through the wadys of the Peninsula, from the borders of Moab to the eastern coast of the arm of the Red Sea, now known as the Gulph of Suez. All branches amalgamated, more or less, in the course of centuries. They were not Ishmaelites, strictly so called, but Ishmaelite was sometimes used as a general term for the peoples of Arabia. Originally wandering herdmen, like the Carthaginians, they blended the pastoral character with the commercial, and at times the military also. The sons of Midian were the merchantmen of the East. Their caravans were the ships of the desert, plying between the more fertile and favoured regions and the rocky peninsula of Sinai. It was to one of these caravans, "bearing spicery and balm and myrrh," *en route* to Egypt, that Joseph was sold for twenty pieces of silver.[4] The account of the spoil which fell to Israel after Gideon's victory, is the evidence of the wealth which the merchantmen secured for the wandering children of the East.[5]

[1] Exod. ii. 16–17.
[2] Judg. i. 16.
[3] Gen. xxv. 4–7.
[4] Gen. xxxvii. 25–28.
[5] Ewald ("History of Israel," vol. ii. pp. 107–108) says of Midian,

88 GIDEON AND THE JUDGES OF ISRAEL.

Many and close are the links which connect the early history of Israel with Midian. After his flight from Egypt, Moses was received by the prince-priest of the Kenites, married the prince's daughter, and for years led the prince's flock towards the west of the desert, "along the mountain ledges green, to glean the desert's spicy stores." It was when thus employed, near the Mount of God, that the great sight of the burning bush was beheld by him, and the commission to go unto Pharaoh was solemnly given him.[1] The wise Kenite chief, when visiting the Israelite lawgiver, sketched the outline of the political constitution of the people;[2] and, when the face of the people was set towards the promised land, Moses invited the chief to cast in his lot with them, "Come with us and we will do thee good."[3] And, as we have seen, a portion of the tribe did so.

Up to this time the worship of the God of Abraham had been maintained, although not in purity, in the Semitic contingent of the tribes. But this worship rapidly deteriorated. The impression made on Jethro by the victories of Israel—"Now know I that Jehovah is greater than all gods, for in the thing wherein they dealt proudly, He is above them"—soon became faint. After the defeat of Sihon and Og, the elders of Midian are found in league with the elders of Moab, with the "rewards of divination" in their hands, inviting Balaam to "come and curse the people that had come out from Egypt."[4] Thenceforth the Midianite appears as one of the prime cor-

---

"This singular Arabian people were in those early times what the Carthaginians, originating in a neighbouring region, afterward became, devoted principally to commerce, but, on favourable occasions to conquest also, for which end they wisely availed themselves of the services of the children of the desert. Distantly connected with Israel by blood and friendship, Midian was really only a small nation. It may have originally occupied only a small territory in North-Western Arabia near Tibûk, for the city Madjan lay on the Arabian gulph opposite and to the east of the southern point of the peninsula of Sinai. No situation could be better adapted for an extensive commerce in all directions. . . . Monarchy was unknown to them, as to the Carthaginians, yet they must, in very early times, have possessed the art of bringing about a great union of Arabian tribes under their own leadership, and even of employing them in war for their own advantage. It ruled in the Sinaitic peninsula over Amalekite Arabs, but, through its allies, the Arabs of the desert, it also ruled over regions far to the East, towards the Euphrates."

[1] Exod. ii., iii.
[2] Exod. xviii.
[3] Numb. x. 29-32.
[4] Numb. xxii. 4 7.

rupters of Israel: the wiles specially of Midianitish women are the occasion of dire calamity. "Vex and smite" is the fierce command of the leader.[1] How sternly the command was carried out may be inferred from a notice in the narrative of the distribution of the cities and plains of the Amorites among the tribe of Reuben. It is said that Moses had slain five princes of Midian who were Dukes of Sihon dwelling in the country.[2]

The Midianites, in great bands, are associated with Amalekites in the invasion of Palestine.

"Amalek," said Balaam in his song, "was the first of the nations."[3] Long before the conquest of Canaan it was one of the strongest of the primitive races. It has been credited even with a temporary mastership of Egypt. For a long period it was the master of Palestine. Driven back to the desert by the Amorite or Canaanite, the consciousness that the land had been the possession of their sires rankled in the mind of successive generations. This may, perhaps, explain the fierceness of the opposition of Amalek. At an early period after the exodus this opposition was shown. Apparently it was unprovoked.[4] It was marked by daring impiety. One of the most striking episodes in the Pentateuch is the battle of Rephidim, when "Moses' hands were heavy, and they took a stone and put it under him, and he sat thereon; and Aaron and Hur stayed up his hands, the one on the one side and the other on the other side, and "—symbol and pledge of victory— "his hands were steady until the going down of the sun." It was at the close of this battle that Moses was instructed to register in a volume and rehearse in the ears of Joshua the purpose of the Eternal that Amalek should be put out from under heaven; and the altar there and then built and named Jehovah-Nissi had particular reference to the holy war against Amalek as the type of Jehovah's enemies from generation to generation.[5]

At the date of the invasion which we are contemplating, Amalek had sunk into the condition of a desert-tribe. Origin-

---

[1] Numb. xxv.   [2] Joshua xiii. 21; see also Numb. xxxi. 1-20.
[3] Numb. xxiv. 20. This may be read, "First of the nations that warred against Israel."
[4] Exod. xvii. 8, "Then came Amalek and fought with Israel."
[5] Exod. xvii. 8-16.

ally powerful enough to rule Midian, Midian now controlled it. The connection between the Kenite branch and the Amalekites had been, for many centuries, intimate. Now a power mightier than the sword has come into play—the power of wealth. Midianite wealth has secured them as allies, and with them a miscellaneous host of the Arabs of the Hauran and Gilead— those Arabs in whom we discern the prototype of the Bedouin of more recent times. In the reign of King Josiah, an outburst of these "corsairs of the wilderness" was sufficiently important to attract the notice of Greek as well as Jewish historians;[1] and Scythopolis, the name into which Bethshean or Bethshan—the point of their entrance into the valley o Esdraelon—was changed, is a witness for the impression left by this visit of Scythian hordes.

It was an appalling spectacle which burst on the view of the inhabitants of the Israelite villages when these confederated tribes poured into the valley through the *Ghor* from Bethshean. The invaders seemed to be without number, "with their cattle and their tents they came as grasshoppers for multitude." The fields were ripening. In Eastern lands, only a short time intervenes between the sowing and the reaping. The harvest is gathered in the early summer; and the sturdy sons of Ephraim, in their homes on the spurs of the hills, had been joyfully anticipating the sheaves filled with golden grain, and the presses bursting with new wine. Alas! all hopes are dashed to the ground. The dark cloud of human locusts spreading through the fair land tells them that "a day of the Lord, a day of gloominess and darkness," has arrived.

What can the affrighted people do? To oppose such a multitude is hopeless. The plain is abandoned to "the corsairs of the wilderness," who eat up its increase, and move onward through the valley of Sharon to the extreme south-west, "until thou come to Gaza."[2] When all has been destroyed they retire, but only to reappear when the next harvest comes round. For seven weary years the scourge is heavy. Peaceful homes are broken up. Men, women, and children fly to the mountainous ranges, and perforate the cliffs, "making them dens and caves, and strongholds." With the disappearance of the material of physical nourishment, the heart of the Israelites dies within

[1] Herodotus (see note in "Sinai and Palestine," p. 340).
[2] Judg. vi. 4.

them. Only one resource is left—their last resource in time of trouble. "The children of Israel cried unto the Lord."[1]

The first instalment of the answer to the cry is the sending of a prophet. The only specification which is given is the phrase, "a man, a prophet."[2] One of the essentials of a prophet is that he be a man, with the sympathy, the force, the fearlessness of the true manhood—vision direct, speech hot and straight—one who is "as lightning out of heaven, the soul of a man actually sent down from the skies with a God's message to us." This prophet speaks in the name of the Eternal. He pierces to the root and cause of the servitude and ruin, and, publishing the mighty acts of Jehovah, he bids the listening villagers reflect on the return which they had made to Him, on their idolatry, neglect, and disobedience. Thus, the preparation for deliverance was laid. It was a token for good that at length "a man, a prophet," had appeared, that a voice which the conscience recognized as the voice of Jehovah again sounded in the ear. The sky was black as midnight, but this was the ray of hope. He had torn Ephraim as a lion, and apparently had gone away. But the coming of His word with power was the pledge that He had withdrawn only until, in their affliction, they sought His face.

"The man, the prophet," is the precursor of the Man, the Saviour. John the Baptist, with his solemn trumpet-call "Repent," was the forerunner of Jesus with His glad tidings of great joy. To nation or to person, the beginning of the gospel is always the preaching of repentance. When this preaching is felt with power, the kingdom of heaven is at hand. So it was in the portion of history before us.

The deliverer belongs to the tribe of Manasseh—one of the two branches of the house of Joseph. The territory of this great house was the central part of the Holy Land, a part rich with "the precious things of heaven, of the dew, and the deep that croucheth beneath, the precious fruits brought forth by the sun and the precious things put forth by the moon, the chief things of the ancient mountains, the precious things of the lasting hills, and the precious things of the earth."[3] The two branches soon moved apart, Ephraim retaining the more central region, Manasseh taking the northern region. Between them they occupied a tract of land which was a meet nurse for

[1] Judg. vi. 6   [2] Judg. vi. 8 (see margin).   [3] Deut. xxxiii. 13-17.

heroic men, for men who might form a national militia, protecting "the outgoings" of the mountain and mediating between the tribes of the north and the south. In the poetic language of the seer, they were "like the horns of the buffalo pushing the people together to the ends of the earth."

The supremacy of power remained for long with the children of Joseph. In their inheritance lay the battle-field of Palestine. In it were the *Ghors*, stretching westward from the Jordan, which were inlets to the places that dropped the fatness which the Bedouin coveted. They held the keys for all the tribes. From their heights they could oversee the valleys, both inland and maritime, rich with rolling grass or waving corn. And in their fastnesses the oppressed could find a refuge and a covert in the time of need. The national sanctuary stood for centuries in one of their plains. Until the era of the royal dynasties of Saul and David, they supplied much of the leading and light of Israel. Joshua was an Ephraimite. From Mount Ephraim, Ehud had led the people to victory against Moab. Deborah, the prophetess, though a native of Issachar, dwelt under the palm tree of Ephraim. In a town of the same mount Samuel was born. Gideon, the greatest of the Judges, is the hero of Manasseh.

We are introduced to him when he is threshing wheat. In ordinary times the threshing would have been done close to the field whence the grain had been gathered, or in the immediate neighbourhood of the village. The "baidar," or "threshing-floor," as the word is translated in the English version of the Scriptures, was an open space or circle in which the wheat was laid. And the instrument used, "sharp, having teeth," was a slab drawn by a yoke of oxen over the corn, the driver sitting or standing in it, until the fruit was separated from the ear, and the straw itself was ground to chaff. But in the case before us the usual process is not followed. The farmer is not in the baidar. He has removed the grain so precious at that time to the wine-press.[1] As little noise as possible must be made. Therefore the oxen, the lowing of which might be heard from

---

[1] "The objects of interest which mainly characterize all the Carmel ruins are ancient olive mills and wine-presses. The wine-presses were nothing more than huge vats, hewn out of the living rock, sometimes above ground in the shape of sarcophagi, sometimes pits eight or nine feet square and the same in depth" (Oliphant's "Haifa," pp. 94-95).

afar, are dispensed with, and the farmer uses the flail. The Hebrew phrase is "threshing wheat with a stick." He plies his stick in a hidden place, and the quantity beaten out is small, sufficient only for the use of the household. For the terror of the Midianites, who are swarming all around, is on him as it is on all. The little that has been saved from their ravages must be guarded. And so he works, softening as much as may be even the thud on the grain laid on the earthen floor; so he works, sad, chafing, indignant in soul. He, the strong man, the son of Israel, to be thus cowering before these children of the East! Has he not heard of the mighty deeds of Jehovah in the past—how He drove the heathen from before the people He had chosen? Do not the fathers of the tribe recall, with bated breath, the grand old times when the terrible shout of Israel made kings and armies quake? And now—woe worth he day!—it has come to this, that the children of these sires must "make them dens and caves," and he must wield his stick with secrecy, hiding from the Midianites.

That such is the nature of his thoughts is evident from the words which he utters when the Divine voice addresses him. "Oh my Lord, if the Lord be with us, why then is all this befallen us, and where be all His wondrous works which our fathers told us of, saying, Did not the Lord bring us up from Egypt? but now the Lord hath cast us off and delivered us into the hand of Midian."[1] A brave, honest soul is in this man, with his eye looking straight before him, though not yet taught, in fulness of trust and hope, to look up. Robust he is, firm and strong as the terebinth which stands beside the wine-press, asking eagerly, communing with his own heart, as to whether nothing can be done to wipe out the disgrace and repair the havoc which has been wrought among his people. He is cast down, he is utterly humiliated, but his courage is not destroyed. The times are calling loudly for the man; here is the man for whom they are calling. Here is the man, not consuming his energy in fevered dreams, or wearing out his spirit like the imprisoned bird beating against the bars of its cage. He is standing in his lot doing the work which lies to his hand in the station to which God has appointed him.

Is not this a feature of all readiness for higher and fuller service? There are persons, not a few, who, conceiving that

[1] Judg. vi. 13.

they have special gifts or special missions, become discontented with their surrounding, fret over their work as unsuitable, as tending to dwarf and cramp their power, and abandon the work, striking wildly out in quest of nobler and more congenial tasks And, no doubt, sometimes the environment is unfavourable to the development of the genius, sometimes the service is unfitted for the man, sometimes the issue justifies the discontent. But may it not safely be said that, in the great majority of cases, the ambition which unfits one for the hearty discharge of present duty is a misleading light? In genuine greatness there is a simplicity of nature, a self-unconsciousness and devotion, widely different from the egotism and impatience which characterize such an ambition. Elisha is no dreamer: he is a practical homely farmer, plowing " with twelve yoke of oxen before him, and he with the twelfth," when the prophet's mantle is thrown [1] around him. David is "taken from the sheepfold; from following the ewes" he is brought to "feed Jacob, God's people, and Israel his inheritance."[2] To shepherds watching their flocks the herald angel announces the birth of the Royal Child, and they hear the symphony of the heavenly host.[3] He of whom they sang lived in lowliness and obscurity until He was thirty years of age; from Nazareth, with its workshop and its simplicities, He goes to the Jordan to receive the baptism in which the heavens are opened and the Spirit of God descends on Him.[4] His apostles are engaged in their craft when the word is spoken, "Follow Me."[5] And here is Gideon, with all the latent possibilities of a kingship over men, threshing his wheat when the angel appears. A beautiful symbol, indeed, of the truth never to be forgotten, that it is ours to take care of to-day's service, and to reckon on God for taking care of to-morrow's opportunity. It has been wisely and pithily said that "we put ourselves in the way of Divine visits when we employ ourselves in honest business. The work Gideon was about was an emblem of that greater work to which he was called, as the disciples' fishing was. From threshing corn, he is fetched to thresh the Midianites."[6]

---

[1] 1 Kings xix 19. [2] Psa. lxxviii. 70–71. [3] Luke ii. 8–11.
[4] Matt. iii. 13–17. [5] Matt. iv. 18–22.
[6] Matthew Henry, "Commentary."

CHAPTER X.

GIDEON : THE CALL AND THE RESPONSE.

The terebinth near the house of Joash—The interest attaching to the oak or terebinth in Holy Scripture—A visitor one day—Who was this angel?—The "deep Providential meaning" of the old Testament Theophanies—*The Call*—It particularizes—The separation and selection of the man—The crisis of his life—The progress in the call—"Learn to labour and to wait"—The call discloses the secret of the power—*Gideon's Response*—The need of inward strengthening—Likeness between Gideon and the Apostle Thomas—The *Ifs* projected by the mind, and the corresponding disciplines—The sign asked—The meal-offering—The angel's commands, and what followed—Anticipation of the Supper of the Lord—The assurance given to Gideon—Yet, there is death to the old man—The resurrection into newness of life.

IN Ophrah of the Abiezrites there was a grove, the seat of its idolatrous worship. But the house of Joash was distinguished by one thing—close to it stood an umbrageous terebinth. The prominence given to this tree in the Old Testament Scriptures has been already noticed. For two reasons, it had a special interest to the Hebrew. Many parts of Palestine are almost treeless. In the highlands of Gilead and the plateau of the Jaulan there is an abundance of timber; but, in other regions, seldom is a grateful shadow cast by the foliage of the terebinth. Hence, as in the narrative before us and elsewhere, the emphasis given to the oak or the palm. Moreover, the oak was the emblem of strength. Ancient prophecy described the olive as one of the chief blessings of the Holy Land, and its value is indicated by the fruit and the oil which it yields, and its richly coloured wood. The palm—tall, straight, elegant—was the emblem of the righteous ; it was a favourite name (Tamar) for the women of Israel. But, as compared with these and other kinds of tree, the oak suggested what is solid, robust, and durable. The seer Amos compares the Amorite to the cedar for height, and to the oak for strength.[1]

One day a stranger sat below the wide-spreading branches of the terebinth, near the house of Joash. On that day Gideon was threshing wheat at the wine-press. And from the conference between this stranger and Gideon came the crisis and the call.

Josephus says, "Somewhat appeared in the shape of a young man."[2] The Biblical narrative is more explicit. It styles the stranger, "An angel of the Lord," or, "The angel of the Lord." In the account of the interview he is called the Lord or Jehovah.[3] It is to one of the Theophanies of the Old Testament that we are introduced; and these Theophanies cannot be set aside as legendary by those who believe that all Scripture is God-breathed. Who is this angel? He is the Great Presence in Israelite history. He appeared to the patriarchs.[4] He appeared to Moses "in a flame of fire out of the midst of a bush."[5] He was the leader of the people when they left the house of bondage.[6] Of the crime and consequences of disobedience to Him they were warned.[7] He was the angel of God's face: the name of the Adorable was in Him: He represented God. Manoah and Gideon feared that, after having conversed with Him, they would die. They felt that they had seen God. And the words used concerning Him, whilst implying distinction from Jehovah, imply also a mysterious unity with Jehovah. Was He the Word who in the beginning was with God, and was God, and who, in the fulness of the time, was made flesh? So said the Christian fathers of the earlier centuries.[8] So say many commentators and divines. Augustine wisely counselled that it is better not to "say positively which of the Divine Persons manifested Himself in this or that instance to patriarchs or prophets, except where some remarkable indications determine our conclusion very decisively."[9] And the words of Canon Liddon suggest the "deep Providential meaning" in the Theophanies: "Whether in them the Word or

---

[1] Amos ii. 9.   [2] "Antiquities," book v. chap. 6.   [3] Judg. vi. 14.
[4] Gen. xxxii. 24–30.   [5] Exod. iii. 2.   [6] Exod. xiii. 21.
[7] Exod. xxiii. 20, 21.   [8] $E\,g$, Justin, Tertullian, Ambrose.
[9] Augustine, "De Trinitate," quoted by Liddon, "Bampton Lectures."

GIDEON: THE CALL AND THE RESPONSE. 97

Son actually appeared, or whether God made a created angel the absolutely perfect exponent of His thought and will, do they not point in either case to a purpose in the Divine Mind which would only be realized when man had been admitted to a nearer and more palpable contact with God than was possible under the Patriarchal or Jewish dispensations? Do they not suggest as their natural climax and explanation some Personal self-unveiling of God before the eyes of His creatures? Would not God appear to have been training His people, by this long and mysterious series of communications, at length to recognize and to worship Him when hidden under and indissolubly one with a created nature? Apart from the specific circumstances which may seem to have explained each Theophany at the time of its taking place, and considering them as a series of phenomena, is there any other account of them so much in harmony with the general aspect of Holy Scripture as that they were successive lessons addressed to the eye and to the ear of ancient piety in anticipation of a coming Incarnation of God?"[1]

God has spoken to us in these last days in His Son, the brightness of His glory and the exact image of His Person. The stars are helpful when the great Luminary is hidden; His coming from his chamber supersedes the use of the more dim and uncertain lights. We who have the revelation of the Father in the Son do not require the occasional and temporary angel to declare God's will; ours is the blessing pledged in the saying of The Truth, "He that loveth Me shall be loved of My Father; and I will love him and will manifest Myself to him."[2]

The appearance of the angel of Jehovah was unexpected and sudden, yet it was not such as to startle the lion-hearted Gideon. The interview which follows is full of meaning. Let us observe the call, and the response.

The call particularizes. "Jehovah is with thee, thou mighty man of valour." So far, the salutation is in accordance with the elaborate courtesies of the Oriental. But in Ophrah the worship of Baal has superseded the worship of Jehovah, and the invocation of the great Name strikes on the ear. Besides, there is a marked force in the addition, "thou mighty man of valour." May we not suppose that to the farmer, hiding at the wine-press from the Midianites, there is a savour of irony in it?

[1] Liddon, "Bampton Lectures," Section ii. p. 58.
[2] John xiv. 21.

Some, indeed, trace a feeling of indignation in the farmer's rejoinder, as if he would show that he resented the language employed. His position was so humiliating, the circumstances of the time were so hard, that mere politeness irritated, and ironical compliments were intolerable. This is going too far. Gideon's words are not indignant; they are sad and earnest; they express the honest doubt and bewilderment of the mind. There is a ring of genuine pathos in them. He at once identifies himself with his people. He is full of the one theme—the condition of Israel. The stranger had said "*thee*"; he replies, "Oh my Lord, if Jehovah be with *us*, why then is all this befallen *us?*" As if he would say, "I cannot be separated from my kindred: if He is not with them, He is not with me. And where are the signs of His presence? Our fathers had the signs; to us they are a mere tradition of the past. Where is the strength which brought the hosts of Israel up from Egypt through the howling wilderness? Brave salutations ill become such a day as this. Why say, 'Jehovah is with thee,' when it is only too plain that He has forsaken us, and delivered us into the hands of the Midianites?"[1]

Thus protests the heart hot within him. But the angel *is* sent to him, and the angel's greeting is in good faith meant for him. God's answer to His crying, sorrowing people is the gift of men. He has no better gift than a man with the full and various play of consecrated power—"His elect in whom His soul delighteth, and in whom He puts His Spirit." The appearance of the angel is the separation and election of the man. It corresponds to the crisis mentioned by St. Paul when he speaks of his apprehension or arrest by Christ Jesus.[2] This is the apprehension of the son of Joash. It is the birth-hour of the new man whose biography is to be hereafter unfolded. The period of chafing without action has passed: now begins the purpose, the life of the hero. Such a birth-hour God-sent men in every age have realized. Is there not, indeed, a moment like it in spiritual history, when the regenerating grace of God's Holy Spirit stirs the pulses, and the mind, thrilling with the consciousness that the Eternal, hitherto unknown, has claimed the life, becomes impatient of mere generalities, and the ear is awakened to hear God?

There is a noteworthy progress in the call. First, we have

[1] Judg. vi. 12, 13.   [2] Philippians iii. 12.

GIDEON: THE CALL AND THE RESPONSE. 99

only the distinguishing, "The Lord is with thee. Awake, arise, thou mighty man, who art fretting and moaning because of the Midianites. He who is with thee is more than all who can be against thee." But, next, the attention having been aroused, there comes the more explicit, "Thou shalt save Israel from the hand of the Midianites." The salutation of the twelfth verse of the chapter issues in the sixteenth verse as a definite promise, "Surely I will be with thee," because now it is linked to a definite charge, "Thou shalt smite the Midianites as one man." The vocation is no longer a thing of hazy outlines; it has become a distinct and positive command. And can we not trace the same progress in many a career? There is nothing more interesting than to observe the way in which, often from less to more, from weakness to strength, and then from strength to strength, men are brought face to face with the "mark for the prize of their high calling," led into the fields in which they are specially to influence their fellows, and complete their ministry to God and His world. May some who perchance shall read these pages learn patience! Have they the capability of higher things than any to which they have attained, or, with their present surrounding, are likely to attain? May they seek grace to "tarry the Lord's leisure," and be wise in the understanding of His will! The poet whispers a needed lesson into the soul when he says, "Learn to labour and to wait." To all who listen whilst they labour, the eye waiting on God whilst hand and brain are toiling, the whole counsel of God's will, and the full measure of usefulness and service, will be gradually declared.

The call discloses the secret of the power. "Impossible," cries Gideon, "that I can save Israel. The thousand to which I belong is among the most mean and impoverished in Israel, and I am the least in my father's house."[1] Estimating the magnitude of the task by his abilities and opportunities, it seemed a cruel mockery to address him as the deliverer of the oppressed people. The Bible, indeed all history, abounds with illustrations of inaptitudes and deficiencies, as beheld from

---

[1] Judges vi. 15. "'My family is poor.' Literally 'My thousand is the meanest.' The thousand was probably a division for military purposes, parallel to the *mishpachoth*, or septs, which were genealogical divisions. It may be compared with the *hundred* or *wapentake* of our English forefathers" (Book of Judges, Cambridge Bible, *cf*. page 18).

a merely human standpoint, so complemented by a Divine fulness that the worm is changed into a "new sharp threshing instrument having teeth." "Poor little monk," said the Saxon knight as Luther confronted the majesty of the empire. God does sometimes choose the wise, the mighty, the noble; yet "not many," says the apostle. How frequently He chooses what the world, judging by appearances, pronounces "the foolish things."

For the might is not in what men are, be their endowments great or small, but in what He is in them. The life is not in the branch, it is in the vine abiding in the branch. "Apart from Me ye can do nothing."[1] "This is the victory that overcometh the world, even our faith."[2]

How beautifully is this set forth in the verse, "The Lord looked on him, and said, Go in this thy might, and thou shalt save Israel; have not I sent thee?"[3] Every clause, almost every word, is expressive. The *Lord* looked. It is not now the angel, it is the Name who is in him. He *looked*. The look flashes the light of the eyes which are as a flame of fire. It is the same look as that which, long centuries afterwards, an apostle, who had denied his Master, met when "the Lord turned and looked on him."[4] But in this latter instance, it was a look mighty towards repentance; in the present case, it is a look mighty towards inspiration, pouring a new life and light into the soul. *Go in this*, is the command. This look is the true might. In the consciousness, in the recollection of it, a man may go anywhere. Everywhere he will feel that the house of God is with him, and the hardest service will be made light. The look and the mission go together—"In this, thy might: have not I sent thee?"

Such was the call; let us observe the response.

Gideon does not resist, but he needs to be "strengthened mightily by God's Spirit in the inner man." Sometimes the first discernment of a higher duty to which the Eternal summons dazzles the sight, almost confounds the reason. It demands a self-renunciation, a devotion to hard and painful service, from which the heart shrinks. Even the meekest and lowliest, "though a Son," needed to learn obedience. It is not therefore to be wondered at that, in the hour when the new vocation burst on the eye of Gideon, there arose fightings and

[1] John xv. 5.
[2] 1 John v. 4.
[3] Judg. vi. 14.
[4] Luke xxii. 61.

GIDEON: THE CALL AND THE RESPONSE.

fears, there was the craving for some evidence that the One who talked with him was not a mere phantasm, the talk itself a mere dream; and that there ensued a dialogue with the visitor in which utterance was given to the emotion that swayed him. He will do anything if only he can be made sure that the mission is a real mission of God, and that he is the man to do it. For courage is often associated with a diffidence which needs to be fought down. Men, seeing the calmness and promptitude of the hero, take little account of the conflict which preceded the action, of the sensitiveness and timidity which had to be overcome by the iron will, and of the reinforcements of strength which, during the action, the will requires. This farmer, one of an impoverished thousand in Israel, "the meanest in Manasseh," himself hitherto only a member of his father's house, must debate the whole matter. The heart of the patriot is burning within him, but there are " wherewiths," and "ifs" which must be dealt with. And this dealing is indicated in the conference with the messenger of God.

There is much in Gideon at this stage which reminds us of "Thomas called Didymus." In both there is a capability of enthusiastic devotion, but in both there is a caution which has no relation to fear, and has no alliance with "the evil heart of unbelief." It is the caution of a genuine manliness; it is the "honest doubt" in which faith lives. "They who begin first to inquire will soonest be gladdened with revelation, and with them Christ will be best pleased; for the slowness of His disciples troubled Him of old."[1] When such inquirers are gladdened with revelation, the whole being—intellectual, moral, spiritual—moves towards the mark; in the unity of all the strength, the soul greets "the vision splendid," "my Lord and my God."

We see the wisdom as well as the patience of the Divine dealing. There are varieties of inflection and meaning in the "if" which the mind projects. And for these varieties there are corresponding disciplines. Read, for example, the answer which Gideon gave to the angel's salutation—"Oh my Lord, *if* the Lord be with us," and so forth. What is the discipline for this kind of *if?* It is, "The Lord looked on him." There is no discussion. The look is enough. That is the assurance of the presence of Jehovah. And how quickly do our reason-

[1] "Unspoken Sermons," by George MacDonald, p. 54.

ings and impatiences vanish, how different seem the point and force of our arguments, when we are really beneath the look! But the second *if*, which is evolved as the interview proceeds, is of another sort than that. In the second *if* there is no question as to the Presence. The authoritative "Surely I will be with thee" has entered into the soul; and, in reverence, in deepest sympathy with the voice, there comes back—"*If* now I have found grace in Thy sight, then show me a sign that Thou talkest with me:"[1] Bishop Hall interprets, "Fain would he believe, but fain would he have good warrant for his faith."[2] He had not been living in the secret of the Presence; much tuning was demanded before mind and soul could make one music. But the instrument is given into the hand of the Lord. And the gentleness of the Lord is evidenced. He will wait, He will help out the struggling faith. Gideon speaks of a meal-offering which he would set before his visitor. And the visitor replies, "I will tarry until thou come again."

Was the meal-offering—the present which Gideon looked to bring forth—a sacrifice set before the stranger as an act of worship? There is a suggestion that it was so.[3] The word used by Gideon is the word commonly employed for one species of sacrifice. Perhaps, as has been remarked, "the double sense which the word may bear of an offering to God or a gift to man, suits the doubt in the mind as to who the visitor might be."[4] The present was, at all events, according to the light which he had. And "if there be first a willing mind, it is accepted according to that a man hath, and not according to that he hath not." Apart from any association with worship, the request of the son of Joash and his action remind us of the manners and customs of hospitality still observed among the Arabian and Bedouin tribes. Still, there is the invitation to the stranger to partake of the meal. Still, for the one whom the host delights to honour, the kid or the lamb is fetched from the flock, and part of it served with soup and cakes. Still, the

---

[1] Judg. vi. 17.   [2] "Contemplations," book ix. chap. 5.
[3] "*Minchah* means sometimes a present made to man, as in chapter iii. 18; but it more commonly means a sacrificial offering (Gen. iv. 3–5), which seems to be its meaning here as explained vers. 19, 20. When coupled with *zwach*, the animal sacrifice, minchah means the meat and drink offering" (Bishop of Bath and Wells, "Pulpit Commentary").
[4] "Speaker's Commentary."

homely villager presents a repast similar to that which was brought forth under the oaks of Ophrah—the flesh by itself in a basket or tray, and the soup or broth in a goblet.

The point which Gideon emphasizes is, "a sign that Thou talkest with me"—a token, that is, that he is not confronted by a mere spectral apparition, but that there is a real conversation proceeding between him and the Lord in whose power he shall be able to smite the Midianites as one man. The belief in ghosts was then, as in the later day of the risen Christ, a prevalent belief among the Israelites; and the man, though in heart obedient to the heavenly vision, needed to be assured that it was indeed the Lord, and that it was to him that the Lord's commission to save Israel had come. It will be to him a sign of special grace if the stranger will remain under the oak whilst he prepares a meal, and if the stranger will accept the meal at his hands. Thus, and then, he will know that for him there is a peculiar and distinguishing favour, and the certainty of help in future enterprise. As to all besides, all subsequent to the setting forth of the present, this must be left to the angel.

The pledge asked having been granted, Gideon hastens to the farmstead, selects the kid, makes ready the cakes, arranges the simple meal, and returns to the terebinth where the angel is seated as before.[1] And, with all becoming deferences and courtesies, the meal is offered. In that which follows, the offerer is at once confirmed and confounded.

The angel command that the smoking flesh and the unleavened cakes be laid on the adjacent rock. He commands further, "Pour out the broth."[2] This second command determines the character of the present. The pouring of a fluid—wine, in some instances water—on altar or stone is one of the most conspicuous features of a sacrifice in Holy Scripture. Jacob set up a pillar in the place where God talked with him, even a pillar of stone, and he poured a drink-offering thereon.[3] So, under the law, the drink-offering was presented as an essential part of the ritual. And even in idolatrous service it was observed. The libation which was ordered at Ophrah transformed what might have seemed an ordinary meal into a sacri-

---

[1] "In this case, the stranger must have waited at least an hour while Gideon made ready the meal which he brought forth" (Kitto, "Daily Bible Illustrations").

[2] Judg. vi. 20.   [3] Gen. xxxv. 14; also Gen. xxviii. 20.

fice. The broth, or juice, denoted the blood, the life of the animal; and this was to flow over the extemporized altar on which the flesh and the bread were laid A rude, but expressive, forecast of the Supper of the Lord—the unleavened bread of sincerity and truth, the Flesh of the Lamb slain from the foundation of the world which is meat indeed, and the Blood poured over the world which is drink indeed!

The sign is immediately given. This angel is the Shepherd of Israel, and the shepherd's staff is in his hand. It is the way of the Lord to use some instrument, to employ some agency. The instrument is only what He makes it; but He is pleased to take account of the earthly creature, and with it, according to His effectual operation, "to do exceeding abundantly above all that we can ask or think." "The end of the staff" is put forth, and it touches the flesh and the cakes.[1] The touch of the lower by the higher, of the natural by the supernatural, of the carnal by the spiritual, is the truth of the blessed Wonderland. What marvels occur in human history when the life is touched from above! The fittest phrase for these marvels which the apostle can find is, "a new creation." What marvels of will-force, of soul-energy, are realized when the Spirit of God appropriates the aptitudes! "Prayers and pains," said Elliot, "through faith in Christ Jesus, can do almost anything." Behold the effect of the touch of the staff, when behind the staff is the might of the Lord! Lo! jets of fire issue from the stone, and flesh and cakes are consumed. To the unsophisticated son of Joash this is a great sight indeed!

Devout thought has traced the shadow of a greater mystery in the sign of Ophrah. As, in the outpouring of the juice of the flesh it has discerned the figure of the libation which, for all the world and for all the ages, is the blood of atonement, so, in the consuming of the flesh it has discerned the figure of the sacrifice of Calvary. And assuredly those to whom the cross of Jesus is the centre of the world find that cross dimly and imperfectly anticipated in the incidents before us, as in many incidents besides. But, to Gideon, the matter certified was the transcendent dignity and inexhaustible resources of the "Traveller unknown." Who he was could not be doubted. And if fire could be made to "rise up out of the rock," could not slumbering potencies in him be aroused? Could not an enthusiasm

[1] Judg. vi. 21.

GIDEON: THE CALL AND THE RESPONSE.

flame forth from even the dull and stolid Israelites? The sign of a Divine energy both to destroy and to arouse had been given: could he not now say, "Surely in that power to destroy the Midianites, and in that power to arouse the oppressed tribes, He will be with me. And I have found grace in His sight."

And yet, under the manifestation of grace and truth, the heart trembles, and fear takes hold of him. Is not the vision too splendid? Is not this person too exalted for mortal man? The vision has gone; the person has vanished.[1] And what of him? He knows that the angel was not a mere angel; that he was the angel in whom is the name of the Eternal. And it is an Israelite conviction that none can see the Eternal and live. "Alas, O Lord God, for because I have seen the angel of the Lord face to face."[2] It *is* death to the son of Joash. It is the hour when the law, "Die and re-exist," is fulfilled. The old idol-clinging, time-serving, enfeebled self has been killed within him. From this moment he is another person. There is a calling distinctly in view. He is henceforth to live not to self, but to God and his country. He is now more than the son of Joash, he is the servant of the Lord—all aims and ends, except the higher, consumed as the cakes had been consumed. And after this death comes peace. Through his soul sounds the voice, friendly and sympathetic, "Peace to thee; fear not; thou shalt not die."[3] The Resurrection-life is working. A fire has risen up out of the rock; and this fire is the power over which death has no dominion. Possessor of God's grace, he is the partaker also of God's immortality; and the secret of the Lord is with him.

[1] Judges vi. 21. In the appearance of the angel to Manoah, it is said that the angel "ascended in the flame of the altar."
[2] Judg. vi. 22.
[3] Judg. vi. 23.

CHAPTER XI.

GIDEON: THE BEGINNING OF THE ENTERPRISE.

The change in the idea and aim of the life—The altar, Jehovah-Shalom—
The sign of a transferred allegiance—"The same night," the time for
action—The illustration given in the narrative of the right witness for
God—Where and how it begins—Three features in the instruction
given to Gideon: First, look to home; Second, build the altar in the
conspicuous place; Third, offer the sacrifice as prescribed—Gideon
obeys, but with fearfulness—The wrath of the villagers—The answer
of Joash—The new name—The story of Jerubbaal spreads.

WHAT a change in the idea and aim of the life has been effected!
The farmer who, a little time ago, plied his flail on the threshing-
floor, his mind a chaos of thoughts and of emotions varying
from utter despondency to fierce indignation, is now conscious
of the call of God and fully in view of a work, the means to
whose accomplishment and the manner of whose fulfilment he
cannot discern. But he has seen the angel of the Lord face to
face, and, with the message of peace brought to him through
the vision, there has come, so to say, a new lease of life for the
performance of the part which has been indicated. In that
hour of awakened energy the first impulse is to build an altar
"there unto the Lord."[1] The same impulse the saints of God,
in days gone by, had felt. Abraham and Jacob and Moses had
built their altars, and through them had endeavoured to give
permanence to the sense of God's presence or help which, in
special circumstances, had been evoked. Abraham, for instance,
named the altar which he had reared *Jehovah-Jireh* when his
son was restored to his embrace as from the dead.[2] Moses
reared his *Jehovah-Nissi* when the fierce onslaught of Amalek

[1] Judg. vi. 24.   [2] Gen. xxii. 14.

was repulsed at Rephidim.[1] Gideon, too, must rear his *Jehovah-Shalom*, his stone-memorial of the peace which had been breathed over him, associating with the memorial the prayer that the Lord who had removed fear from his own breast would send the peace, which the bleeding and distracted people needed, through the smiting of the Midianites as one man.

The altar thus erected was the sign of a transferred allegiance. Hitherto, though not formally renounced, Jehovah had been only the traditional God; the actual homage of the villagers, including, it is to be feared, the family of Joash, was rendered to Baal, whose altar and grove were the conspicuous features of Ophrah. In the pile of stones hastily and loosely thrown together Gideon virtually said, " The Lord, the God of Israel, will I serve, and Him will I obey." This shrine is the token of personal dedication, of a solemn and explicit surrender to the Voice which had spoken to him from heaven. The new sight has taught him a new name—Jehovah-Shalom. In the strength of this name, he will go.

What follows? "Bid God welcome, and He will come again." "The same night" the Voice a second time reaches him. Ah, would it not be well to wait, to consider the matter in all its bearings, to discuss with himself the ways and means, to take some chosen friends into his confidence, and have some preparations made for the critical hour? There is a time to wait. Jesus waited at Nazareth until " He began to be about thirty years of age."[2] And, even after the descent of the Holy Ghost, He waited forty days, "being tempted of the devil."[3] Nor can we forget that after the ascension the apostles were commanded to "tarry in the city of Jerusalem until they were endued with power from on high."[4] But the time to wait is sometimes longer and sometimes shorter. " When it pleased God to reveal His Son in me," writes St. Paul, "immediately I conferred not with flesh and blood."[5] And in the character of of the true soldier there is a promptitude which we delight to honour. " When can you start for India?" the veteran general was asked. " To-morrow," was the reply. The demand was urgent and the obedience was instant. In the case before us, when the name is learned and the might in which the work is

[1] Exod. xvii. 15.   [2] Luke iii. 23.   [3] Luke iv. 2.
[4] Luke xxiv. 49.   [5] Gal. i. 15 16.

to be done is confessed, the period for action is "that same night."

Let it be understood that whosoever in distinct personal experience knows Jehovah-Shalom, is called to be the witness for Him. Thenceforth self, in its shrinkings from toil and pain, in its timidities, in its own preferences, is to be dead, and the life is to be hidden in God. This Old Testament story is a beautiful illustration of the right kind and manner of witness for the kingdom of God.

Observe where and how the witness begins. "Throw down the altar of Baal that thy father hath, and cut down the Asherah that is by it."[1] The stamping out of the idol is the point of departure for the hero. He must be the reformer of the evil within if he would be the deliverer from the foes without. He had asked, "Why is all this woe befallen us?" He is reminded that the worship of the Phœnician Baal is the why. The fathers who had told him of the miracles of the past might have told him of the Song in which the great lawgiver had testified against the people that, in sacrificing "to gods whom they knew knew not, to new gods that came up of late that their ancestors dreaded not,"[2] they were kindling a fire which should burn to the lowest pit. The war against Midian must be preceded by the crusade against Baal.

Three features are noticeable in the instruction given with regard to this, the initial work of Gideon.

He is commanded to look first to his father's house. The Baal-altar belonged to Joash, either as its owner, or its custodiar. The son of Joash might have asked of himself in what form he should set about the task assigned to him. This starting-place would not have occurred to him. But the Divine injunction points the moral which, in the search for some great thing to do, we are apt to overlook—that the part of wisdom is to work outwards from the circle next us. A man's first theatre of action is the place in which he lives. There or nowhere is his ideal; there or nowhere is his duty. We may be mistaken as to leadings of Providence or spheres of labour, but there can be no mistake as to one sphere. "Return to thine own house,"[3] said the Lord to a man whom He had healed. Ah! it is far more easy to go to the street and preach there than to preach faithfully and effectually to one's own flesh and blood. But let

[1] Judg. vi. 25.   [2] Deut. xxxii. 17.   [3] Luke viii. 39.

GIDEON: THE BEGINNING OF THE ENTERPRISE. 109

none think of throwing down Baal-altars here and there until they have thrown down the Baal-altars in their own home or circle. "They are a growing sort of men," says Carlyle, "who valiantly do the work that lies to their hand, and withal prepare for that which is before."

Further, Gideon is commanded to "build an altar unto the Lord his God upon the top of the stronghold in the orderly manner."[1] The phraseology of the chronicler is doubtful. Attaching the more obvious meaning to the clause "in the orderly manner," it might be supposed that, in the injunction given, the hero is charged to comply with the prescribed rules or order as to the erection of altars. And much, in this view, has been written on the duty of observing every part of a Divine ordinance, and of seeing that, in all circumstances, the way which God Himself has marked out be followed. The Old Testament, in the word to the son of Joash, has been regarded as anticipating the New Testament precept to the Churches, "Let all things be done decently and in order." But the use of the Hebrew term translated "in the ordered place," or "in the orderly manner," in other passages will scarcely warrant this interpretation. It must be held as referring to the disposition of the material for the sacrifice, the pile of wood to be laid on the altar.[2] And the chief point of the command is, that the altar thus to be prepared for the burnt-offering shall be erected in the most conspicuous situation in Ophrah, on the top of the citadel—the place which had been fortified for the protection of the community. It is to be recollected that this is the second altar reared on the day on which the angel of Jehovah appeared. The first was *a private memorial*, not intended for sacrifice; it symbolized the personal separation of the one on whom Jehovah had looked, and to whom He had said, "Peace to thee." The second is *a public testimony;* it is intended for sacrifice; and the scene of its erection is the public place, the "strong tower within the city," destined for shelter in the evil day. Cresting that tower, the altar witnessed, "God is our refuge and strength." Probably the idol of Astarte had stood in close proximity. In the altar surmounting the tower the fuller Voice was sounded: "There is none like to Thee,

[1] Judg. vi. 26.
[2] See Gen. xxii. 9: "Abraham built an altar and laid *the wood in order.*"

O Lord. The Lord is the true God: He is the living God and King of eternity."[1] The light of such a testimony must go forth "with the ripple and the radiance" of a brave, "I am not ashamed," flashing on the vision of all from the summit of the fortress.

Finally the sacrifice to be offered is prescribed—"Take thy father's young bullock, even the second bullock of seven years old, and throw down the altar of Baal that thy father hath. And take the second bullock and offer a burnt sacrifice with the wood of the Asherah which thou shalt cut down."[2] It is not clear whether two bullocks are pointed to, whether we are to read "*even*" or to read "and" in the former of the quoted clauses. The weight of opinion preponderates in favour of the conjunction "and," making the command equivalent to the taking of two bullocks, and the sacrifice of the one of the two which was seven years old. Why two should be specified we can only conjecture. It may have been that only the two had been spared from the ravages of the Midianites, or that the two indicated were specially kept for the purposes of husbandry, or that the two were devoted to sacrificial rites in honour of Baal. No doubt "the labour of both would be required for pulling down and removing the altar of Baal, and for bringing the materials for building the altar of Jehovah."[3] The younger to be laid on the altar is not young. The years of its age parallel those of the Midianite oppression. And the fuel for the offering is to be obtained by the cutting down of the posts or pillars set up in honour of the idol. "The earth is the Lord's and the fulness thereof;" that which had been desecrated is to be reconsecrated, the abuse is to be changed into the use, wrested from the service of the false for the service of the true.

Gideon obeys the instructions. But, as well he might, he obeys with fearfulness. He is the one man against the world. He is virtually severing the future from the past—marching into a future that is full of peril and difficulty. And the first consequence of the step to be taken will be the wrath of his fellow-villagers, the indignation, perhaps the fierce retribution, of his father's house. But he has put his hand to the task, and he cannot look back. We imagine the trepidations of the morning next after the night in which the Voice of the Lord found him. Must he set about the dreaded reformation? How

[1] Jer. x. 10. [2] Judg. vi. 26. [3] "Speaker's Commentary."

GIDEON: THE BEGINNING OF THE ENTERPRISE. 111

is he to do so? Hour follows hour, and it seems more and more hopeless in the full light of day to accomplish the part to which he is pledged. At length the plan takes shape. He will impart his design to some reliable men, and wait for the cover of night. He selects ten stalwart servants of his family,[1] and tells them to be ready for action; and when the sable curtain is drawn across the outer world, and the village is asleep, the daring farmer, with his little band, noiselessly but effectually fulfils the words of the Lord. The irrevocable deed has been done, and the most lion-hearted of mortals could not without some misgiving abide the issue.

Lo! in the early morning, the excited townsmen observe an altar reared on the fortified place, and on it the remains of the bullock that had been offered! More still—more appalling still!—the altar of their village god is demolished, and the Asherah cut down. He sees the folk of Ophrah in eager discussion over the catastrophe. He hears the angry roar as they sway hither and thither, and demand, "Who has mocked our mighty one, who has done this?" Perhaps he was a suspected person; perhaps in bygone days he had shown some zeal for Jehovah; perhaps his silence or his absence attracted the suspicions of the people. For soon the cry rang forth, "This ravager and destroyer is Gideon the son of Joash." And fierce and hot becomes the demand, "Joash, bring out your son that he may die."[2] It is a dark, critical moment. Gideon has only one hope—Jehovah-Shalom.

But what happens? That which Gideon feared might be his ruin turns to his salvation. He has dreaded the anger of his father's household. Behold, the anger is turned away. The boldness of the son has supplied courage to the father. The father is a man of fertile resources, nimble wit, and decision. Very likely the son in many conversations had sown the seeds of doubt as to Baal's right and Baal's might, and the father, made sceptical, needed only a moment such as this to give force to his scepticism. He will not surrender the hero of his

---

[1] Judges vi. 27. In this verse there is a distinction between "the men of his father's house"—*i.e.*, of the Abi-Ezrites, "the thousand" to which Gideon belonged—and "the men of the city"; from which it has been conjectured that there was a Canaanite population, apart from the Israelite, in Ophrah.

[2] Judg. vi. 28-30.

house, and he is ready with his keen, incisive satire. His sharp tongue stands him in better stead than sharp sword would have done. It is the same kind of satire as that which, generations afterwards, flashed from Elijah in his famous conference on Carmel with the priests of Baal.[1] Shrewdly, cleverly, he turns the tables on the men who are clamouring for the punishment of Gideon. "You, to be vehement on behalf of Baal, you playing the part of his protector: is this befitting? If he is a god, is he beholden to you? Will he not protect himself? Does he need your vengeance? Will he not avenge himself of the one who has thrown down his altar? Gideon die indeed! Rather let him die this very morning who will thus set himself above the god, and virtually deny the power of the god?"[2] Thus protests the bluff old chief to all who stood before him, and the bold, happily conceived speech disarms the opposition. On that day, Gideon is styled by popular acclamation Jerubbaal, as the one with whom Baal may settle the quarrel caused by the overthrow of Baal's altar.[3]

Such is the beginning of the enterprise. Gideon has, "with the seeing of the eye," beheld the Power who is with him. He has learned that the only obstacle in the way of this power is the unreformed evil of his people. He has learned the new name Jehovah-Shalom. He is himself the owner of the new name Jerubbaal. He has secured the confidence of the Abiezrites and of his father's household. A national party is already formed. The feeling has spread, "He who can do what has been done is the very captain whom we need." Far and near the story of Jerubbaal spreads. It finds its way into the tents of the Midianites, awakening fear. It is told in the dens and caves in which the children of Israel hide themselves, awakening hope. Is not the Lord about to visit His people in remembrance of His mercy?

[1] 1 Kings xviii.   [2] Judg. vi. 31.   [3] Judg. vi. 32.

CHAPTER XII.

GIDEON: THE TRUMPET-BLAST.

The return of the Midianites—The clothing of Gideon with the Spirit of the Lord—The trumpet-blast—The response of Abi-ezer—The summons to the northern tribes—The junction of the forces—The emotion of Gideon—Weak, but not faithless—Two differences between his pleading and the reluctance of Moses—We must do justice to him—The patience of God—The craving for a sign—The signs asked intended for the confirmation of his own faith—Signs which would naturally occur to him—Two points from which to regard them—The previous sign and the two to be regarded—What these two, reversed, said to Gideon—Their effect on him—Their symbolical meaning—More than an idealization of the qualities which characterized him—The fleece a symbol of Israel, and the dry ground a symbol of the nations—Their significance for and beyond the immediate moment—A prophetical meaning—A parable of the Church of Christ—Teaching many lessons bearing on personal religion.

THE man is ready, and the moment of action is not long delayed. The wild Bedouin tribes, after gathering the produce of the earth and plundering the luckless inhabitants of hill and dale, had withdrawn to their several regions—there to await the return of summer. With the ripening of grain and fruits, the cloud of human locusts reappears. They cross the Jordan at Bethshean; they stream through the gorges; their tents are pitched in the fair and fertile valley. In previous invasions, the honest farmer had observed their occupancy of the plain with indignation, but with the hopelessness caused by the overwhelming numbers of the invaders, and by the evidences of their wealth and power. He had only hung his head when the men and women of the village appealed to Baal; in his soul the question always sounded, "Why is all this befallen us, and where be all the wondrous works of Jehovah of which our fathers told us?" There is another emotion now burning within him.

"The Spirit of the Lord came upon him,"[1] or, as the phrase may be rendered, "*clothed* him." What is signified is, the possession of will and mind by a purpose which brooks no delay, a purpose through which the tides of a Divine energy flow into the channels of thought, purifying and intensifying the will to act.

> "Whoso has felt the Spirit of the Highest,
> Cannot confound nor doubt Him nor deny.
> Yea, with one voice, O world, though thou deniest,
> Stand thou on that side, for on this am I."[2]

The result of this investiture is—A GRAND TRUMPET-BLAST.[3] Shrill and clear, it is heard in the homes of the Abiezrites. They have already saluted their great man; now, instead of skulking into dens and caves, they rally around him, infected by his own intrepidity. A man's foes are sometimes they of his own household. The prophet has sometimes little honour in his own country. It is not so on the present occasion. The division of the tribe of Manasseh to which Gideon belonged is united in the voice, "Thine are we, and on thy side, thou son of Joash."

This is a token for good: and the new leader follows it up by an immediate and urgent call to the northern tribes to arm. The messengers by whom "the fiery cross" is sent have an inspiriting tale to tell. They can tell of all that has happened in Ophrah, and of that which has been demonstrated by the occurrences there, viz., the force of Gideon's personality. They can tell, too, that already the nucleus of a patriotic movement has been formed, that those who know him best have responded, as one man, to the trumpet which he blew. And the enthusiasm catches. All Manasseh is ablaze. Deborah, in her song, complained that "Asher sat still at the haven of the sea and abode by his creeks;" Asher now wipes away the reproach, it sends its thousands to the help of Jehovah against

---

[1] Judg. vi. 34. [2] T. N. Myers, "Saint Paul."
[3] Judg. vi. 34, "He blew a trumpet, and Abi-ezer was gathered after him."

the mighty. Zebulun, as in the day of Barak's campaign, "jeopards the lives" of its sons; and Naphtali claims the high places of the field. Other tribes are not mentioned. For Issachar, the apology has been offered that probably "it was unable to join him because the Midianites were encamped in the heart of their country."[1] The great midland tribe of Ephraim, afterwards, demands why no call had been sent it. But the four northern tribes contributed a gallant army; from the fortress crowned by the altar of Jehovah, Gideon beholds a mighty host pouring towards him with shouts that recall the old shout of a king which Israel's enemies knew and feared.[2]

A grand spectacle! A supreme moment! But how is it with the hero himself?

There is something awful in a great success, especially when the success brings the man face to face with the issue, with the crisis which, hitherto, he has contemplated through the haze. He has yielded himself to the dominating purpose: the work to be done, in its general scope and aim, has been clearly enough outlined, and the way towards its accomplishment has been seen and followed. But now he is precipitated on the event; the instruments and the means of action are in his hand; how are they to be used? how are the forces at disposal to be marshalled? Beheld from afar the battle seemed grand and exciting; but when it is imminent, when the enemy is right in view, and the raw, undisciplined, material needs to be ordered and arrayed, ah! the stoutest heart will quail, the boldest and strongest faith will have its shrinkings and fears. Is it to be wondered at that, with the thousands of Israel's chivalry waiting for his word, ready to fight but, for the most part, those "who before knew nothing thereof," Gideon, also an untried soldier and ignorant of methods of warfare, invested suddenly with a tremendous responsibility, should pause, should retire from the noise and glare of the host, and pour out his heart before the God whose call he had obeyed?

Shall it be said that he was faithless and weak? He was

---

[1] "Speaker's Commentary." So also Dean Stanley ("History of Jewish Church," lect. xv.), "Isachar, overrun by the Arab tribes, is absent."
[2] Judg. vi. 35. It is said of the three tribes, Asher, Zebulun, and Naphtali, that "they came up to meet them"—probably the men of Manasseh previously mentioned. The object of the "coming up" was to effect a combination of the forces.

weak. Let it be remembered that it is to those who have no might that the increase of strength is promised."[1] We may assume that none of the men who had responded to his summons saw the glance or heard the word which savoured of a craven fear. It is in standing before God that the hero knows his own weakness; it is to God that he confesses it, and it is in waiting on God that he changes his strength. Those who are led know not the secret struggles of those who lead, their sense of the awful burden of power and command and their "beseeching thrice" that they may know the sufficiency of an almighty grace. Do we blame Gideon for falling back on the *ifs?* He who knows what is in man does not blame him. His may be a scanty and imperfect faith, but it is faith. The *ifs* are not bred by doubt of God, by a distrust which prompts the desire to be relieved from the task. There is a manifest difference between his pleading and such reluctance as that of Moses to undertake the commission to Pharaoh, which kindled the anger of the Lord. We can trace the difference in two respects. In the first place, to Moses there had been a full and various revelation of God in anticipation of, and in answer to, the questions and timidities of the human heart. The great sight of the burning bush had been vouchsafed, the Divine commission had been explicitly given; and then, one by one, the objections of the mind of the flesh had been most graciously and patiently met. The "blank cheque"—the *I am* of the Eternal—which faith can fill up as the occasion calls, and which, however great the amount, is always honoured, had been given for his operation; he had been presented with the Covenant Name and memorial to all generations; signs had been wrought and promised to evidence the Power in which he was to go. and when, still, Moses urged the slow speech and slow tongue, God Himself had said, "Go, and I will be with thy mouth and teach thee what thou shalt say."[2] All this varied, one might say exhaustive, dealing on the part of the Eternal Wisdom and Love, this marvellously patient lovingkindness, had been the experience of Moses; and his backwardness in accepting the service marked an obstinacy which passed the bound of humility, and entered the region of the evil heart of unbelief. In the case of Gideon, the assurances of a Divine presence and strength, although distinct and ample,

[1] Isa. xl. 29. [2] Exod. iii. and iv.

neither in form nor in fulness approached those granted to the prophet of the older time; nor was there, on his part, the craving for release from the duty to which he was designated. "If thou wilt save Israel by mine hand," is another kind of speech to God than "Send, I pray thee, by the hand of him whom thou wilt send"—only, it is implied, *not by me*.

And this suggests the second point of difference between the opposition of Moses and the fearfulness of Gideon. Moses in the transaction of the desert was too busily occupied with self. His estimate of capability for the work was the measure of his own gifts and aptitudes. He could not find in *them*, the justification of the mission. In himself, he wanted that which seemed to him the insurance of success. To arouse and lead his countrymen?—had not he failed before, when " he supposed that his brethren would have understood how that God, by his hand, would deliver them"? If he had failed then, how could he be confident that he would succeed now? Years had passed since the failure on account of which he had fled from Egypt: and these years had made him more distrustful of himself. To go to Pharaoh!—had not his residence at Court taught him that the man to gain a monarch's ear must be subtle, dexterous, and persuasive of speech?—the very qualities in which he was lacking. Oh no; he was not the man for the mission. "I am not eloquent, neither heretofore, nor since Thou hast spoken to Thy servant."[1] In vain came the word, "I will be with thy mouth." The mouth, with its stammering speech, was more to him, at the moment, than the Presence with it. This refusal to look away from self and trust God alone, and find in God, not self, the reason of the mission and the fitness for it, to go in the faith that He is "able to make all grace abound always as an all-sufficiency in all things," was the dishonour put on God which, in the homely phrase of the sacred writer, "kindled His anger." True humility does not consist in thinking meanly or otherwise of self: it consists rather in putting self aside, as reason of service or measure of fitness, and closing, simply and fully, with God in His will and power. Now, weak as Gideon may have been, he has learned to look off from self. He is God's instrument. What is to be done will be done by God. "The Lord had looked on him, and said, Go in *this* thy might." And the *Look* or the revelation of the might was ever with him.

[1] Exod. iv. 10.

We shall see how, more and more as the campaign advances, the demonstration of the only effectual might is made. At the present stage, we recognize the modesty, the genuine humility of the speech, "If Thou wilt save Israel by mine hand."[1] He is not the Saviour; he is only the hand by whom the Saviour is pleased to act.

Gideon is not hasty. Since God is to be the all in all, he is anxious, over anxious we might say, to be certified that God will work by his hand. Let us do justice to him. He is not to be subjected to tests appropriate to us, with our fulness of revelation, and in the conditions of our religious and social life. There was then no word of the Lord. The national oracle was far away at Shiloh. He had grown up in a semi-heathen community, and his views were narrow and confused. God bears and forbears with the man whom He has caused to approach to Him. Very beautiful is the patience by which He makes good the promise, "To this man will I look, . . . even to him that trembleth at My word."[2] The exhibition of this patience in the sacred narrative is interesting and suggestive.

The craving for a sign, for some portent in the heavens or some departure from the ordinary course of nature, is noted in the New Testament as a characteristic of the Hebrew. Jesus Christ accused His brethren according to the flesh of a stubbornness of mind in this matter, "Except ye see signs and wonders, ye will not believe."[3] And St. Paul writes: "The Jews require a sign."[4] Gideon illustrates this craving; though in his case it was the evidence of an excess of caution, rather than of positive unbelief. It has been conjectured that the request for signs additional to those already vouchsafed was prompted by the wish to have his mission fully authenticated to the people whom he was to lead.[5] This is not the motive which a study of his words and action suggests. The dealing with God is a private dealing. It is his personal attitude to the call that is emphasized. And the signs selected were such as fell within his cognizance only. The fleece was disposed by him at night; its moisture or its dryness was observed by him in the morning. The historian's statement is most naturally interpreted when it is accepted as the record of a transaction between him and the Eternal.

[1] Judg. vi. 36. [2] Isa. lxvi. 2. [3] John iv. 48.
[4] 1 Cor. i. 22. [5] Dr. Kitto, "Daily Bible Readings."

GIDEON: THE TRUMPET-BLAST. 119

He feels that he is bold, almost to the extent of presumption. When the reverse sign is asked for, he uses language similar to that of Abraham when he stood before the Lord interceding in behalf of Sodom.[1] It is even more intense "Oh let not Thine anger be hot against me, and I will speak but this once." The Lord is very merciful, when there is faith even like the grain of mustard seed. And "more things are wrought by prayer than the world dreams of."

The sign which Gideon ventures to indicate is one which naturally occurred to the honest farmer of Ophrah. In Palestine, the dews are heavy,[2] and the nights are often cold.[3] A sheepskin or fleece may have been sometimes worn by him as a protection against the cold of night,[4] and he may have observed that the fleece in the morning was saturated with dew, and may have wrung the moisture out. Thence is suggested the token which he proposes to his Heavenly Counsellor. We may regard this token from two points. First, what it was and said to him; and, second, its symbolical or didactic significance

1. The son of Joash had a twofold mission. He was the Jerubbaal—the one called to confound Baal and overthrow the idolatry which had become dominant among the Abiezrites. He had to cleanse the Church before he attempted to deliver the State. For this aspect of his work, the most appropriate sign was one associated with sacrifice, one which would show that all homage is due to Jehovah, that with Him is the consuming fire, that the touch of His rod can transform the meal into the meal-offering, and the meal-offering into the burnt-offering. And this was evidenced by the visit of the angel of the Lord, and by that which happened when the meal "brought out under the terebinth" was, by the angel's command, transferred to the rock.[5] The sign, then and there given, belongs to the region of worship.

But the double work now to be regarded relates more

---

[1] Gen xviii. 32

[2] So David (2 Sam. i. 21) in his lamentation over Saul and Jonathan's appeals: "Ye mountains of Gilboa, let there be no dew." And the Psalmist (Psa. cxxxiii. 3) compares the unity of brethren to "the dew of Hermon, and that which descends on the mountains of Zion."

[3] So Jacob, replying to Laban (Gen. xxxi. 40), says, "In the day, the drought consumed me, and the frost by night."

[4] "As in Afghanistan," Lord A. Hervey, "Pulpit Commentary."

[5] Chapter vi. 19-24.

specially to the second aspect of the mission—the deliverance of Israel from the yoke of the oppressor. The previous wonder said "Jehovah is God"; the wonders now recorded say, "This God will save His people by thy hand; thou shalt go in His strength." Their immediate object was to demonstrate the Divine favour for him . to prove that, for all emergencies, the grace of God is sufficient. "Heaven's real miracles will endure turning, being inside and outside both alike."[1] The miracles of the two nights before the march are testimonies as to the commission of the hero, and are pledges of all-embracing might.

"If Thou wilt save Israel by mine hand, as Thou hast said, behold, I will put a fleece of wool on the floor, and if the dew be on the fleece only, and it be dry upon all the earth beside, then shall I know that Thou wilt save Israel by mine hand as Thou hast said. And it was so, for he rose up early on the morrow, and thrust the fleece together, and wringed the dew out of the fleece, a bowl full of water."[2]

This is certainly extraordinary. The fleece is so permeated with the dew that it seems to have received not its own share only, but all that would have fallen on the earth around it which is dry. It has received the whole abundance of the grace, the environment is sterile and parched. Still, with characteristic caution, Gideon thinks, "It is extraordinary, but it is explicable. For it is the property of wool to attract and absorb the moisture in the atmosphere:[3] the opposite of that which has taken place—the wool not attracting, but repelling, whilst the soil attracts and receives all the dew—would be the extraordinary and, on natural lines, the inexplicable circumstance." And it is this that he dares to ask of God.

"O let not Thine anger be hot against me, and I will speak but this once; let me prove, I pray Thee, but this once with

---

[1] Matthew Henry, "Commentary."

[2] Judges vi 36-38. The word rendered "bowl" occurs in chapter v. 25 The line in Deborah's song translated in A. V. "She brought forth butter in a lordly dish," is literally "in a bowl of mighty ones" It was probably "a shallow drinking cup, usually of brass" (Van Lennep, "Bible Customs," p. 475). "A bowl full of water"—"A detail highly characteristic of a true narrative" (Lord A. Hervey, "Speaker's Commentary")

[3] Lord Bacon in his "Natural History" says, "Sailors have used every night to hang fleeces of wool on the sides of their ships, towards the water; and they have crushed fresh water out of them in the morning."

GIDEON: THE TRUMPET-BLAST. 121

the fleece; let it now be dry only on the fleece, and upon all the ground let there be dew."[1] The prayer is granted. The order of nature is not so rigid as to forbid the exercise of the Divine Sovereignty, and He who hears prayer listens to the voice of a man. On the second night, the sign is reversed; when the second morning dawns, "it is dry upon the fleece only, and there was dew on all the ground."[2]

The timidity of Gideon was dispelled. For him, there could be no well of trembling. We never again read of a sign asked. He knows whom he is trusting. The lesson taught him in Jezreel is that which the warrior of the Cross afterwards declared in the great words, God is "able to do exceeding abundantly above all that we can ask or think, according to the power that worketh in us."[3] Henceforth he is

> "One who never turned his back, but marched breast forward,
> Never doubted clouds would break;
> Never dreamed, though right were worsted, wrong would triumph,
> Held we fall to rise, are baffled to fight better,
> Sleep to wake."[4]

2. The incident which confirmed the faith, and stimulated the courage, of the leader of Israel is so striking, that a symbolical and prophetical character, variously interpreted and applied, has been traced in it.

By some, indeed, it has been regarded as only the idealization of the qualities most characteristic of Gideon. It is nothing more, in their view, than a poetical representation of that which he was—" Warm and overflowing with zeal, when all besides are indifferent and dry, and, on the other hand, maintaining the greatest coolness and dryness when all other hearts are overflowing with unreasonable impatience and excitement. This once granted, it is easy to see how legend may have reported of Gideon, the great commander, that he wore on his breast a fleece which was moist when all around was dry, and dry even when all else was moist. And if Gideon, as a general, was distinguished by this spontaneously varying fleece, a narrator of a poetical turn might represent him before his entrance on his mission as supplicating from Jahveh, the

[1] Judg. vi. 39.   [2] Judg. vi. 40.
[3] Ephes. iii. 20.   [4] Browning's "Asolando."

wondrous fleece as a sign and pledge of his fitness for the arduous campaign. And so runs our existing account."[1]

The "existing account" may not thus be explained away. The indications of "a poetical turn" in the narrator are not so obvious to those who discern a supernatural operation in the history of Israel from the Exodus onwards, who feel that this history is one of special providence and special grace. The signs are unquestionably out of the ordinary course of events, but the story of Gideon, and a great deal besides in the annals of the chosen people, is also extraordinary. If wonderland is to be waved out of sight at subordinate points of the chronicle, it may as well be waved out of sight at the principal points also: and then it will be difficult to determine where the "poetical turn"[2] ends and where the prose of historical fact begins.

One of the notes to be insisted on with regard to a "real miracle" of Heaven is that a sufficient cause for a modification of the order of the universe must be shown.[3]

Was there such a cause for compliance with Gideon's request? The Christian believer cannot separate the history of Israel from the purpose of God to reveal His will as the will to bless all the families of the earth. That history is to him the channel through which the grace afterwards to be brought at the revelation of Jesus Christ flowed from generation to generation. Now, the moment which we are regarding was a critical moment. Defeat by the Midianites might involve the crushing out of the national life, and, with this, the crushing out of the true worship. All depended on the success of Gideon's mission. The sufficiency was not in himself. The comfort, the strength, was beyond himself. For the campaign that was imminent, it was of the utmost consequence that he should be assured of the Invisible Force behind him. And God, the Highest, stoops to give the assurance, in answer to the prayer of faith.

---

[1] Ewald's "History of Israel," vol. ii. p. 500.

[2] There are "poetical turns," rather poetical quotations, in the ancient books of Scripture   The account of the sun standing still is apparently a quotation from a book called the Book of Jasher, which is held by Keil to have been a book of national songs. But the source of the poetry is expressly indicated in the history.

[3] Horace gives as a canon of art, "Nec Deus intersit, nisi dignus vindice nodus inciderit."

Assuming, then, that the portion of the narrative which records the signs is genuinely historical—is not an interpolation of one with a "poetical turn"—what is the symbolic worth of the signs? All interpreters are agreed that they connect, more or less directly, with Israel and the peoples around it. The fleece of wool is the symbol of Israel—small as compared with "all the earth beside." Midian, for the time, is the symbol of all the earth. Looking to the immediate event, we see, in the first place, the vast host dry and unblest; the vital force, the sap, is with Gideon's band. The dew on the fleece is the pledge of an energy able to restore and revive the nation. Again, when the token is reversed, when the earth, not the fleece, is wet, there is an anticipation of the excitement in Midian; the soil whence spring the thought and action of the great host is clammy and moist, and the heart of the multitude becomes like water. Contrary to all that might have been anticipated, the consternation is where the resources are apparently inexhaustible, whilst the small army of Gideon, though raw and undisciplined, is calm and powerful. And, looking beyond the immediate event, the question may be put, Is not the condition of the fleece on the two successive nights, the representation of the two great periods in the history of Israel? There is no more beautiful image in Sacred Prophecy than that in which Jehovah says, through the Prophet, "I will be as the Dew unto Israel."[1] The people around were sunk in idolatry and manifold social and moral debasement. No benediction seems to fall on them. Israel called out of Egypt, separated from ignoble thraldoms, and from the manner of the nations, in the solitude of Sinai, hedged around by law, sanctified to Jehovah, is the heir of the promises. "What could be done more to the Lord's vineyard that He did not do in it?"[2] "The Spirit was poured upon it from on high, and the wilderness became a fruitful field, and the fruitful field was counted for a forest."[3] The Lawgiver, contemplating the fleece on which the Spirit had been poured, exclaims, "Happy art thou! who is like unto thee, O people saved by the Lord?"[4]

Gideon besought that the moisture might be on the ground, not on the fleece. The entreaty is granted. Was he not, unconsciously, the occasion of a prophecy? In the reversal of

[1] Hos. xiv. 5.
[2] Isa. v. 4.
[3] Isa. xxxii. 15.
[4] Deut. xxxiii. 29.

the token, are we not reminded of the consequence of apostacy from covenant grace and standing? That the fleece, not the earth, attract the moisture, is in the Divine ordering. So, it is in the Divine ordering that Israel receive and retain the blessing, not for herself but for the world. But when the elect people departs from its sphere of worship and life, it loses the privilege of the dew. That which should have been the fountain of blessing to the nations is dried up and withered, and the nations receive what passes away from it. They have the moisture; it becomes arid. Not that God will "cast away His people which He foreknew";[1] but He will bring it to realize that its strength and hope perish when they are cut off from the Lord. Israel now seems like the dry land. Yet, there is hope for the man of God. He who watered the ground from His chambers can bring life where there seems only death. He who can do this otherwise than in the way of nature, can do beyond all expectation, and even otherwise than in the way of all appearance.

And in this, whoso is wise will read a parable of the Church of Christ—its place, the secret of its vitality, and the condition of its power. Nor will he fail to learn many lessons bearing on personal religion. Each of the signs has, in these connections, its special significance. The fleece, taken from sheep or kid which has been slain, perhaps the very kid which had been offered to the angel, may remind us of the covering for human sinfulness which God, through the sanctified life of Christ, has provided.

> "Jesus, Thy blood and righteousness,
> My beauty are, my glorious dress."

It is the one thus covered, the one abiding in Christ, who realizes the power of the Spirit poured from on high. On the other hand, God, who is able "even of stones to raise up children to Abraham,"[2] God, "who quickeneth the dead, and calleth those things that be not as though they were,"[3] can bless even the hard apparently unproductive earth: the surrounding of the Church may receive the grace, whilst the Church itself is cold and dull. For it is the conjunct testimony of the two signs that, without the descent of the Higher Force, that which outwardly possesses the advantage will

---

[1] Rom. xi. 2 [2] Matt. iii 9. [3] Rom. iv. 17.

count for little; with that descent, what is externally unfavourable and unlikely may be rendered capable of great things. "Not by might, nor by power, but by My Spirit, saith the Lord of Hosts."[1] And this is the matter of the object-lesson which Gideon received. He got the "strong consolation" which he desired. May we imitate him in his holy importunity! Wonders such as he craved are among the things left far behind. God has provided some better thing for us.

> "The childlike faith that asks not sight,
>   Waits not for wonder or for sign,
>   Believes because it loves aright—
>   Shall see things greater, things divine."[2]

But the essence of the prayer of the mighty man is the essence of all true prayer in every time—"Let me prove, I pray thee" —this is the essence. And the invitation and promise run— he that hath an ear, let him hear !—" Prove me now herewith, if I will not open you the windows of heaven, and pour you out a blessing, that there shall not be room enough to receive it."[3]

[1] Zech. iv. 6.
[2] Keble's "Christian Year," Hymn on St. Bartholomew.
[3] Mal. iii. 10.

CHAPTER XIII.

GIDEON: TESTS AND SIFTINGS.

"Jerubbaal, who is Gideon"—The well of Harod, where was it?—The situation of the opposing armies—"God's thoughts not our thoughts"—The main interest of the history of Israel a religious interest—The protection against "vaunting"—The proclamation enjoined by the Law—The effect of the proclamation at the spring of Jezreel—The conduct of the Israelites has its counterpart in that of many Christians—The additional command—The second test and its effect—A sign of the quality of the man—The lessons taught us.

THE historian, beginning the narrative of the campaign, is careful to give both the name and "the new name" of the leader of Israel. "Then Jerubbaal, who is Gideon."[1] Both the mission and the might are indicated. The son of Joash goes forth, not as a mere patriot at the head of patriot-bands, but as the champion of the Lord of Hosts, warring against the domination of Baal, with the degrading servitude and the manifold evil which that involved. And the strength by which he is inspired is not his own. "The Lord has looked on him." How different is he from "the people that were with him." In a letter to his beloved Melancthon, Luther writes of "a common-place not in your books, Philip, the common-place of faith." This common-place is now "writ large" in the book of Gideon's life. He sets forward as *Jerubbaal*, the man who has received the white stone bearing the name of the Prince who has power with God and men and has prevailed — an Israelite indeed, who has learned the lesson taught to Jacob at the fords of Jabbok.

He has been fitted for his part by the transaction on which we have dwelt. The fearfulness and trembling are past. They

[1] Judg. vii. 1.

GIDEON: TESTS AND SIFTINGS.

have been set in the view of the Almighty, and the look bestowed on him, and the signs vouchsafed to him, have dispelled them. The soldier of faith has received his weapons; he is anointed with the power to wax valiant in fight. It is now the time to act.

> "Think not of rest, though dreams be sweet;
> Start up and ply your heavenward feet."

And before the sun has risen with burning heat—in early morning—the Lord's host is encamped "beside the well of *Harod*."

So the well or fountain was named in consequence of the event in Israelite history with which it is associated. That event is its sole association. The only reference in later Scriptures to it is in the list [1] of "the mighty men whom David had." Two of the thirty-seven in the latter part of this list are called Harodites. We cannot identify the fountain with any particular spring; but "it was possibly the same as that elsewhere called the spring of Jezreel,"[2] and now known as Ain Jalûd, "at the base of the mountain range of Gilboa, about half an hour's walk east of Zerin,"[3] the ancient city of Jezreel.

The situation of the opposing armies is partly described; and the description is one of those traits which stamp a narrative as genuine and authentic. Gideon is represented as leading his people along the southern branch of the plain of Esdraelon; the Midianites, and Amalekites, and the children of the East are represented as occupying a portion of the northern branch, near to a hill called Morêh,[4] perhaps the Little Hermon or one of the slopes which overlook the valley. The Israelites had thus a full view of the great force against which they were moving, and which was not more than two or three miles distant. And the prospect of the vast multitude caused many a hitherto stout heart to quail. How insufficient even the thirty thousand warriors of the northern tribes seemed for the gigantic task which they had undertaken!

[1] 2 Sam. xxiii. 25.
[2] Stanley's "Sinai and Palestine," chap. ix.
[3] "The Land and the Book," Central Palestine, chap. vi.
[4] Not the place called "the plain of Moreh" in Gen. xii. 6, and the "plains of Moreh" in Deut. xi. 30. There is a hill overlooking the valley of Jezreel, called Mutsillim, which Dr. Robinson thinks may have been Moreh.

They thought themselves too few; God thought them too many. For "His thoughts are not our thoughts, neither are our ways His ways." The deliverance was to be in the line of all His past dealing. The fathers of Israel "got not the land in possession by their own sword, neither did their own arm save them: but His right hand and His arm, and the light of His countenance, because He had a favour to them."[1] The main interest of the history of the chosen people is a religious interest. This was secured by the manner of all the triumphs recorded in their annals. What these, in connection with other features, proved was that the great constructive and aggressive forces are those of religion. Religion—the acknowledgment of the living and true God—was always manifested as the essence of well-being, and every great emergency contributed to the enforcement of the lesson. God was the All. He was the Judge, the Lawgiver, the King. The Midianites trusted in horses and chariots: the Israelites must remember only the name of the Lord their God. On the ear of the captain falls the message—a strange one it must have seemed to him—"The people that are with thee are too many for Me to give the Midianites into their hands, lest Israel vaunt themselves against Me, saying, Mine own hand hath saved me."[2]

Gideon was the champion of Jehovah against Baal. He had thrown down Baal's altar. But a victory which would have given occasion for self-glorifying might have led to the erection of another altar to another type of idolatry—the idolatry of self—equally, perhaps more dangerously, misleading. There must be no room for vaunting: the day must declare, "I am the Lord thy God which brought thee out of the land of Egypt, out of the house of bondage. Thou shalt have no other gods before Me."[3]

A great reduction in the number of the host must be effected: but it must be effected in the orderly manner.

There was a unique provision in the law of Israel. How far the practice conformed to the law we cannot say. But the ordinances to be observed on the eve of battle are thus stated: First, the priest, in the name of the Eternal, is to address the army, bidding all realize the imminence of the struggle, but exhorting them to preserve an undaunted front—no fainting, or trembling, or terror—in the assurance of the Divine power going with them to fight for them against their enemies. But, this

---

[1] Psa. xliv. 3.   [2] Judg. vii. 2.   [3] Exod. xx. 2, 3.

charge delivered, the officers are to announce that liberty to withdraw from the host is given to those who have built a new house and not dedicated it, or who have planted a vineyard and not eaten of it, or who have betrothed a wife and not been married; and farther, and more generally, to any who are fearful and faint-hearted, lest the cowardice might be infectious among the troops.[1] A resolute and courageous few, it is implied, are better than an irresolute and ill-compacted multitude. Jehovah could save with many or with few; only let all taking part in His wars be valiant and faithful.

But never was such a spectacle witnessed as that witnessed at the spring of Jezreel. The instruction to Gideon is that the proclamation enjoined be made; and it is made in the form customary with the northern tribes.[2] What does the heroic commander behold? In the early morning, he had looked on thirty-two thousand men apparently eager to be led on: before the day has far advanced, he sees twenty and two thousand taking advantage of the liberty given and hastening back to their homes. A panic, it was evident, had seized a vast majority of those who had obeyed his trumpet-call. Is it to be wondered at? They had been enervated by years of servitude; they were, many of them, half-starved; morally as well as physically their strength had gone. Not in such a rabble was to be found the stuff out of which a brave army could be formed. Better that the craven hearts should depart from Mount Gilead.

Nor let us be too ready to cast the stone at the cowardly Israelites. Their conduct has its counterpart in the conduct of many who "profess and call themselves Christians." How brave are purposes and protestations when the danger involved in executing or adhering to them seems a thing of distant courses! Peter was sincere, and felt the courage of his resolution, when he declared his readiness to accompany his Master to prison and

---

[1] Deut. xx. 1–8.
[2] The proclamation is, "Whosoever is fearful and afraid, let him return and depart early from Mount Gilead." There is no mountain of this name in the neighbourhood of Jezreel. Gilead was beyond Jordan. It has been supposed that *Gilead* is a copyist's error for Gilboa, the letters of the two words being similar. It has been supposed, also, that the form given was the customary form in Manasseh, or, at least, among the Abi-ezrites. Some of Gideon's kindred (Josh. xvii. 3) dwelt beyond Jordan, near Mount Gilead.

to death: that any doubt should be thrown on his zeal and ability to do so pained him. When the shades of the prison and the possibility of death were to be reckoned with, he followed the precedent set by the Hebrews of Gideon's day. And so it is with many; let each reader of this chapter ask whether it may not have been so with him or her, at some past moment when the severe test was applied. Ah! we speak largely. We are full of resource until "the host of the Midianites is seen on the north side" of us. In the trial hour undisciplined strength is mere weakness. Impulse is of little worth until it is consolidated in principle. The worth of impulsiveness is shown in the action of the twenty-two thousand at the Fountain of Trembling.

Surprise follows surprise. What are the ten thousand in comparison with the army of the enemy, like the sand for number, and with a huge array of chariots and horsemen? Gideon may well have grave misgivings as to the issue of the campaign on which he has entered—the odds against him are so great. But what a tax is laid on his faith when the Divine voice is heard within, "The people are yet too many"? Yet too many! What can this mean? What farther weeding out must be done? Surely, now, he has under his command the very pink and flower of the northern chivalry! No; and a second trial of a remarkable nature must be imposed. The remainder of his army, after the departure of their comrades, continued in the position taken up in the morning, on the rising ground above the spring with its deep pool, and the marshy soil about it. There they had been exposed for some time to the heat of the sun, and their thirst was aggravated by the fatigues of previous marches. "Bring them down unto the water," was the command, "and I will try them for thee there: and it shall be that of whom I say unto thee, This shall go with thee, the same shall go with thee; and of whomsoever I say unto thee, This shall not go with thee, the same shall not go. So he brought down the people to the water."[1]

What was the method observed in the selection of the warriors? What was the truth evidenced in the second of the tests prescribed that day?

The thirsty soldiers come to the pool. Now is the moment. The Lord says to Gideon, "Every one that lappeth of the water

[1] Judg. vii. 4.

GIDEON: TESTS AND SIFTINGS.

with his tongue as a dog lappeth, him shalt thou set by himself; likewise every one that boweth down upon his knees to drink."[1]

A curious mode of selection! a strange principle of classification! All to depend on the one thing—who took, or who did not take, the water in the palm of the hand and sip it. But that one thing had a significance. It was a sign of the quality of the men.

"The number of them that lapped, putting their hand to their mouth, were three hundred men: but all the rest of the people bowed down upon their knees to drink water."[2] The three hundred are the resolute, self-denying, soldierly men, "patient of labour and thirst, willing to stoop, content with a little."[3] The rest of the people are the self-indulgent and rash. They will have a great gulp of the cooling water; all is forgotten except the gratification of the appetite. They reflect not on the possibility of a surprise by the enemy; the need of the moment, the craving of the moment, overbears all considerations; they throw themselves down at the brink of the pool and greedily drink. And the Lord says, "By the three hundred that lapped will I save you, and deliver the Midianites into thine hand: and let all the other people go every man unto his own place."[4]

May we not say of this incident what St. Paul says of the events of the history of Israel in general, that it happened unto them for a type or picture of truth in which all future generations are interested, and that it is "written for our admonition upon whom the ends of the world are come"?[5]

Think of the people who take the greedy drink "bowing down on their knees." Are we not familiar with their countenance? Is it not sometimes only too plainly evidenced in ourselves? There is no feature in moral discipline more slowly learned, and more intermittently practised, than self-restraint. A repression, at times even effacement, of self is indispensable to the highest kind of work. "Strait is the gate, and narrow is the way which leadeth unto life."[6] And, even in regard to things in themselves lawful, there are circumstances in which the good soldier will put a curb on appetite, will even refuse the pleading of natural human desire. "It is sometimes expedient," writes the saintly Thomas à Kempis "to use a restraint even in good desires and endeavours, lest through importunity thou

[1] Judg. vii. 5   [2] Judg. vii 6.   [3] Bishop Hall's "Contemplations."
[4] Judg. vii 7   [5] 1 Cor. xx. 11.   [6] Matt vii 14.

incur distraction of mind : lest by thy want of self-government thou beget a scandal to others ; or again being by others thwarted and resisted thou become suddenly confounded and so fall. Sometimes, thou must use violence, and resist manfully thy sensual appetite—not regarding what the flesh would or would not : but rather taking pains that even perforce it may be made subject to the Spirit."[1] Now, in this self-tutoring, the great mass of the Israelites was shown to be deficient. An incident apparently trivial will sometimes reveal the inner spirit and temper of a life. And the mode of using the water showed the capability of the men whom Gideon led to the pool. Those who bowed on their knees are not blamed; they are only proved to be wanting in some of the noblest traits of character. As they rushed to the water-edge to slake their thirst, so would they rush on the spoil in the day of victory, and be corrupted by so doing. They do not form the most select circle of God's warrior-bands : it is by the three hundred, not by them, that He will save Israel.

For the test which shows a tendency to self-gratification, and remissness in holy vigilance in the many, shows that these features are present in the three hundred, who only take the sips of water which their hands can hold. They can be sparing in the use of even necessary things. They will not be off their guard, even in moments of ease. There is a work before them, and they are "straitened until it is accomplished." They will not go down to the earthly thing, they will lift the earthly thing to them. There is an unbending loftiness in the aim, an immoveable mightiness in the will. It is they who continue to the end; they who, though faint, can and will pursue until the victory is fully won. Such moral control is a sign of the manhood according to God's own heart. There is a moment in the career of David which illustrates it. In one of his numerous wars against the Philistines, " he longed and said, Oh that one would give me to drink of the water of the well of Bethlehem which is by the gate." Three of his mighty men, fired with devotion to their chief, broke through the host of the Philistines and brought a jar full of the water longed for. But he refused to drink it, because it seemed to him the blood of the men who had gone " in jeopardy of their lives."[2] The lower craving was neutralized, was denied, through the pressure of a

[1] "Imitation of Christ," book iii. chapter 2.   [2] 2 Sam xxiii. 15-17.

thought which dominated his soul. Those of whom it is possible to say this, who stand out from others, distinguished by a toughness of moral fibre, a special faculty of endurance at the behest of a sacred purpose, are the men by whom the Lord wills to save His Church and world.

Would that the impression of the three hundred were multiplied! Thermopylæ and Jezreel are not solitary instances of the force with which the Almighty can clothe the three hundred In the wars of the kingdom, as in the affairs of life, the proverb holds good, "Better is little with the fear of the Lord than great treasure and trouble therewith."[1] The hordes of Xerxes were powerless as against the few with God for them. The hordes of the Midianites were scattered before the breath of Gideon and his handful. "Fewer Christians and better ones," has been indicated as a desideratum of our day. This, at least we may learn from the chapter on Providence before us—that numbers, organizations, methods, occupy only the second rank in the ordering of God. There are occasions in which He dispenses with them, lest His "Israel vaunt themselves against Him, saying, Mine own hand hath saved me." He will recognize the human instrumentality; but it must always be held as subordinate. For ourselves, let us realize the lessons of Gideon's band. One of the great questions of life is that which the thought of this band at the well of Harod suggests. —Is the man above the circumstances, or are the circumstances more than the man? Will he go down to the stream, or will he lift what he needs of the stream to him! Will he conjoin the "sober and holy," with the thankful, use of comforts, and in all be true to the nobler warfare of the heavenly kingdom? Not by those who are ready to throw themselves down on their knees and take full draughts when the river of human pleasures offers itself, will any good cause be strengthened, or any signal victory be won. The likeness of the three hundred is manifest in the elect of every time who "climbed the steep ascent of heaven, through peril, toil and pain." May ours be the breathing—

> "O God, to us may grace be given
> To follow in their train."

---

[1] Prov. xv. 16.

CHAPTER XIV.

GIDEON: "THE CAKE OF BARLEY BREAD."

The equipment for the campaign—The necessity of immediate action—Rapid and bold movements a traditional policy of the Israelites—The command, and the offer of a sign—The nocturnal expedition—The camp of the Midianites—The dream—Its terms and its matter—The interpretation—What this betokened to Gideon—His grateful recognition of God—His return to the three hundred, and his call to arise.

So the great army which Gideon led to the hill of Moreh has melted away. At dusk, the thousands whom he dismissed left the Israelite encampment—many of them, no doubt, remaining not far apart, and ready to rejoin their comrades when the call to do so reached them. The leader is left, facing the immense multitude of "Midianites, Amalekites, and the children of the East," with the paltry three hundred "who had lapped." Apparently, they had reserved for themselves a sufficiency of food for present use, and a supply of the trumpets with which the Israelites were provided.[1] And this was the equipment, in

[1] The meaning of chapter vii ver. 8 is obscure. It seems strange that the three hundred should be called "the people" in one clause, and in a following clause it should be said, "He sent all Israel, every man to his tent." The Seventy, followed by some commentators, reads, "They took the victuals of the people in their hand," *i.e.*, the three hundred took the victuals of the 9,700 who had been sent away. But this is not a satisfactory explanation; for such a quantity of provisions would encumber the few who were left, and it is not a correct rendering of the Hebrew text. "Why not understand that the people took their trumpets as well as their victuals, all the people, both the three hundred that remained and the multitude that went away, yet who were not to go off as fugitives, but to deceive the enemy by keeping up their military order and discipline?" (Principal Douglas, "Handbook on Judges," p 45)

GIDEON: "THE CAKE OF BARLEY BREAD." 135

men and means, for the campaign! Good Bishop Hall says that "the strongest faith will ever have some touch of infidelity":[1] if the captain of the Lord's host, as he reflected on the situation, felt some touches of infidelity, could any one be astonished?

One thing is clear: whatever is to be done must be done quickly. To delay would be fatal to the enterprise. It would take the heart out of the small band of the Hebrews; and it would give additional force to the action of the enemy by showing the wretchedly small resources of the insurgents. In the wars of the Conquest, and in other wars, the great victories of Israel were the result of sudden and bold movements, causing panic and confusion in the ranks of the heathen. Such a movement is necessary now. The only hope is in starting at once, trusting God that the blow will be effectual to the salvation of the land.

Gideon understood this. Clear and articulate in his own breast is the Divine oracle, bidding him not wait for the morrow, but "that same night" march on the host. He could hear the promise sounding within, "I have delivered it into thine hand."[2] But, whilst ready, he is cautious; and the God whom he serves knows the man whom He has chosen. The man pled for signs, when the Lord bade him go in His might; he pled for assurances, even after the tribes had rallied around him. Now, his invisible Guide offers him an aid to his faith, a "token for good" which would scatter any lurking fear: "Go thou with Phurah thy servant down to the host: and thou shalt hear what they say; and afterward shall thine hands be strengthened to go down unto the host."[3]

We see the two—the hero and his trusty Phurah—stealing forth undiscerned from the encampment. There is nothing recorded of the follower, except that he is "his servant," rather his "young man."[4] A loyal, valorous henchman, we take him to have been—perhaps one of the few who had helped the son of Joash to overthrow the altar of Baal in Ophrah. On, silently, master and young man move. It is dark. They descend the

---

[1] "Contemplations," book ix.   [2] Chap. vii. 9.
[3] Ibid. vers. 10, 11.
[4] The same word is applied to Joshua (Exod. xxxii. 11). So also the "young man who bare his armour" accompanies Jonathan in his attempt to go over to the Philistine garrison" (1 Sam. xiv. 6).

hill slope; they pass the spring henceforth memorable as the Spring of Trembling—but no trembling with them; the two miles which separate the camps are soon traversed. Loose, apparently, is the discipline of the Midianite army; for, unchallenged by sentinels, they are allowed to approach close to the ranks of the armed men.[1] We may suppose that some appearance, at least, of the order usually observed by an army would characterize the disposition of the enemy "lying along in the valley like locusts for multitude, and their camels without number like sand by the sea side." The women, children, camel-drivers and camels, would have the centre of the interior; in front and in rear, and as wings on either side, would be the companies of the armed men. Protected by the black night, the Israelites get so near one of such companies that they can overhear the conversation of two men, possibly on guard—awake at least while the locust-like multitude is at rest.

It was about a dream which one of these two, who had been asleep, had dreamed. "Lo," says the Arab, "a cake of barley-bread tumbled into the host of Midian, and came into the tent, and smote it that it fell, and overturned it, that the tent lay along." The matter of the dream, and the terms in which it is related, are noteworthy. A cake of barley-bread was the most poor and common kind of food[2]—"such as could hardly be eaten by men, it was so vile," says Josephus.[3] We may infer from its being in the dream and the parlance of the Midianite that it was frequently in use at that time among the oppressed children of Israel. A traveller describes the misery of the Syrian peasants in a recent year in the words, "They are everywhere reduced to a little flat cake of barley or doura."[4] This kind of cake is beheld tumbling into the host of Midian, as if from a height. Nay, the word *tumbling* is

---

[1] The expression in ver 11 is, "outside the armed men." Revised Version, "the outermost part of the armed men." The word translated "armed men" may be otherwise rendered "Ranks by five." "It probably means in battle array, which usually is in five divisions—the van, the centre, the two wings, and the rear" (Lias, "Book of Judges").

[2] Barley as distinguished from flour. The cake was round, baked hastily on coals, or on stones laid in a shallow hole in the soil.

[3] "Antiquities," chap vi.

[4] Volney, "Travels in Egypt and Syria," vol. ii. p. 412.

even more emphatic. It has the force of *brandishing*—a cake becoming like a sword, flashing and moving as if it would hew and destroy. And so, in point of fact, it is conceived of as doing. It comes into, not merely *a* tent, but the tent, the tent of the king or general;[1] and then phrase is heaped on phrase to bring out the direness of the catastrophe. The tent is smitten; it falls; it is overturned; it lies along, levelled to the ground.

Surely this dream is a proof of the appositeness of the wise man's saying that "in the multitude of dreams there are divers vanities."[2] But a thread of truth may run through divers vanities. In the confusion of ideas there may yet be a thought worthy of attention. The Latin poet writes of "the time when true visions are wont to be seen";[3] and the Arab soldier's dream was one of the kind to which Lord Byron refers, as

> " in their development having breath,
> And tears, and tortures, and the touch of joy,
> They leave a weight upon our waking thoughts,
> They take a weight from off our waking toils,
> They do divide our being; they become
> A portion of ourselves as of our time."[4]

The dreamer had been influenced as many a dreamer has been before and since; and he tells his vision eagerly to one sharing with him the duties of the outpost. The companion at once finds an interpretation; in this instance the interpretation belongs to God.

The interpreter is haunted by a fear of this Israelite revolt. Many sneer at it. The great host to which he belongs is wrapped in the security which comes through the consideration of overwhelming numbers and commanding wealth and power. The Abiezrite and his undisciplined, half-starved peasants, what of him and them? Nevertheless, there is something of the prophetic soul in the rude Arab; and his thoughts and misgivings at once suggest to him the significance of the dream. The cake of barley-bread—the mean, wretched-looking thing—that answers to the Israelite. The tumbling and brandishing of the cake—that is the descent of these poor feeble Hebrews;

---

[1] The word is emphatic, and may be understood as applying to the royal tent. [2] Eccles. v. 7. [3] "Ovid," Ep. 19.
[4] Lord Byron's Domestic Pieces, "The Dream."

and the smiting of the tent—oh, there is no doubt what that means! "It is nothing else save the sword of Gideon, the son of Joash, a man of Israel: for into his hand hath God delivered Midian, and all the host."[1]

This is what "the awful listener" and his armour-bearer hear. It is enough. It shows that there is in the vast multitude before him a temper, a condition of feeling, which is a preparation for panic and rout. Dean Stanley sees in this feeling a resemblance to the consternation which fell on the Arabs, centuries later, when the name of Richard was mentioned, the belief being that his shadow caused even horses to start at the sight of a bush.[2] We are certainly reminded by it of the terror which filled the Canaanites before the invasion of their territories by Israel, and which made the conquest of the territories more easy.[3] The conversation also shows that Gideon's name has penetrated into the hostile army, and that the keen edge of his sword is known there. He accepts the omen. His faith receives a new anointing. It may not seem much; but "when we are going, a little thing drives us on." To him it is not a little thing. He pours out his gratitude in the worship of that Shepherd of Israel whose hand he can recognize in the incident. "A wise Providence had prepared a dream in the head of the Midianite, an interpretation in the mouth of another, and brought Gideon to be an auditor of both, and made his enemies prophets of his victory, encouragers of the attempt, and proclaimers of their own confusion."[4] He worships. Anew before Jehovah he accepts the mission; and then he hastens back to "his little flock." Now or NEVER. "Arise, for the Lord hath delivered into your hand the host of Midian."[5]

[1] Chap. vii. 14.
[2] "Lectures on the History of the Jewish Church," Lect. 15.
[3] Josh. ii. 24.
[4] Bishop Hall's "Contemplations," book ix.   [5] Chap. vii. 15.

CHAPTER XV.

GIDEON: TRUMPETS AND TORCHES.

The boldness of Gideon—The reason for the restriction as to number of men—The stratagem—The instructions given to the three hundred—The march under cover of night—The quiet of the camp rudely and suddenly broken—The panic and confusion—The action of the men—The flight—Israel "cried together"—Similar stratagems, but none so completely successful—The passages of the Jordan occupied by the Ephraimites—Oreb and Zeeb—The traces of this flight in the Old Testament—The small and inadequate means, and the issue—The trumpet: its significance—The torch and the pitcher—The excellency of the power is of God.

CAUTIOUS, even timid, before the hour comes, Gideon is resolute when the clouds have rolled past, and the way of God's choosing is clear. The conversation of the two soldiers, overheard by him, has dispelled every doubt. In his mind, there is no perhaps; the shadow of the "ifs" and "wherewiths" has vanished. His word to the three hundred is the bold, "Arise, for the Lord hath delivered into your hand the host of Midian." In that hour of illumination, he understood the reason of the restriction as to the number of the people appointed to go with him. It was not to be a question of human force against human force: it was to be a question of Divine power against the enemies of the Divine order—and if God be for the few, it matters little how many are against them. Even as regards the kind of result to be realized, there is a noticeable wisdom in the employment of only a small band. It was a band of picked men, all to be thoroughly relied on, all capable of heroic self-control, no craven among them. Silence and secrecy were essential to the accomplishment of his plan; these were assured by the selection which had been made. His small host was perfectly disciplined, and in perfect readiness for any bold and daring stratagem. He and they must, and can, act in thorough sympathy.

The stratagem is of the simplest possible character. Gideon divides his three hundred into three companies or battalions, each numbering a hundred men. One of these companies he commands in person. The troops are really unarmed. In the one hand of every soldier is placed a trumpet—Josephus calls it a ram's horn [1]—such as that which was used by the Israelites at the storming of Jericho. The other hand grasps a pitcher, or earthen jar, very brittle, in which it was customary to carry water; [2] and, within the jar, there is a torch or firebrand, of the same kind as the firebrands which, at a later period, Samson, in one of his many freaks, attached to the tails of the jackals which he let loose among the cornfields of the Philistines.[3] The brand will be invisible until the jar is broken, when it will suddenly flame out on view. This, apparently, is the entire equipment of the diminutive army: swords may have been slung to their side, but the only sword to be wielded in the critical time of the day is "the sword of Jehovah and Gideon."

The instructions given to this singularly arrayed army are peculiar, but definite. No mention is made of "sharpening spears and fitting armour." [4] The sole charge is, "See in me what you are to do. March alongside of me down the height on to the outside of the camp. Not a word. Only observe my movement, and follow it exactly. When you reach the outposts, one of your companies will defile to the right, and another to the left, so that at the moment of action it may seem that the camp is surrounded. Your positions taken, you will await the signal. Do not stir until I stir. As I do, so shall you do. 'When I blow with a trumpet, I and all that are with me, then blow ye the trumpets also on every side of all the camp, and say, The sword of the Lord and Gideon.'" [5]

---

[1] "Antiquities," book v., chap. 6: "They had also each of them a ram's horn in his right hand, which he used instead of a trumpet."

[2] So Gen xxiv. 14, 16, 18, 20.

[3] Judg xv 4. The torch or brand was made of resinous faggots.

[4] Bishop Hall's "Contemplations," book ix : "When we would look that Gideon should give charge of whetting their swords and sharpening their spears and fitting their armour, he only gives order for empty pitchers and lights and trumpets."

[5] Judg. vii. 17, 18.

GIDEON: TRUMPETS AND TORCHES. 141

Under cover of night, the battalions, thus appointed and instructed, march. It is near midnight. Approaching the enemy, the Israelites can hear the change of sentries. The second of the watches is set:[1] those who have been relieved from duty join their comrades in that which was to be the last sleep of the vast majority of the vast host spread over the plain of Esdraelon. All is quiet. The plan, fixed beforehand, is fully and successfully carried out. The three companies take up their places at the centre and the right and left wings of the camp.

The night is still. On a sudden a blast and yell which seem unearthly startle all. With the utmost possible clang the trumpets peal forth. The Midianites spring to their feet, seize their arms, and rush hither and thither. The blast waxes louder and louder; a crash is heard; and, as if by magic, the blackness of darkness is illumined by flaring lights, fierce and lurid like the flames of hell itself. Orientals are easily excited; all the more easily that night because the bond which unites Midianite, Amalekite, and the children of the East, is only a mercenary one. There is no underlying principle of cohesion. For self-interest they are associated; if self-interest seem to demand, they can be separated. An indescribable panic seizes all.[2] They can distinguish a terrific cry, "For Jehovah and Gideon;" and from it they judge that the Hebrews have descended from their heights in full strength. They run, in the hurry and darkness they know not whither; they trample one upon another; they mistake friend for foe, and "every man's sword is against his fellow."[3] All the time the men of Israel are stationary. The trumpets continue to blow; the torches to flash; the battle-cry rings forth; they themselves keep their ranks unbroken, and their strength is conserved.[4] Jehovah is fighting for them. The proud army of the hour before becomes utterly demoralized, and is routed and scattered. A Hebrew psalmist, having this and other deliverances in view, begins one

---

[1] At this period the Israelites divided the night into three watches, each watch lasting four hours. The first was from six to ten p.m., the second from ten to two a.m., the third, or the morning watch, from two to six a m This suggests that the time of the attack would be between ten and eleven p.m. At a later period the Roman division of four watches was accepted. [2] There might be a suspicion of treachery.

[3] Judg. vii. 22. [4] Ibid. vii. 21.

of the grandest of the national hymns with the strain, "Let God arise, let His enemies be scattered; let them also that hate Him flee before Him. As smoke is driven away, so drive them away; as wax melteth before the fire, so let the wicked perish at the presence of God. But let the righteous be glad; let them rejoice before God; yea, let them exceedingly rejoice."[1]

Strategy, similar to that of Gideon, has been frequently employed. Hannibal rescued his army from the snares into which the Roman general had drawn him in the plains of Campania by a *ruse*, in some features analogous to the Hebrew's. And other illustrations might be cited. But never was a result so great accomplished by means so inadequate. It was Jehovah's doing, and it was marvellous in the eyes of His people. But we admire the intrepidity, the unflinching courage, the fertile resource of the untrained soldier of Ophrah not the less, but indeed all the more, that he recognized himself as only the instrument of a higher Power, that, as the mere lieutenant under the real Captain of the host, he gave as the battle-word, "The sword of Jehovah, and of Gideon."

The deliverance was complete. The camp of Midian was wholly broken up; all the wealth of the host was left to the impoverished Israelites; prince and private fled, pell-mell, in the direction of the Jordan, to places which cannot now be ascertained; one of them called Beth-shittah, the House of the Acacia, probably near the narrower part of the river; and another, Abel-meholah, the Meadow of the Dance, afterwards celebrated as the birthplace of Elisha—not far, probably, from Beth-shean.[2] The object, of course, was to cross the river and escape to the eastern country. Their intention was frustrated by the conduct of the men who had been disbanded, and the patriotism of the sons of Ephraim.

Many of those who had been sent away lingered in the neighbourhood of the theatre of strife. The blast of the trumpets, borne through the still night air, might awaken them also. Anyhow, the tidings of the rout of the great army soon spread, and the men "were cried together out of Naphtali, out of Asher, and out of all Manasseh,"[3] and pursued after the flying Midianites. To cut off their retreat, to intercept their escape, it was necessary to occupy the lower fords of Jordan. And Gideon despatched messengers to Mount Ephraim be-

[1] Psa. lxviii. 1-3.   [2] Judg. vii. 22.   [3] Judg. vii. 23.

GIDEON: TRUMPETS AND TORCHES. 143

seeching the hardy mountaineers to seize the passages or fords unto Beth-bara, and to guard the Jordan. As we shall see, the Ephramites had their own grudge against the successful leader But this feeling was overborne by the enthusiasm of the day o victory, and they responded to the call. When the portions o' the routed host, which were headed by two princes or emirs o highest rank, reached the fords, they found the men of Israel waiting for them. And in the chase and slaughter which ensue the two princes were captured.[1]

In connection with these princes we notice a feature of som interest. Their names, Oreb and Zeeb, signify respectively the Wolf and the Raven. In uncivilized tribes, the practice of giving a name which associated the person with an inferior creature, on account of some real or fancied possession of qualities belonging to the creature, was, and is, common But, not among savages only. In the England and the Germany of earlier times, names which have now become common refer to birds and beasts.[2] One of the noblest of the patrician families of Rome—that of the Gracchi—perpetuated some remote connection with a jackdaw. The names Aquinus and Corvinus were historical; they speak of the eagle and the crow. Thus, in the Midianite aristocracy, we distinguish a noble of the highest rank as the wolf, and another as the raven. Then capture was an event of consequence only second to the capture of the kings; and the rocks on which they were put to death were named after them in future ages.[3] With their heads in charge, the Ephraimite chiefs did homage to the victorious leader.[4]

So ended the great event of the valley of Jezreel. It rescued the north and the centre of Palestine from an oppressive bondage. In the history of the nation it ranked as one of the mighty acts of Jehovah. When the Israelite, of a later time wished to pour out the vials of his wrath on his enemies, the de sire through which he breathed his hatred was, that the accursed confederacy might meet the fate of the Midianites, and "their nobles be made like Oreb and Zeeb; yea, all their princes a Zebah and as Zalmunna, who said, Let us take to ourselves th

---

[1] Judg. vii. 24, 25. [2] Wolf, fox, &c. [3] Judg. vii. 25
[4] The historian says, "They brought the heads of Oreb and Zeeb to Gideon on the other side Jordan." Gideon, in his pursuit of the enemy, had crossed the river.

houses of God in possession."[1] When the Assyrian threatened destruction to the people of God, the prophet bade them be of good cheer, assuring them that the Lord of Hosts would "stir up a scourge for the invader, according to the slaughter of Midian at the rock of Oreb."[2] Indeed, to the mind of psalmist and seer, the "day of Midian" seemed to be typical of all deliverances, and even to foreshadow that Messianic triumph which should not be like the warriors' battle with confused noise and garments rolled in blood, but should be the breaking of a yoke or burden through "the Child to be born, the Son to be given, whose name shall be called Wonderful."[3]

Thus the dream of the cake of barley bread which tumbled from the heights into the Arabian camp was fulfilled. As pitted against the huge host of a hundred and thirty-five thousand warriors, how insignificant and contemptible were Gideon and his three hundred men? By the power of the Eternal, this cake overturned the royalty of Zebah and Zalmunna. Another illustration was given of the principle which St. Paul expressed in the aphorism that God has "chosen the foolish things of the world to confound the wise, and the weak things of the world to confound the things which are mighty, and base things of the world, and things which are despised, yea and things which are not, to bring to nought things that are."[4] Who could have foretold a victory, the means to which were a few trumpets and torches! Who would have invented the narrative of such a victory? In the way of God to men, we find many such surprises. Who would have thought that a shepherd-boy, watching a few sheep in the plains of Bethlehem, should be the founder of a Royal Dynasty which extended through many generations, and of which, as concerning the flesh, the Christ of God should come! Who would have thought that one who lived and toiled at Nazareth should attract the homage of nations, east and west and north and south, and, in this year of 1890, be hailed by more than four hundred and thirty millions as the Son of God who has the words of eternal life! Who would have thought that the few tracts and historical books in which the best part of Hebrew literature has been preserved, should form the larger portion of the Book which has been translated into nearly four hundred languages, and which is read by peoples in their own tongue

---

[1] Psa. lxxxiii 9-12.
[2] Isa. x. 26.
[3] Isa. ix. 4-8.
[4] 1 Cor. i. 27, 28.

as the Book of books, God-breathed and "profitable for doctrine, for reproof, for correction, for instruction in righteousness, that the man of God may be perfect, throughly furnished unto all good works"![1] Very pertinent to this aspect of Divine procedure and providence are the words of Mr. Gladstone with reference to the Bible: "In proportion as the means are feeble, perplexed, and to all appearance confused, is the marvel of the results that stand before our eyes. And the upshot may come to be that, on this very ground we may have to cry out with the Psalmist—absorbed in worshipping admiration, 'Oh that men would therefore praise the Lord for His goodness, and declare the wonders that He doeth for the children of men!' Or 'How unsearchable are His judgments, and his ways past finding out.' For the memories of men and the art of writing, and the care of the copyist, and the tablet and the rolls of parchment, are but the secondary or mechanical means by which the Word has been carried down to us along the river of the ages; and the natural and inherent weakness of these means is but a special tribute to the grandeur and greatness of the end and of Him that wrought it out."[2]

In the achievement for which the Most High used Gideon and his men, there is a suggestion with regard to moral and spiritual victories to which it may be interesting to refer. The three hundred, as it has been pointed out, were practically unarmed. The one hand held a trumpet, the other hand held the earthen vessel which contained the torch. Now, in this we may discern the nature of the warfare and of the triumphs of the kingdom of God.

The trumpet occupies a conspicuous place in the Old Testament order, and in the New Testament imagery. In the long years of the wilderness, the calling of the assembly of Israel, and the journeying of the camps, were regulated by the blast of the silver trumpets which Moses was commanded to make "of a whole piece." And the use of the trumpet "over burnt offerings and peace offerings, and sacrifices of peace offerings, in the day of gladness, and in solemn days, and in the beginning of months," was enjoined as "an ordinance for ever throughout the generations of the people."[3] In the wars of the

[1] 2 Tim. iii. 16, 17.
[2] "The Impregnable Rock of Holy Scripture"—*Good Words*, April, 1890.
[3] Num. x.

conquest, the first and most decisive of all successes was accomplished through the solemn investiture of the city by the priests preceding the ark of the Lord bearing "seven trumpets of rams' horns," and "a rereward coming after the ark," which consisted of priests also blowing with trumpets. Armed men headed the procession; but not a spear was couched, not a sword drew blood. When the priests blew, and the people hearing the blast shouted, "the wall fell down flat."[1] Thus, "the great sound of a trumpet" formed part of the Israelite imagery for all that spoke of solemn crisis, of special interposition of God. Christ employed the figure in His discourse on the dispensation of the second coming.[2] The apostle repeats the figure in the same connection.[3] In the apocalypse of St. John, the seven angels who stand before God are presented with seven trumpets; and the sounding of each trumpet heralds the developments of the eternal purpose to which each is specially related.[4] When the seventh angel sounds, the mystery is finished,[5] and great voices in heaven exclaim, "The kingdoms of this world are become the kingdoms of our Lord and of His Christ, and He shall reign for ever and ever"[6]

A representative significance thus attaches to the triumph of Jezreel. The blowing of the trumpets is in the line of ordinance and prophecy. The Lord of Hosts has another kind of battle and of victory than those which are with confused noise and garments rolled in blood. The proclamation of truth, the announcement of a Divine will which is stronger than all the conspiracies and confederations of men, the man sounding or declaring the word of the Eternal—this, not the man slaying and killing, this, rather than the prowess of armies with chariots and horses, is the idea of the kingdom of heaven. Hence, the trumpet has been held to denote that "foolishness of preaching"[7] by which it pleases God to save them that believe. "Christ overcame the world," says a Christian Father, "by unarmed apostles bearing the trumpet of preaching, and the torch of miracles."[8]

But there is more than the trumpet. Its blast is loud and shrill, but the effect must be completed by the flashing of the

---

[1] Josh. vi.   [2] Matt. xxiv. 31.   [3] 1 Thess. iv. 16.
[4] Rev. viii.   [5] Rev. x. 7.   [6] Rev. xi. 15.
[7] 1 Cor. i. 21.   [8] Theodoret, quoted in "Pulpit Commentary."

GIDEON: TRUMPETS AND TORCHES.

light. If the good soldier of Jesus Christ has the trumpet in the one hand, to sound the alarm, to summon the ungodly to surrender, to proclaim the acceptable year of the Lord, he has the torch in the other hand, to flash with full force on the darkness and confound it, to indicate where and with whom the salvation is. The light is hidden in the pitcher; it is a treasure in an earthen vessel, a vessel of inferior stuff indeed, because the excellency of the power is only and wholly of God. And the light is concealed until the earthenware is broken. The carnal must die. The mere fleshly life must be given away. It is out of this death that the power of the torch comes: from this losing of the life, that the true life force proceeds. The dying of the Lord Jesus must be borne about in the body, that the life also of Jesus may be made manifest in the body.[1]

The trumpet and the torch are the two emblems of the fight of faith. Yet, let it ever be remembered that the efficacy is not in them, not in him who administers them—it is in the Living God. The cry which rang through the camp of Midian was the cry of Israel—" For the Lord and Gideon."

[1] Cf. 2 Cor. iv. 7-12.

CHAPTER XVI.

GIDEON "FAINT, YET PURSUING."

The one rallying cry for the time—What of Gideon and his three hundred?
—The tale of their enterprise now resumed—The pursuit to the river—
The escape of the kings with a remnant of the army—The pursuit
into the Hauran—The power of a supreme purpose—Held up to the
light of the word applied to the hero and his men, how many characters are shown to be wanting in unity and consistency—Some sketches
of John Bunyan—The contrast between the spirit and the flesh illustrated—The picture of Gideon, a stimulant to perseverance and energy.

THUS, the men of Israel, assembling "out of Naphtali and
Asher and all Manasseh," followed the panic-stricken
Midianites. Thus, too, the men of Ephraim cut off the
possibilities of retreat for the great mass of the disorganized
host by "taking the waters unto Beth-bara and Jordan." It
was a splendid outburst of the old national spirit. In the
enthusiasm of the hour, in the consciousness of the opportunity
which had come, all grudges and jealousies are forgotten.
Nothing is present to the view except the need of the common
fatherland. For the time, the one rallying cry is, "The sword
of the Lord and of Gideon."

But what of the leader himself and his gallant three hundred? We saw them standing in the lots which had been
marked out for the companies, sounding their trumpets and
flashing their lamps, whilst the children of the East "ran and
cried and fled." Did they remain in the routed camp, exploring
its wealth, and, after their long strain and scanty fare, gorging
themselves on its abundance? No; these water-lappers will not
throw themselves on their knees to gratify their appetite: the
parched mouth may be moistened, but this is all. Neither

slothful bed nor epicure's feast can tempt them. They reappear in the historian's statement—"Gideon came to Jordan and passed over, he and the three hundred men that were with them, faint, yet pursuing."[1] The tale of their prowess has been intermitted to complete the description of the flight of the enemy and the action of the tribes now it is resumed, and an impressive word-picture of their condition and of their energy is presented.

We seem to trace their movement after the scattering of the great army. The trumpets and pitchers and lamps have done their part, and are laid aside. We may suppose that the soldiers seize their weapons, or provide themselves with the completer armour left by the Midianites. The heroic captain will not leave his work incomplete. He wishes to stamp out the confederacy, so as to prevent the possibility of its being formed again. He wishes, especially, by the capture of the kings to strike at the centre of the whole combination. Therefore, without halt, without taking even the rest which nature demands, he and his band march, through broiling heat, in pursuit of the enemy, until the river is reached.

They arrive there to find that, whilst by far the greater part of the Midianite host has been slain, a remnant headed by the kings, had effected a passage across the river before the men from Mount Ephraim had taken the fords. This remnant must number several thousands. Is it prudent to pursue such a multitude? The men are exhausted; will it not be wise to wait, to recruit the wearied frame, to reorganize the companies and secure reinforcements, and thus move *en masse* against the kings? No, for in the meantime the defeated royalties will escape; and, burning with the sense of shame and the passion for revenge, they may organize fresh bands of mercenaries and return to wipe out the disgrace which has befallen them. While the terror is on the heathen hordes, while the prestige of the victory is undimmed, Gideon must push his advantage to the uttermost. The timidity of former days has vanished. The lesson that feebleness, with God behind, can do all things, has been thoroughly learned; and conferring not with flesh and blood, he pushes at once to the other side of the river, into the Hauran, a region comparatively unknown—"faint, yet pursuing."

[1] Judg. viii. 4.

The illustration of the energy and patience which mark the highest kind of heroism, and the word which interprets these qualities, are noteworthy. Any purpose that commands the interest neutralizes the action of fleshly cravings and shrinkings, lifts a man above the level of even pressing want, and leads him on, in spite of hindrances and difficulties, to the end which he contemplates. It need not be a purpose intrinsically great, or one which connects with great issues. What an amount of force, impelling and controlling action, is manifested in those who, year after year, insist on climbing the Alps or performing other gymnastic feats! Only let the will in a man become concentrated on some object, and it is scarcely possible to set a limit to the faculty of endurance or the power of accomplishment. "You can have only half-willed," said Suwarrow to some who had failed in doing what their hand found to do.

But how elevating, how ennobling, is this will-power when the gaze is steadfast towards a mark of light, when the aim is one that associates the life with "things lovely and of good report"! Down the stream of time there come many voices which articulate the perseverance so grandly exemplified in Gideon; none more lofty and sustained than that of the apostle and prisoner of our Lord, as expressed in the immortal lines, "I count not myself to have apprehended, but this one thing I do, forgetting those things which are behind, and reaching forth unto those things which are before, I press towards the mark for the prize of the high calling of God in Christ Jesus."[1]

"Faint, yet pursuing"—it is the word of the hero. Held up to its light, how wanting in a certain unity and consistency are the characters of many—some most amiable, most likeable, with good intentions, and good parts both intellectual and moral! They have no "chief end" which proportions other ends, and is like a magnet to the filings of their force, attracting and causing them to cohere, and giving solidity to the disposition. And so they keep oscillating, like the pendulum of a clock, between almost opposite sets of things; only, unlike the pendulum, theirs is not the oscillation which secures the keeping of time. For they lose the time. They make little headway. They fail to grasp the opportunity, as all do who

[1] Phil. iii. 13, 14.

merely look out for opportunity instead of making it. They drift rather than act. They are impelled and then are driven back — mere jelly-fish, whose motion depends on tides and currents around them. Not by such can any work be performed which, through well-doing, furthers well-being. They have no part with Gideon and his three hundred.

John Bunyan introduces us to some who form an outer circle. We remember Little Faith, who lived in the town of Sincere, and who, "going on pilgrimage, chanced to sit down in Dead Man's Lane, and slept there." And, so sleeping, he was espied by "three sturdy rogues, Faint-Heart, Mistrust, and Guilt (three brothers)," who came up to him and bade him stand — Faint-Heart exclaiming, "Deliver thy purse," Mistrust pulling a bag of silver out of his pocket, and Guilt knocking him down. The poor man was robbed, and would have been murdered but for a sound which the robbers feared might be the steps of "Great Grace."[1] For "Faint-Heart" is often the robber, and, but for "Great Grace," ready with reserves for even the feeblest faith, would often be also the murderer of Little Faith. What prayer more appropriate than the prayer of the apostles, "Lord, increase our faith, so that, though faint, we may not falter, or sit down and sleep, but always pursue"!

We remember too that good man, Mr. Ready-to-Halt and the word of Christiana to him, before she went to the river: "Thy travel hither has been with difficulty, but that will make thy rest the sweeter." And Mr. Feeble-Mind, apt to fear and doubt of God's goodness, but who, when the errand from the King was brought to him, exclaimed, "As for my feeble mind, that I will leave behind me; when I am gone I desire that you Mr. Valiant bury it."[2] It is better, surely, like Mr. Ready-to-Halt, to go on crutches than not go at all; better, even with Mr. Feeble-Mind, to be the pilgrim, than, with strength of mind, to refuse the pilgrim's staff. But why keep to the crutches? Why doubt and tremble when the Lord calls, and gives us the resources of Omnipotence? No task can be too hard, no burden can be too heavy, no cross can be too crucifying, if only we are sure that His grace is sufficient, and that we are really following Him. It is for us to press with the little strength which we have: in pressing, the strength is increased. "They

[1] "Pilgrim's Progress," First Part.   [2] Ibid. Second Part.

who wait on the Lord change their strength. 'Faint, yet pursuing,' they run and are not weary, they walk and are not faint."[1]

"Faint, yet pursuing." The contrast suggested between the spirit willing and the flesh weak is often very striking. The three hundred are footsore. They have scarcely slept for nights. They have given themselves no leisure to eat. They are tired and ready to lie down. But their look is onward. The joy of the Lord is their strength. And has not the same triumph of mind over matter, of faith over sense, been frequently evidenced in men and women of all sorts and conditions? "He was simply the bravest man I have known," writes Dr. Samuel Cox of the late Mr. Lynch; and the story he tells is this: "To think, to compose, was an unfailing delight to him: the treasuries from which he drew his thoughts seemed inexhaustible; but to *write* was an agony which no words can fully utter. Hardly was he seated at his desk before he was assailed by the rending, suffocating pangs of his cruel disease. As the work went on, the anguish grew, until the intolerable agony compelled him to fling himself on the floor, where he lay patiently and stedfastly enduring the pressure of his great pain. No sooner was the fierce spasm past than he rose, seated himself once more at his desk, and resumed his labour till seized by another intolerable spasm. And thus the day would wear on, labour and anguish alternating many times; until, at last, utterly exhausted by the weary conflict, he would lie still and prostrate on the ground."[2] Courage such as this is interpreted by the words applied to Gideon and his band, "*Faint, but pursuing.*"

What time our hearts are overwhelmed, we may recall the picture of the sturdy band — Gideon and his helpers in the war. Faint, weary in well-doing, we are apt to become. As the years pass, the ideals become dim, we sink down into a dull contentment with low levels, we count ourselves to have apprehended. We are sometimes disappointed too. Expectations are belied. We sow, but there seems little or no harvest. The fruit is blighted. For one reason or another, we begin to ask, What profit is there in such service or toil? When, thus, our hearts turn coldly on themselves, the recollec-

[1] Isa. xl. 31. [2] "Sermons for my Curates," Preface, pp. 11, 12.

tion of the old-world story may greet us like a vision of angels beckoning nearer God, and breathing into our hearts the assurance that

> "We rise by the things that are under our feet,
> By what we have mastered of good and gain,
> By the pride deposed and the passion slain,
> And the vanquished ills that we hourly meet."

CHAPTER XVII.

GIDEON: THE PURSUIT AND CAPTURE OF THE KINGS.

The flight of the kings eastward—Gideon on their track—The conduct of the Israelites to whom he appealed for help—Ephraim, and its arrogance—The tact and self-control of Gideon in his dealing with Ephraim—The opposition of the men of Succoth and Penuel of another type—Difficulty of tracing the route of the Hero—The places mentioned, Succoth, Penuel, Nobah, Jogbehah, and Karkor—How the request for bread was met at two of these places, and the threats of cruel punishment—The circuit taken by Gideon—His surprise of the host which thought itself secure—Capture of the kings—The vengeance taken on Succoth and Penuel—Gleams of moderation of spirit—The fate of Zebah and Zalmunna—The ornaments—The return to Ophrah.

THE kings, with a remnant of their huge host, had fled in an easterly direction. They had effected a passage across the Jordan before the Israelites had taken the fords, and they had pushed through the territory of Gad, either due east, or east with a bend towards the south. Their object was to reach a place which would provide a cover for the panic-stricken troops, and would render them secure from "the sword of the Lord and of Gideon." On the track of the Midianite royalties, Gideon and his three hundred cross the river, "faint, yet pursuing."

It might have been supposed that a great wave of enthusiasm would break at the feet of the Hero of Israel, whose wonderful daring and faith had been the means of national deliverance. Alas for human nature! the conduct of Israelites, to whom he appeals for help in the time of need, verified the reflection of the Preacher, "I considered all travail, and every right work, that for this a man is envied of his neighbour."[1]

[1] Eccles. iv. 4.

GIDEON: THE PURSUIT AND CAPTURE OF THE KINGS 155

The first sign of this envy was given by the men of Ephraim. When they presented the heads of Oreb and Zeeb to Gideon, "they did chide with him sharply;" the matter of their sharp speech being, "Why hast thou served us thus that thou calledst us not when thou wentest to fight with the Midianites?"[1] This is not a solitary example of the arrogance of the great central tribe. The same chiding was encountered by Jephthah, the hero of Gilead, when he returned from his successful campaign against the Ammonites.[2] And indeed the tribe was notorious for its "pride and stoutness of heart."[3] In later times, allegiance to King David and King Solomon was only half-hearted, because by the glories of their dynasty pre-eminence was given to Judah. When the schism of the ten tribes occurred, Ephraim became the leading unit in the northern kingdom. Hosea, identifying it with this kingdom, speaks of it as "a cake not turned,"[4] as "like a silly dove without heart,"[5] as "a heifer taught and loving to tread out the corn."[6] In the day when the Lord will be to Israel as the dew which saturated Gideon's fleece, Ephraim will say, "What have I to do any more with idols."[7] And Isaiah represents the traditional feeling between it and Judah, in the word in which he forecasts the blessed days of a Messiah's reign, "The envy also of Ephraim shall depart; Ephraim shall not envy Judah, and Judah shall not vex Ephraim."[8]

Verily, "by pride cometh contention." There is a haughty scorn in the sharp speech. One of the half-tribe of Manasseh, and he a member of one of the poorest thousands, thus to treat the great neighbour! Why should it have been slighted by not being summoned to take its part in the great warfare against the common foe?

The tact and gentleness of Gideon are illustrated in his reply. It breathes the air of that charity which "vaunteth not itself, and is not easily provoked." It was not a time for fierce recrimination between those who had been partners in a great enterprise, and had contributed to a notable victory. His self-control on this occasion strikingly contrasts with the impetuous temper of Jephthah when the same provocation was offered.[9] We cannot but admire the moderation of the son of Joash. Instead of meeting "words of high disdain" with words also of high dis-

[1] Judg. viii. 1.   [2] Judg. xii. 1.   [3] Isa. ix. 9.   [4] Hos. vii. 8.
[5] Hos. vii. 11.   [6] Hos. x. 11.   [7] Hos. xiv. 8.   [8] Isa. xi. 13.
[9] Judg. xii. 4.

dain, and thus precipitating a contention which would have issued in bloodshed, he disarms the wrath of the Ephraimites by a sweet reasonableness, nay, by a graceful self-depreciation. He magnifies the exploit of the exasperated Israelites. The heads of the two nobles in his view, recalling the great battle of the rocks near Jordan, invited and gave point to the magnanimous "What have I done in comparison with you?" The part he himself had played, when measured by the slaughter which they had effected, and the service which they had rendered, seemed like the poor hills of Manasseh in contrast with the rich slopes and plains of the other branch of the House of Joseph. "Is not the gleaning of the grapes of Ephraim better than the vintage of Abiezer? God hath delivered into your hands the princes of Midian, and what was I able to do in comparison of you."[1]

It was this wit, wisdom, graciousness which won the day. The outbreak of passion in others will never be conquered by the outbreak of passion in ourselves. He is the conqueror who can rule his own spirit. Gideon might have threshed the Midianites, and been threshed and beaten by his own irritation. He was enabled to practise the art of self-repression; and the enmity which had swelled like a flood-tide, soon subsided and ebbed. "Then," adds the historian, "their anger was abated towards him when he had said that."[2]

But the opposition afterwards encountered was of another type. In Milton's "Samson Agonistes," the fallen champion is represented as saying that "in nations grown corrupt, and by their vices brought to servitude," nothing is more common than

> "To despise or envy or suspect
> Whom God hath of His special favour raised
> As their deliverer. If he aught begin,
> How frequent to desert him, and at last
> To heap ingratitude on worthiest deed."

And the chorus of Danites responds—

> "Thy words to my remembrance bring
> How Succoth and the fort of Penuel
> Their great deliverer contemned,
> The matchless Gideon in pursuit
> Of Midian and her vanquished kings."[3]

[1] Judg. viii. 2, 3.   [2] Judg. viii. 3.   [3] "Samson Agonistes."

GIDEON: THE PURSUIT AND CAPTURE OF THE KINGS.

This ingratitude, this base contemning, is set before us in the history. And the bearing of "the matchless Gideon" towards those who were guilty of it is wanting in the nobleness which he manifested when replying to the pride of Ephraim.

It is impossible to trace, with accuracy, the route of the Israelite leader in his pursuit of the fugitive kings. The sum of the Biblical narrative is that he came to Succoth, then to Penuel; that, thereafter, he "went up by the way of them that dwelt in tents, on the east of Nobah and Jogbehah," and swept down on the Midianite host encamped in security at Karkor. This route, these places, offer a problem whose solution has hitherto baffled interpreters of Holy Scripture.

The impression naturally conveyed is that all these places were on the east side of the Jordan, over which it is said that "Gideon and his three hundred men had passed." But this impression has been challenged. The site of the first of the places, the Succoth whose rulers were so false to every generous instinct, is looked for by some topographers on the west side of the river, at ruins ten miles south of Beisan or Beth-shean.[1] Others, again, who admit that the old city is to be sought for on the east side of the river, identify it with an ancient town called Sûkkôr, a little way farther south than Beth-shean.[2] But these views separate the Succoth of Gideon's history from the Succoth of Jacob's; and the conjunction of the one, as of the other, with Penuel, makes it more than probable that the same town is mentioned in both histories. The Succoth of the Book of Genesis was near the Jabbok, west of Mahanaim, "in the valley."[3] It was there that Jacob rested after his memorable interview with Esau.[4] The name was bestowed in recollection of the booths which he had made for his cattle. In subsequent times, it was noted for its thick, deep soil of clay, out of which Solomon cast the vessels of bright brass which he consecrated to the service of the Lord in the temple which he built.[5]

Penuel was only a short way from Succoth. It was on the height overlooking the valley in which Succoth was situated. Close to it, was the scene of the wrestling of the Angel of God's

---

[1] Robinson, Van de Velde, Tyrwhitt Drake, Major Conder, identify the ancient Succoth with the ruin Sakût.
[2] Burkhardt. Jerome also mentions a Sochoth in the same region.
[3] In Joshua xiii. 27, Succoth is described as "in the valley."
[4] Gen. xxxiii. 17.
[5] 2 Chron. iv. 17.

face with Jacob, on the night before the meeting with Esau, when the new name Israel was given to the patriarch. "As he passed over Penuel, the sun rose on him, and he halted on his thigh."[1] After the conquest, it was distinguished, like some cities which occupied important strategical positions, for its lofty tower.[2] From that tower, the eye could sweep the territory of the trans-Jordanic tribes. It was a point of so much consequence, that Jeroboam rebuilt it after the kingdom of the ten tribes had been formed.[3]

These places were on the high road from the Jordan through the inheritance of Gad. Jacob, in his journeying from "the land of the people of the East," came first to Penuel, and next to Succoth; Gideon, reversing the route, came first to Succoth.

It was a city with an imposing organization of rulers and elders. No fewer than seventy-seven are mentioned; seventy councillors or elders, and seven princes or rulers at their head.[4] It had not sent any contingent to the national army: surely, in the hour of triumph, it would gladly contribute of its abundance to the gallant band which pursued the common foe, though hungry and thirsty. He appealed to the men of Succoth, "Give, I pray you, loaves of bread unto the people that follow me, for they be faint, and I am pursuing after Zebah and Zalmunna, kings of Midian."[5] It was an appeal both to their humanity and their patriotism. The appeal was dishonoured.

Their conduct was selfish and cowardly in the extreme. The people following Gideon seemed, in point of numbers, wholly inadequate to the purpose contemplated. They had, perhaps, seen the array of Midianite troops, camels, and chariots, imposing even though a mere remnant of the great host; and these paltry three hundred, weary and feeble-looking, what could they avail? The probabilities were that they would never capture the kings, that they would be ignominiously routed, and their quixotic enterprise would prove a failure. If so, the victorious Midianites might retaliate on them for any help given at that juncture. It was safer not to risk this vengeance, even though refusal might irritate Gideon, than to close with his request and thus risk the wrath of the foe. The fever of national enthusiasm burned very low in these Gadites. Practi-

---

[1] Gen. xxxii. 31.
[2] Shechem, see Judg. ix. 46, and Sion, see 2 Sam. vii. 9.
[3] 1 Kings xii. 25. [4] Judg. viii. 14. [5] Judg. viii. 5.

GIDEON: THE PURSUIT AND CAPTURE OF THE KINGS. 159

cally, the river had divided them from their brethren according to the flesh; and this isolation meant pettiness of feeling and local selfishness.[1] There was no chivalry of sentiment, there was no sense of piety or honour, there was no bond of covenant in these calculating wise-acres, as they answered, "Are the hands of Zebah and Zalmunna now in thine hand that we should give bread unto thine army?"[2]

The beautiful self-control which distinguished Gideon on the occasion previously referred to, is absent on this occasion. After all, the case of the Ephraimites was very different from that of the churlish Gadites. The former had manfully borne the brunt of a great fight. They had taken their part as became men of Israel and worshippers of Jehovah; and, though they might be arrogant, the arrogance was charged with the consciousness of their position as in the front rank of God's sacramental host. They were men of Israel first, and men of Ephraim second. The people of Succoth were practically disavowing their responsibility to their brethren; they were withdrawing themselves from the national league; they were closing their eyes to the great things which God had done for His people: they were magnifying Baal, not Jehovah. And the wild beast in the mighty Abiezrite was aroused. It broke loose from the retreat to which the look of the Lord had sent it. It was the savage, rather than the man of God, who answered the baseness of the seventy and seven with the threat, "When the Lord hath delivered Zebah and Zalmunna into mine hand, then I will tear your flesh with the thorns of the wilderness and with briers."[3]

From the valley, Gideon ascended the slope to Penuel which, with its tower, seemed to invite the weary men. But the same request was answered in the same spirit and in the same terms as at Succoth. The elders had gone into their famous tower, and from it hurled their refusal. Again the wild nature of the irritated man dictated his rejoinder. With a defiant, "When I come again in peace, I will break down this tower,"[4] he passed on.

[1] The answer of the men of Succoth and Penuel strikingly contrasts with the answer of the children of Gad to the heads of the thousands of Israel, reported Josh. xxii. 21-29
[2] Judg. viii. 6. The word translated "the hands of Zebah and Zalmunna" is literally "the palms." In some old versions (*e.g.* Wycliff's) the distinction is preserved, "the palmes of the hoondes ben in thine hond." A reference to the firm *grasp* of the Midianites is traced by some commentators.
[3] Judg. viii. 7.
[4] Judg. viii. 9.

He had ascertained that the Midianite princes, surrounded by their fifteen thousand troops, "all that were left of all the hosts of the children of the East,"[1] were encamped at a place called Karkor. Where and what was this Karkor? "It was far in the desert, beyond the usual range of the nomadic tribes,"[2] says Dean Stanley. A more definite description cannot be given. We know of an ancient town named Karkaria, not far from the Dead Sea, and only a day's journey from Joktheel or Petra.[3] But this is too far south. It is to be observed that the article should be used in connection with the word—*the* Karkor. Now, etymologically, Karkor signifies a walled or enclosed place; and possibly the shelter which the kings had found may have been an extensive walled enclosure erected by the Gadites for the protection of cattle or sheep. And it is interesting in this connection to recall that, in the notice of the fenced cities of the children of Gad in the Book of Numbers, we find the Jogbehah mentioned in the narrative of Gideon's pursuit among the cities; and immediately after the cities there is added the phrase, "folds for the sheep."[4] The Karkor whose security the Midianites appropriated may have been a fold in the neighbourhood of the Jabbok so extensive as to be distinguished as *the* Karkor.

Be this as it may, the camp of the enemy had been fixed at a spot far enough from the high road towards the east to set the Midianites at ease. "The host were secure,"[5] says the historian. Gideon, to escape the observation of outposts, made a wide circuit. "He went up by the way of them that dwelt in tents" —following, we infer, a route familiar to the Bedouin, and leading to Bedouin settlements—"on the east of Nobah," a city belonging to the half-tribe of Manasseh, which formerly was called Kenath, but had received the name of one of the families of Machir;[6] and then re-entering the territory of Gad, east of Jogbehah, one of the fenced cities of that territory.[7] The sites of Nobah and Jogbehah cannot be identified, but the cities

[1] Judg. viii. 10.
[2] "Lectures on the History of the Jewish Church," Lect. xv.
[3] So Eusebius and Jerome, Ewald also favours the view.
[4] Num. xxxii 36.   [5] Judg. viii. 11.
[6] Numb. xxxii. 42. The place is now called Kunawât. Nobah has been supposed to be Nawa, a place on the road to Damascus. But the probabilities are that it was the old Israelite town on Mount Bashan.
[7] Num. xxxii. 35.

GIDEON: THE PURSUIT AND CAPTURE OF THE KINGS. 161

were on the eastern frontier of the land of the Israelites; and the intrepid warrior selected a route which skirted their fields, in order that, unnoticed, he might approach and surprise the army which was wrapped in security. The attack is dismissed in a single clause, "He smote the host."[1]

Zebah and Zalmunna are the names of the two kings who were at its head. In the Book of Joshua it is said that Moses smote the kingdom of Sihon king of the Amorites, who reigned in Heshbon, with five princes of Midian, who were "dukes of Sihon, dwelling in the country."[2] These vassal princes of the Amorite king were so independent that they are called kings in an earlier historical book;[3] and probably, after the dismemberment of the kingdom of Sihon, their successors, or some of them, assumed regal rank and power. The two kings who had fled from Jezreel are presented to us as still surrounded by the state and dignity of Eastern potentates, even their dromedaries being richly caparisoned, and having strings of jewelled moons or crescents hung around their necks. With Oriental indolence and *abandon* they are at rest in Karkor, little thinking of the "Jehovah who is terrible to the kings of the earth." In a moment, "the stout-hearted are spoiled; they have slept their sleep; none of the men of might find their hands."[4]

The assault on the host was made at night. We may suppose that the tactics of the previous surprise were, to some extent at least, repeated. The repetition would strike terror, would awaken the superstitious dread which still clung to the Midianites. On a sudden, in the darkness, again the blare of the trumpets is heard. Again the cry rings forth, "The sword of the Lord and of Gideon." Panic seizes the troops; they rush hither and thither; they scatter and fly in wild confusion. Gideon and his warriors penetrate into the interior of the camp, searching for the two monarchs. The two monarchs have also fled. He gives chase, and soon arrests them: and he so terrifies the disorganized army that all resistance is dropped, the only care being to save dear life.[5] The triumph

---

[1] Judg. viii. 11.
[2] Joshua xiii. 21, "The princes of Midian, and Evi, Rekem, and Zur, and Hur, and Reba, which were dukes of Sihon, dwelling in the country."
[3] Numb. xxxi. 8.　　[4] Psa. lxxvi. 1-5.
[5] It is written (chap. viii. ver. 12), "He discomfited all the host." The verb "discomfited" means "terrified."

is complete. The confederacy, once so terrible, is now and for ever broken. Victory has crowned the march of the brave water-lappers, "faint, yet pursuing."

Will they not rest now? What means the sentence, "Gideon, the son of Joash, returned from battle before the sun was up"?

The Chaldee Targum renders the phrase, "Before the sun went down." Modern opinion inclines to the view that the word translated sun, *Heres*, should be regarded as a proper noun.[1] It is pointed out that, although it is sometimes, it is not generally employed to represent the sun.[2] It is pointed out also that the adverb *up* is not used in the Hebrew Scriptures to denote sun-rise, and that, as in "the going *up* of Akrabbin,"[3] it is used of ascent in a mountainous country. Two additional considerations are urged—the one, that Heres is a name given to places and mountains, as Timnath-Heres, the residence of Joshua; and the other, that Heres was the name of a mountain north-west of Judah, close to the border of Dan, which, against the efforts of the children of Dan, the Amorites retained as a mountain fastness.[4] The suggestion, therefore, is pressed that, in the clause quoted, the historian indicates the return of Gideon to a mountain or hilly upland for the purpose of recruiting after the exhausting fatigues of the expedition.[5]

It may be so, but there is much to be said in favour of the ordinary reading. "The sun went down" is a Hebrew phraseology; if we translate "the sun was up," we keep to the same line of figure—the line, indeed, which is observed in Genesis, where it is written that "the morning *arose* when the angels hastened Lot,"[6] and that "the sun was *risen* or gone forth on the earth when Lot entered Zoar."[7] And it is in harmony with the swiftness of all Gideon's movements to suppose that, having captured the two kings, and broken up the Midianite encampment, he would at once return to the places on which he had declared he would empty the vials of his wrath when the Midianite chiefs were in his possession. Assuming that his attack was made in

[1] The Septuagint and the Syriac and Arabic versions so regard the word.
[2] It is used to denote the sun in poetry: seldom in prose, though it is thus used in chap. xiv. 18. [3] Judg i 36 [4] Judg. i. 35.
[5] "Dr. Cassel remarks that, as we have the *splendour of the dawn* (Zareth-Shahar) as the name of a town on the same side of Jordan (Josh. xiii. 19), we need not be surprised at an *ascent of the sun* as the name of a mountain" ("Cambridge Bible").
[6] Gen. xix. 15. [7] Gen. xix. 23.

GIDEON: THE PURSUIT AND CAPTURE OF THE KINGS. 163

the second watch of the night, the prey would before long be "in the hands of the mighty." We assume that Penuel and Succoth were not far distant. Before the day had been fully ushered in he may have led back his three hundred men, no longer pursuing, and the sense of faintness neutralized by the elation of glorious victory.

The demon of revenge was raging in the breast of Gideon. Very different was his spirit from that of the Leader of Salvation when He prayed for His enemies, " Father, forgive them, for they know not what they do."[1] But he was an Abiezrite, who lived eleven centuries before the day of Christ; the time to which he belonged was a half-savage time; his upbringing had been semi-heathen; and the dastardly conduct of the men of the Israelite towns had stirred into fierce indignation both the resolution of the patriot and the zeal of the Jerubbaal.

Yet, grim and ghastly as was the punishment threatened and inflicted, the severity of the vengeance is lightened by some gleams of moderation.

It is to be noted, for instance, that he furnishes himself with a carefully prepared list of the seventy elders, and the seven princes, or rulers, of Succoth. A young man of the town is caught, who, on being interrogated and commanded, writes the names of the threescore and seventeen.[2] Gideon's desire is to save the townsmen; his only quarrel is with the chiefs. When it is said that "he taught (or corrected) the men of Succoth," the reference is not to the entire population, but, as is implied in the language of the chronicler, to the elders.[3] And we are at liberty to infer this also as to the case of Penuel. Resistance to him there, it would seem, was given by the headmen, and it may have been by others, from the tower. The tower was battered down; and "the men of the city"—the same expression as that applied to the elders of Succoth, presumably their chief men—were slain. At all events, in both places the women and children were spared.

Gideon's threat, when the men of Succoth refused to give his little army bread, was, " I will tear your flesh with the thorns of

---

[1] Luke xxiii. 34.
[2] Judg. viii. 14. In the A V. the phrase is, the young man "described the princes of Succoth." Literally it is "wrote."
[3] Judg. viii. 16, "He took the elders of the city, and thorns of the wilderness and briers, and with them he taught the men of Succoth."

the wilderness and with briers." The verb translated "tear" might be otherwise rendered "thresh," and we are asked by some critics to interpret the threat as meaning that he would correct the churlish Israelites by threshing instruments with sharp points, like thorns of the wilderness and prickly briers. David subjected the Ammonites of Rabbah to a similar cruelty when "he put them under saws and harrows of iron," harrows meaning "threshing instruments having teeth."[1] Is there a sufficient reason for questioning the more obvious interpretation of the words? Thorny branches in abundance might be obtained from the acacia groves of the country, and the briers were a common kind of scrub. A revoltingly harsh revenge he could take, with the use of these thorns and briers. "The probability is that the naked bodies of the men were laid in the midst of a heap of thorns, briers, and prickly bush, and then threshing sledges or other heavy implements of husbandry were drawn over them. In Northern nations where the body is completely covered, the idea of such punishments with thorns on the naked person seems a far-fetched device; but in the East, where the clothing leaves much more of the person exposed, and where, in consequence, men are continually lacerating their skins by passing through thickets, the idea of such laceration is always kept present, either by the actual experience of suffering, or by the constant observation of it. Thus, tearing the flesh with thorns comes to be a familiar idea of penal infliction, and, as such, is still popularly mentioned as among the punishments which evil-doers deserve or will obtain, not only in this life, but in the life to come."[2]

Another gleam of gentler feeling is evidenced in the address of Gideon to the two captive kings.

Their execution was not the result of that blood-thirstiness which makes the annals of warfare, especially in earlier times, so painful. It was the act rather of the avenger of blood, as recognized in Israelite law, than of the ruthless and merciless conqueror. Brothers of the Deliverer of the people had, at some period either before, during, or after the campaign, been put to death. It may have been after the victory of Jezreel; it may have been at the beginning of the strife when they were endeavouring to join the army assembling at Ophrah; it may have

---

[1] Such instruments are mentioned in Isaiah xxviii. 17 and xli. 15.
[2] Kitto "Pictorial Bible," Judges viii.

been in the days when the Hebrews were obliged to hide in dens and caves of mountains. But, at or near Tabor, they had been put to death. Of this the question put to the kings informs us. And it has justly been remarked that the incidental notice of this hitherto unreported event reminds us how much has not been related which, directly or indirectly, concerns the crisis, and the knowledge of which would have made the antecedents and the circumstances of the war more intelligible to us.[1] The chronicles of Israel are so brief; the tale of transactions and deeds is so curtly told, that we miss important links in the chain of narrative.

"What manner of men," demands Gideon, "were they whom ye slew at Tabor?"[2] The kings reply with Oriental obsequiousness. They give him a regal dignity, and intimate that the slain men resembled him—the same beaming countenance and native majesty. "As thou art, so were they; each resembled the children of a king."[3] Their answer explains the disappearance of his brothers. Where members of the family circle having the same father might have different mothers, those who had the same mother were specially attached to each other; and these lion-like men were Gideon's uterine brothers, whom he had dearly loved. "As the Lord liveth," he exclaims, "if ye had saved them alive, I would not slay you."[4] But to put the murderers of his kindred to death seemed, according to the notions of the period, a duty demanded of him. And he turned to his young son, Jether, "his firstborn," and commanded, "Up, and slay them."

The boy hesitated; he was "yet a youth."[5] His heart revolted from the task assigned to him. Too gentle, it may be, for these rough days, Jether has no place in subsequent history; and in the light of his "fear to draw the sword"[6] we can understand why. The unhappy Midianites entreat that the father, in the fulness of his vigour, should himself be their executioner. "Rise thou, and fall on us: for as the man is, so

---

[1] In chap. x. 11, 12 reference is made to deliverances not recorded in the historical books of Scripture "Such references show the existence of a real history in the background of that which has been preserved in the Bible" ("Pulpit Commentary"). [2] Judg. viii. 18.
[3] Or "the king." The marginal reading is "according to the form of a king." [4] Judg. viii. 1.
[5] See Numbers xxxv. 19. [6] Judg. viii. 20.

is his strength."[1] Their request is granted; and the lifeless corpses of the once puissant Zebah and Zalmunna are the token that the servitude under which Israel had so long groaned is ended, and that the emancipation of the national life is complete.

Here we might have wished that the story ended. But Holy Scripture is always faithful to fact. The men of the Bible are only men; and faults and errors are never concealed. And the closing portion of Gideon's biography shows how insensibly the evil steals into the soul, even through what in itself is natural, or is allied to a purpose good and pious. The beginning of the deterioration has been traced to the action with regard to the men of Succoth and Penuel. That, it is held, indicated the relaxation of the spell by which the look of Jehovah had bound the mighty man. He ceased then to be the man of faith; he fell to the level of the man of sense. And no doubt this is so far true. But the decline (let us not exaggerate it; there is the stamp of the "Israelite indeed" to the end) may rather date from the moment when the covetous glance was cast on "the ornaments that were on the camels' necks."[2] These ornaments, as has been remarked, were a part of the Arab royal state. They were small crescents, or moons, of gold and silver, with chains and bronzes.[3] He on whom Jehovah himself had gazed and sent him forth in His might; he who, through summer heat and notwithstanding manifold privations, had toiled, intent only on his God-appointed service; he who had headed the water-lappers, himself the most abstinent of all, bestows longing glances on these little moons. And they are stripped from the necks of the dromedaries, and borne away in triumph by him and his three hundred. The wiles of the Midianites had conquered Israel in the past; the gold and the wealth of the Midianites were now an evil and a curse to the people redeemed from the hand of the enemy. This we shall presently see.

---

[1] Judg. viii. 21.   [2] Judg. viii. 21.
[3] In the 26th verse of the chapter, "chains about the camels' necks" are mentioned. Ornaments were also taken from the person of the kings. In Isaiah iii. 18, among the signs of female vanity are mentioned "round tires like the moon." "The custom of adorning the necks of their camels with gold chains and ornaments prevailed among the Arabs so late as the time of Mahomet, and part of the Prophet's booty after the taking of Caibar consisted of such jewels" ("Speaker's Commentary").

Thus, after a short, brilliant, and decisive campaign, Gideon, surnamed Jerubbaal, returned to Ophrah. We can imagine the welcome which awaited him there! We can imagine the emotion with which he would visit the wine-press where he had threshed the wheat, and the terebinth under which had sat the Holy One who looked on him. What a change! Jehovah was God. He had remembered His people, and had, through him and by the strength which he had communicated, raised up "an horn of salvation." At the altar which his own hands had reared, the patriot presented his *Laus Deo*.

CHAPTER XVIII.

GIDEON: THE JUDGESHIP—LIGHT AND SHADE.

The national sentiment reflected in the offer of a hereditary rule—The new sense of national unity—Considerations favourable to the idea of a succession of rulers in Gideon's family—Monarchy contemplated in the Book of the Law, and the conditions prescribed there—The attitude of Samuel when the elders of Israel demanded a king—The dominating reason of his displeasure—The answer to his prayer, and what this answer implied — Gideon's feeling similar to that of Samuel — The offer of the crown a great temptation—Two kinds of ambition—Gideon's election—A grand decision, but tokens in the narrative of a royal state, and of moral deterioration—Three such tokens: First, his house with its surrounding; many wives and children. Second, the name *set* to one of his sons, Abimelech. Third, his request when he declined the hereditary rule, willingly yielded to by the men of Israel—The ephod · its symbolical significance—Why Gideon determined to make and put the ephod in Ophrah Gratitude, Piety, Policy—The result of the act deplorable—The current of movements sometimes bears men beyond, even contrary to, their original intention—Israel made to sin—The snare to Gideon and his house—Gideon's rule and its beneficial character—The close of the life, and the burial in the sepulchre of Joash.

TRIUMPHANT, and bearing splendid trophies of his triumph, Gideon recrosses the Jordan. Whether he was the object of a great popular enthusiasm, and in what manner any such enthusiasm was expressed, we are not informed. The narratives of Holy Scripture omit much that bulks largely in other narratives. What does not seem essential to their purpose finds no place in the page. But one thing is mentioned, and in it we see the reflection of the national sentiment. He is asked to accept the position of ruler. The word "king" is not used; but

GIDEON: THE JUDGESHIP—LIGHT AND SHADE. 169

the reality signified by the word is formally and solemnly offered. And not for himself only, but for his family also. For the first time in Israel's history the idea of a hereditary, dynastic government is articulated. Possibly an assembly of the tribes, as represented by the princes and elders, was summoned and was held, the result of whose deliberation was the unanimous request: " Rule thou over us, both thou, and thy son, and thy son's son also: for thou hast delivered us from the hand of Midian."[1]

In that hour of recovered freedom and prosperity, the nation felt that its urgent necessity was a strong and continuous central power. It is " the men of Israel" who ask the son of Joash to constitute this power. The phrase " the men of Israel " is to be interpreted in harmony with the phrases previously used, " the men of Succoth " and " the men of Penuel." It points to the head-men, the princes and elders of the people; and not the Manassites only, the Ephraimites and others;—the men represent Israel. The success of the great leader has drawn them for the time together; it has softened the pride of Ephraim, has touched the commercial spirit of Dan and Asher with a new emotion,[2] has quickened the valour of Zebulun and Naphtali,[3] has even drawn Gilead out of its seclusion beyond Jordan.[4] A spirit of fellowship, the *esprit de corps* which, under the years of servitude, had almost died out, is stirred into vitality; and to all it seems obvious that he who had ventured so much, and had planned with such marvellous wisdom and boldness, is the true Heart, and the true Head also, of the land. He shall be the visible bond and pledge of union; his authority shall be supreme over all; his trumpet shall be the call to arms; his judgment shall be the arbiter of disputes; his genius shall be the inspiration of all that is free and chivalrous. He has proved his right to be thus enthroned, and the enthronement seems the condition of that order which is both truth and liberty And the presumption is that the children of such a head will inherit some measure of the father's force and spirit. They will at least

---

[1] Judg viii. 22.
[2] In Deborah's song (Judges v. 17) it is written, "Why did Dan remain in ships? Asher continued on the sea shore, and abode in his creeks."
[3] Judg v. 17, "Zebulun and Naphtali were a people that jeoparded their lives unto the death in the high places of the field."
[4] Judg. v 17, " Gilead abode beyond Jordan."

perpetuate the tradition of his noble daring, and thus be, in themselves, an embodiment of imperishable memories. Moreover, the succession of rule delegated to them will save from the chaos which must follow the ruler's death. The acknowledgment of that succession will prevent intrigues on the part of ambitious and unscrupulous men, and tribal jealousies with all the evils which must appear in their train. Is it not better at once to extend the call to the generations to come? To do so marks the fulness of their confidence in Gideon, and interprets the hope of a continuity of national policy: "Rule thou, and thy son, and thy son's son"

In the Book of Deuteronomy, the establishment of monarchy when Israel should come into the land given it by the Lord is contemplated and provided for. The day would come, it is announced, when the people would desire to be like all the nations around them, and, it is added, that the wish should be acceded to. The stipulations are laid down that the king elected must not be a stranger, must not multiply horses, must not multiply wives, must not multiply silver and gold, and must "write him a copy of the law," and "diligently observe the law."[1] Does not the election of Gideon and his house to the sovereignty of the land prove that the clock has struck the hour predicted in the Scripture of the Hebrews? Is not the *Vox populi* in this instance the *Vox Dei?*

Very striking is the attitude of Samuel when, at a later period, the Israelites did demand that they should have a king like the nations around them. Before we regard Gideon's declinature we may observe this attitude, and the Divine word concerning it. We shall thus be reminded of the standpoint of the Israelite indeed—that of Gideon in the declinature.

"The thing," we are told, "displeased Samuel when they said, Give us a king to judge us. And Samuel prayed unto the Lord."[2] No doubt a personal feeling was an element of this displeasure. The demand was ungracious; apparently it ignored the faithful service which Samuel had rendered to Israel. It implied the exclusion of his family from government: it implied that his function as a judge should cease.[3] To a man who had given his whole strength to his work, who had defrauded none, op-

---

[1] Deut. xvii. 14-20.   [2] 1 Sam. viii. 6.
[3] The elders, indeed, say, "Thou art old, and thy sons walk not in thy ways; now make us a king."

GIDEON: THE JUDGESHIP—LIGHT AND SHADE.

pressed none, whose hand had never received a bribe to blind his eyes therewith,[1] this could not be otherwise than painful. But the personal feeling was only an element; it was not the chief determining cause of the prayer to Jehovah. The dominating impulse of the appeal to Heaven was the instinct of the true prophet—the instinct afterwards interpreted by Elijah, when he said, "I have been very jealous for the Lord God of hosts."[2] The conduct of the Israelites seemed to be a denial of the first principle of the Theocracy—that the King of Israel was Jehovah, and none besides.

And the answer returned to the prayer confirmed the impression—"They have not rejected thee, but they have rejected Me, that I should reign over them."[3] The petition of the elders of Israel, in the form in which it was presented, ignored the real seat and source of the Kingly Power. They wished a king to judge them after the fashion of the heathen nations by which they were surrounded. They wished a general to lead their armies, and arbitrate in all their concerns. In their desire there was no acknowledgment of the Invisible Ruler, no consultation of Him, no expression of faith that He could and would raise up a prophet like to Moses and Samuel; no craving that their leader might be a different kind of person from a leader of the heathen, that he might be the reflection of the Higher Lordship in respect of which they were separated from all other peoples. The Divine Oracle told Samuel to recognize in their actions the tendency which had been manifest from the beginning of their history—the tendency to substitute the visible for the invisible, to lose the ideal truth of Israel, and sink to the level of the nations. Their conduct in pleading for a king was "according to all the works which they had done since the day that the Lord brought them out of Egypt unto that day, wherewith they had forsaken Him and served other gods."[4]

The error consisted not in the substance, but in the manner of the request. To wish a more stable government—one which gave greater securities for vigour of administration, promptitude of purpose, and unity of tribal action, was right and patriotic. But the elders of the people broke loose from the basis of the nation, when they failed to recognize the Supreme King, and to ask for one who should be the captain of the Lord's host,

[1] 1 Sam. xii. 3.
[2] 1 Kings xix. 10
[3] 1 Sam. viii. 7
[4] 1 Sam. viii. 9.

responsible to Him, and judging in His name. The throne of the king whom they asked was to be to them a substitute for the Mercy Seat, as the throne of the Unseen Ruler, where He met and communed with His flock through His ministers. The mercy seat, the tabernacle, the priesthood, the sacrifice, the Urim and Thummim—theoretically the centre of the whole people —had ceased to be so. The lamp of God was dim and low in the temple of Jehovah, where the ark of God was,[1] and the importunity for a warrior-king, like the king of the heathen nations, was virtually the sign that the popular mind had lost sight of the real foundation and strength of Israel. "They have not rejected thee, but they have rejected Me." Nevertheless, the instruction was to hearken to their voice, protesting solemnly, and showing the manner of the king for whom they pleaded. A strong will and arm had come to be necessary: they sought what was necessary in a wrong way; but it must be conceded; and, out of royalties, some of which would be a travesty, some a dark counterfeit, some a feeble likeness of the true king, would emerge the Reality, whose pattern is in the heavens; the man who reigns in righteousness, and who is "an hiding place from the wind, and a covert from the tempest; as rivers of water in a dry place, and the shadow of a great rock in a weary land."[2]

Gideon, at the period of our present contemplation of him, is the Israelite indeed. He has the same consciousness as that mirrored in the prayer of Samuel: his self-denial, when pressed to mount the throne and become the "father of kings," is one of the noblest incidents of history; it has been remarked, and not without cause, that "we may almost look in vain for parallels to it."[3] It was a great temptation; one which proved the quality of a man's mind, which divided asunder soul and spirit, joints and marrow, and was a discerner of the thoughts and intents of the heart! "There are two kinds of ambition,"

---

[1] *Cf.* 1 Sam. iii. 3.   [2] Isaiah xxxii. 1–2.

[3] Cambridge Bible: "Moses and Joshua might have made themselves kings, but they were never invited to do so. Cincinnatus returned quietly to his farm when his dictatorship ended, but it was never offered to him as an hereditary dignity. Cæsar's refusal of the crown was dictated by policy rather than principle. The same may be said of Oliver Cromwell. To Washington the opportunity of founding a dynasty was never given. Gideon's conduct displays not only disinterestedness, but faith of a high order."

writes Carlyle, "one wholly blameable, the other laudable and inevitable. The selfish wish to shine over others, let it be accounted altogether poor and miserable. 'Seekest thou great things for thyself,' seek them not—this is most true. And yet there is an irrepressible tendency in every man to develop himself according to the magnitude which nature has made him of, to speak out, to act out what nature has laid on him. This is proper, fit, inevitable; nay, it is a duty and even the summary of duties for a man. The meaning of life here on earth might be defined as consisting in this—to unfold *yourself*, to work what thing you have the faculty for. It is a necessity for the human being—the first law of its existence. Coleridge beautifully remarks that the infant learns to speak by the necessity it feels."[1] Gideon is tested by the summons of the men of Israel. Shall he leap into the hereditary ruler's chariot, and thus hug the blameable ambition, "seeking great things for himself"? We could not have said that to have done so was "*wholly blameable*." There was much not only to excuse, but, it might be affirmed, even to justify it. He had not sought the great thing. Rather, the great thing had sought him. And its acceptance would give him a vantage ground which could not be challenged. But he had beheld the vision of the Eternal. He had seen the angel of God face to face. He had gone in the strength of the look which Jehovah had fixed on him. He had been only the instrument of the King of Israel. He dared not assume the purple of potentates like the Zebah and the Zalmunna whom he had captured. No: "According to the magnitude which nature"—and grace—"had made him of," he would develop himself. He would rule, but only as Jehovah's servant. The reply, swift and straight as his movements were wont to be, is given, "I will not rule over you, neither shall my son rule over you: the Lord shall rule over you."

It was a grand decision. But poor human nature can seldom tarry long on the heights of such grandeur. A hereditary principality was declined; but Gideon did not retire to his farm like the Roman Cincinnatus. He did not continue to judge Israel under a palm tree, like Deborah. On the contrary, there are tokens, in the brief notice of his latter days, of a state and importance bordering on the regal, and tokens, it must be added, of a tendency to overstep the bounds of rule in the fear

[1] "Lecture on Heroes," Lect. vi.

of God, and of that moral deterioration which too often follows great prosperity. Let us notice these tokens.

"Jerubbaal, the son of Joash, went and dwelt in his own house."[1] Hitherto, he had lived under the paternal roof. But now a residence of a more pretentious character is built—it may have been by the direction and at the cost of the men of Israel. And there he lives with the style and surrounding of a prince. We have seen that one of the prohibitions contained in the ordinance regarding the king who might be chosen was directed against the multiplication of wives. This was a way of heathen royalties. Parents were always willing to give their fairest daughters to the monarch; and, for political reasons, as well as for pleasure, it was sometimes regarded as expedient to enlarge the alliances of the monarch. Israel's history is a standing testimony to the evils of polygamy. Solomon's huge array of wives and concubines turned away his heart after other gods.[2] David's life was overshadowed by sin caused through the multiplying of wives; and out of his family life came the direst troubles and calamities of his reign. Gideon, who had resisted the attractions of a throne, could not resist other attractions. His harem was magnificent as that of an Oriental royalty. A very township must have grown up around his own house, to contain his many wives with their many children. We read of "threescore and ten sons of his body begotten,"[3] and we are told of at least one son not included in this enumeration, and no doubt there were daughters besides. Tragedies, in this wide circle, were inevitable; these tragedies brought lamentation and woe to the country after his decease.[4] And the ruler was himself morally enervated. He who headed the water-lappers at Jezreel becomes corrupted by sensual indulgence; and, possibly, the idolatry which, under an altered guise, again stole into the life of Israel, was encouraged with the view of providing for the enormous expense of the household and establishment which transformed the once simple rural Ophrah into the seat of both a court and a temple.

An incident in the brief chronicle of the judgeship of Gideon suggests that, though the kingly title was not claimed, there was a craving after the kingly position. A woman of Shechem, perhaps a Canaanite, and not therefore ranking among wives of

[1] Judg. viii. 29.
[3] Judg. viii. 30.
[2] 1 Kings xi. 4.
[4] *Cf.* chapter ix.

the first degree, bore a son to Gideon, "whose name he called Abimelech."[1] The verb translated "called," literally means *set*. It was not, we may suppose, the circumcision name; but one set to him at a later period. It was not assumed by the young man himself; nor was it given to him by the people of Shechem; nor yet by his mother's family.[2] Gideon *set* the name, which was the official name of a line of kings of Gerar,[3] and which may be rendered either "Father of a king," or "My father, a king." If we accept the former rendering, it may signify the projection of the father's thought about his son— "He shall be a king, and the new designation will remind him of the fatherhood, whence came the patents of the royalty." If we accept the latter, it may have been intended to indicate that, though uncrowned, he, the father, had been the king. In either case it is at least striking that the son who afterwards did grasp at the throne which Gideon declined for his family as for himself, should, by Gideon's act, be formally charged with a name associated, both in etymology and history, with the conception of royal power and dignity.

A third notice concerning Gideon, in the period subsequent to the capture of the king, is of special significance. When he declined the crown which was offered him, he "desired a request" of the men of Israel. Well had it been for him, well for them, well for the whole country, if that request had never been made, or if it had been denied, and if he had returned to the poverty of his family in Manasseh. The request was that every one would give him the prey which he had taken from the vanquished Midianites. To explain why the prey was so great and costly, it is said, "They had golden earrings because they were Ishmaelites."[4] They belonged to regions famous for cattle, and for gold and precious stones.[5] The love of rings for

[1] Judg. viii. 31. The position of this woman, called by Josephus ("Antiquities of the Jews") Drumah, was similar to that of Hagar in Abraham's household. But it is said that this inferior wife of Gideon resided in Shechem.

[2] *Cf.* Neh. ix. 7: "Thou didst choose Abram . . . and *settest* him the name of Abraham." The suggestion is, a surname, or a name additional to the one given in infancy. *Cf.* also 2 Kings xviii. 34; Dan. v. 12.

[3] Gen. xx. 2.

[4] Judg. viii. 24. The "Children of the East" were sometimes comprehended under the name Ishmaelites.

[5] Arabia had its gold mines—"The gold of Ophir."

ear or for nose was a characteristic feature of Arab peoples,[1] and the spoil which the Israelites had gathered in the deserted camp was immense. Gideon asked that this spoil be surrendered to him, and the answer returned was, "We will willingly give it." A garment—may we suppose the ruler's military cloak?[2] —was spread, and into it every man cast his share of the golden rings.

A most valuable pile! The weight of the nose-rings which formed it was "a thousand and seven hundred shekels of gold," equal to more than £3,000 sterling.[3] Besides, there were small crescents similar to those which had been stripped from the dromedaries of the kings, and pendants or ear-drops, and chains[4] which had hung around the necks of camels; and, rarer than all, a variety of the costly purple which was worn only by kings.[5] Never had such wealth been gathered and presented to a son of Israel as the wealth that day gathered and presented to the son of Joash.

What was his object in "desiring the request" thus complied with? It has been said that "in this desire for gold, he falls to the level of ordinary men."[6] But his was not an ordinary craving for gold. He asked it as a means to an extraordinary end, and one which probably, in its inception in his own mind and in his original intention, did not aim at the mere enrichment of himself and his family. "He made an ephod" of the gifts of the elders, "and put it in his city, even in Ophrah."[7]

The ephod was the part of the priestly dress which, in the popular imagination, was most intimately associated with the priesthood. It was always worn by the high priest when he asked counsel of the unseen Judge by Urim and Thummim.

---

[1] It is characteristic of Arab peoples still. Even the Bedouin of the desert have their ear or nose rings and other ornaments.

[2] It is the outer garment—the shawl or cloak, that is pointed to. Dean Stanley (Lect. xv.) writes, "His vast military mantle receives the spoils of the whole army."

[3] The ring presented to Rebekah weighed half a shekel (Gen. xxiv. 22). The shekel was more than twice the weight of a sovereign in sterling money. Assuming that the rings were as heavy as Rebekah's, those thrown into the pile would represent rings taken from 3,400 bodies.

[4] Chains are mentioned as ornaments of woman's and man's necks—Cant. iv. 9; Prov. i. 9.

[5] The renowned Tyrian purple, made from a shell-fish found in the Mediterranean.

[6] "Speaker's Commentary." [7] Judg. viii. 27.

GIDEON: THE JUDGESHIP—LIGHT AND SHADE. 177

There was a beautiful symbolism in all its prominent features. The onyx stones which connected its two parts—the one covering the front and the other the back—were set "in ouches of gold," "graven as signets are graven with the names of the children of Israel;" the breastplate fastened "by wreathen chains" to the ouches on the shoulders and bound "with a lace of blue" that it might never be loosed, with its four rows of precious stones, each row consisting of three stones, and the twelve tribes memorialized on the stones; the "curious girdle," below which hung the bells and pomegranates, "round about the hem of the robe"—the bells to ring and make music as the priest ministered and went into the holy place;—these, the marked points of the garment, appealed to the eye and the imagination of the Israelite.[1] The son of Manasseh had only a slight acquaintance with Shiloh and its sacrifices. To him the priest, in his function and service, was almost an unknown person. But the ephod was the outstanding sign of acts in which some relation to the Invisible was established. It seemed to be necessary to this relation. The suggestion, indeed, was that it—not the one who was clothed with it, or the office which it expressed, but itself—constituted a medium between God and man. Micah, of Mount Ephraim, made an ephod for the house of his gods: he assured himself of the favour of Heaven when the wandering Levite entered that house arrayed in the ephod.[2] Gideon, with visions of worship and of responses by Urim and Thummim, utilizes the nose-rings and ornaments, and eardrops, and purple raiment, once worn by Midian's kings, in making an ephod and putting it, or setting it up, in Ophrah.

Three reasons may have operated in the determination to make this ephod;—these three, Gratitude, Piety, Policy.

This Ophrah was a memorable place to him. Bethel, one of Israel's primitive sanctuaries, was the scene of Jacob's dream, and the place in which he reared the altar, El-Bethel. Was not the Abiezrite village a place equally hallowed? Had not God appeared to him there? there sent him? there pledged the deliverance of the people? The two altars told a wondrous tale: the one spoke of Jehovah-shalom; the other was the witness for the work perpetuated in the name Jerubbaal. Is not this the house of God? His experience answers, Yes; his

[1] Exod. xxviii. 4-36. [2] Judg. xvii. 13,

soul says, Yes. Let it be distinguished then as a holy place; there let the ephod, the sign of the house of God, be set; let it wait for the priest whom God will send. He must suitably memorialize the great events which have occurred; and what memorial can be more suitable than the vestment which belongs to the worship of Jehovah, and testifies to Him as against Baal and those that are no gods?

Thus, the making of the ephod was a pious work. Let us believe that it was the interpretation of a genuinely pious feeling. The connection of the statement of the desire for the earrings with the refusal of the hereditary rule on the ground that Jehovah was the only Ruler over Israel, suggests that, in this desire, Gideon had regard to Jehovah's glory. He may have thought that, by devoting the spoil to a religious purpose, he was teaching the people that their homage was due to the Unseen King, that by Him the victory had been gained, and to Him its fruits should be dedicated.[1] His experience, too, of God's favour, and of the blessedness of the man whom God caused to approach to Himself, may have prompted the wish to have the constituted means of communion with God—the Urim and Thummim—at hand. The ideal of a ruler, as sketched in the instruction concerning Joshua, was that he should stand before the priest and obtain counsel through the priest "after the judgment of Urim before the Lord."[2] Are we not at liberty to infer that Gideon wished to realize this ideal? And, with regard to the people, in placing the richly jewelled and beautifully constructed ephod in Ophrah, was it not practically a way of withdrawing their interest from the false worship, and binding them anew to the covenant which had been established with their fathers, and laid down for their obedience in the ordinances of Moses?

No doubt, a political consideration entered into his resolution. Shiloh, where the tent of meeting was placed, was in the territory of the tribe of Ephraim; and though the anger of the men of that tribe had abated towards him, Gideon knew how uncertain their temper was. His access to the priest at Shiloh

---

[1] In Numbers xxxi. there is the account of a great spoiling of the Midianites. And the officers come to Moses, and say, "We have brought an oblation for the Lord, what every man hath gotten, of jewels of gold, chains, and bracelets, rings, earrings, and tablets, to make an atonement for our souls before the Lord." [2] Numb. xxvii. 18–21.

could not be constant and direct. It was, probably, part of his policy to reduce the pretensions of the haughty Ephraimites, and to keep more fully within his own control the power exercised by the national religion. Politicians, from a purely political point of view, have in all times recognized that forces so strong and penetrative in their action as religious forces should be under the influence of the State, that there should be an alliance in some form between religion and authority. Gideon, who was a statesman as well as a warrior, may have been guided by this view; and, in taking the step he took, he was aided by the neglect of the tent of meeting which had become prevalent, and by the absence of the priesthood from all that marked the enterprise of the nation. No priest had read to his troops the prescribed proclamations before battle. No priest had asked counsel for him before the Lord. After the death of the illustrious Phinehas, the high priest had almost disappeared from public view. Possibly Gideon resented the apathy of the priests and Levites to him and his mission. More probably, he felt that a new impetus must be given to the national worship if it was to direct the national life, if it was to mark the visibility of Jehovah's rule over Israel. And, with the view of promoting such an impetus in a manner which would at the same time increase his authority and make his Ophrah the seat of a new power, Gideon, we conceive, put the ephod in *his* city.

Whatever his motives may have been—and it is only justice to him to suppose that they were not selfish or sinister—the result of his action was deplorable. He made Israel to sin, though his intention assuredly was opposed to this. The good intention is not sufficient. Human nature, in its wilfulness, is sometimes too strong for its teachers. Movements, when once originated, sometimes bear those who are in their current far beyond, indeed in directions never contemplated by, the thought of the originators. Sometimes the originators are themselves led whither, in the beginning, they protested against its being possible that they could go. This has been abundantly verified in both ecclesiastical and political history. The evidences of it are most conspicuous in our own day. To glance at only one. No more touching and, in many ways, noteworthy book has been published within the last half-century than Dr. Newman's "*Apologia pro Vita Sua.*" The history of the religious opinions given in it is fitly interpreted in the words to be found in its preface. Referring to the vague impression that his conduct towards the Anglican Church, while he was a member of it, "was inconsistent with Christian simplicity and uprightness," he says: "An impression of this kind was almost unavoidable under the circumstances of the case, when a man who had written strongly against a cause and had collected a party round him by virtue of such writings, gradually faltered in his opposition to it, unsaid his words, threw his own friends into perplexity and their proceedings into confusion, and ended by passing over to the side of those whom he had so vigorously denounced."[1] Dr. Newman has drawn the outline of a picture which, with more or less variety of detail, has been frequently realized. Jerubbaal is not a sinner above all others. He who had overthrown Baal prepares, through his inconsiderate, though well-meant, zeal, for the return of his nation to the service of Baal. His personal influence and his widespread fame drew the people to the ephod which he had placed, and the ministrations conducted in connection with it. He himself meant that the sanctuary of Ophrah should lead to God: gradually it led away from God. Superstition, like a deadly serpent, coiled around the cult he had established. Farther and farther this cult departed from the ritual and the truth of Israelite worship. For a time, he might not observe the departure: if he observed, he might doubt as to the way of its growth. From protest he might slide into acquiescence, and gradually into a more positive sanction of usages which, at an earlier period, he would have condemned. And thus, having misled others, he and his became themselves misled. He had effected a political unity: he was guilty of a great religious schism. In the emphatic language of the Scripture, "All Israel went a whoring after his ephod: which thing became a snare unto Gideon, and to his house."

Very striking is the phrase, "which thing became a snare."[2]

---

[1] "Apologia pro Vita Sua," p. 4.

[2] In chap. ii. 3 the angel of Jehovah protests to the Israelites, "The gods of the people of the land will be a snare to you." There, as in other passages (Exod. x. 7, xxiii. 33, 1 Sam. xviii. 21), the snare involves such a complication as leads to destruction. The idolatrous worship of the ephod, with the image or the teraphim with which probably it was associated, led to the ruin of Gideon's family.

GIDEON: THE JUDGESHIP—LIGHT AND SHADE.

The rich ephod trapped the wise man. His wisdom could not keep him out of the trap. He had lost the consciousness of the look of Jehovah. Wisdom, with will-worship, is powerless against the seduction of idolatry in one form or another. And the ephod speaks of will-worship. He deviated from the Divine order; and such deviations, however slight at first, increase and widen, until the original idea is parted from. Even what, in itself, should point beyond itself is corrupted into an end. The serpent of brass which memorialized a notable event of the wilderness became, in the course of years, a snare, because an idolatrous character was attached to it, and to it the people burnt incense. And the good king called it *Nehushtan*—meaning a mere piece of brass—and he broke it into fragments.[1] The best things may ensnare, unless the mind is prepared to obey God, and observe His ordinances in the way of His appointment. It is never safe, though there be much to encourage and even justify it, to swerve from the path of precept. Precept and promise are in closest neighbourhood: when we wander from the one, we lose the key of the other. "Never man," writes Bishop Hall, "meant better than Gideon in his rich ephod; yet this very act set all Israel a whoring. God had chosen a place and a service of His own. When the wit of man will be overpleasing God with better devices than His own, it turns to madness and ends in mischief."[2]

And now the story of the life hastens to its close. Of the judgeship of Gideon and the development of Israel under that judgeship scarcely anything is said. The only notice taken is the brief sentence, "The country was in quietness forty years."[3] No band of Midianites was seen on the fertile plain of Esdraelon; no enemy from north or south disturbed the repose of the land. "The sword of Jehovah and of Gideon" could not be forgotten. A moral cancer was eating out the pith of national well-being; but its work was unobserved. The wise and good might feel that for the quietness in which they rejoiced they were, under God, indebted to the one man whose sway was acknowledged by all; that his decease was certain to bring about disunion and chaos. But, during the four decades of

---

[1] 2 Kings xviii. 4.   [2] "Contemplations," Book ix. cap. 7.
[3] Judg. viii. 28. The frequent employment of the numeral 40 suggests that it may not record the exact number of years, but may be "a round number."

Jerubbaal's ascendancy, "Israel dwelt safely: the fountain of Jacob was on a land of corn and wine; also his heavens dropt down dew."[1]

But the inevitable did come, though not until many years had passed over the head of the deliverer of his people. "In a good old age" he died, his children surrounding him, the nation weeping, "My father, my father!" Pious hands laid the remains of the once mighty man in the sepulchre of Joash; and Ophrah was left, with its ephod, with the house in which he had lived, with the family; but without the one whose prowess had shed lustre on what would otherwise have been a village of the Abiezrites, unnoticed and unknown. Its renowned person was a man never to be forgotten—one who, in his far past time, and in the narrow theatre which Palestine afforded, shone like a star in the firmament of God—[2]

> "One of those great spirits
> Who go down like suns,
> And leave upon the mountain-tops of death
> A light that makes them lovely."

---

[1] Deut. xxxiii. 28.

[2] "There is a sweetness and nobleness blended with his courage, such as lifts us into a higher region: something of the past greatness of Joshua, something of the future grace of David" ("Lectures on the History of the Jewish Church," Lect. xv.).

CHAPTER XX.

The ingratitude of the people connected with forgetfulness of God—Significance of Abimelech's history—Shechem: its beauty and associations—Abimelech made king there—How his ambitious designs were promoted—The money given him out of the house of Berith, and the use made of it—Wealth of heathen temples illustrated—Wholesale murder—Jotham on Gerizim—Could he be heard from that altitude?—Parable and fable—His fable, and its meaning—His running away—Fulfilment of his prediction—Insurrection in Shechem—The siege and destruction of the city—The tower of Shechem: how it was burnt—Thebez, where was it?—What happened there?—The retributions of Providence illustrated in Abimelech's end—The witness of the Scriptures for righteousness—The changing and the abiding.

THE historian anticipates the course of events when, before tracing the career of Abimelech, he associates "forgetfulness of God with ingratitude to the memory of Jerubbaal."[1] Under these two heads, he sums up the infatuation of the people. Ingratitude, as has been remarked, is not a vice to be charged against Israel. "In the time of the Judges, by one great service a man—from whatever rank in life—so secured the gratitude and respect of the people that he remained in power, as their governor, all the rest of his life, however long that life may be. In the case of Gideon they went farther; ... they were anxious that the government should be made hereditary in his family."[2] It was under the influence of evil counsels that their hearts were turned against the family of their deliverer. And, no doubt, the lapse from faith in the Covenant-God, with the consciousness that thereby they broke from all that was most

[1] Judg. viii. 34, 35.
[2] Kitto's "Daily Bible Illustrations," twenty-fourth week, seventh day.

The narrative seems to imply that the disturbance of political order and social harmony, caused by the usurpation of Abimelech, did not occur for some years after the death of Gideon. We can scarcely suppose that a sanctuary of Baal, so near to Ophrah as Shechem, would have been allowed, or that this sanctuary would have been endowed with the gifts and votive offerings of people, during his rule; and therefore, when we read of a house of Baal at Shechem, from which the men of the city took "threescore and ten pieces of silver" to aid the usurper, it is inferred by some writers that the erection and enrichment of the house were subsequent to the decease of the overthrower of Baal. If so, we must allow for the lapse of a considerable time, during which the seventy sons continued to live in Ophrah, and the people to dwell in security under their vines and fig-trees. But the absence of the strong arm was slowly but surely felt. When there was no king in Israel, the tendency was for every man to do what was right in his own eyes. And the history sets before us the operation of that cause of disorganization and evil with which we are only too familiar — the apostacy from the Covenant God into the idolatry of a Deity of Covenants, a type of Baal-worship signified by the phrase Baal-berith.

As has already been indicated, Gideon had prepared for this apostacy by the great mistake of his life. A strange inconsistency, indeed, that he who had destroyed the worship of the false should yet have provided for the return to that worship! In the national priesthood and the sacrifices of the tabernacle lay the securities for the acknowledgment of Jehovah and His law. Instead of strengthening, Gideon had weakened these securities. The priesthood had, before his day, lost its power: it had ceased to be the accepted medium between the people and the Eternal Wisdom and Holiness. It was still further obscured by the *simulacrum* which he set up in the Holy Place beside the terebinth. Shiloh was displaced by Ophrah, with its ephod and teraphim. These offered a visibility of the Divine. And Israel craved for some visibility.[1] The worship of the

---

jectured, by way of accounting for the exclusive use of the Jerubbaal name in the ninth chapter, that the biography of Abimelech is taken from another source than the previous history.

[1] As illustrated in the idolatry of the golden calf in the wilderness. When Moses "delayed to come down out of the mount, the people gathered

true God was too severe, too sublime. It went a whoring after the vestment, with the images which were possibly connected with it. It was on the down-grade to the service of the Baalim and the Asherah.

"And it came to pass that, as soon as Gideon was dead, the children of Israel turned again."[1] "As soon as he was dead"—the one man who had stood between them and the sin! His personal influence was the only preventive. Israel, like other nations, was a hero-worshipper. It kept in the right way so long as the hero was spared and he led in that way. But the bent was towards the evil. It was prone to go *quickly* out of the Divine path. It had been turned to God, but the repentance was not after a godly sort. It did so, following its hero. The hero gone, the reaction at once set in. Does not the ancient chronicle sound a warning for all times? The apostle apprehended the warning when he protested that he would not have the faith of those whom he had begotten through the gospel stand in the wisdom of men, but in the power of God,[2] when he besought them not to glory in men, not to magnify those by whom they believed, but to see that the ground of all their confidence was the entire surrender of themselves to the Holy Spirit of the promise. His seal, he would teach us, is the only effectual authentication of the message; His work is the only earnest and confirmation of the inheritance. They who would possess the truth must be possessed by the truth—must have it, not for the sake of another or on the word of another, but for the truth's own sake. The human soul is not the property of any, however mighty or noble or wise. It is the property of the Eternal. "All things are yours; whether Paul, or Apollos, or Cephas. . . . And ye are Christ's; and Christ is God's."[3]

"The children of Israel made Baal-berith their God."[4] "Baal-berith" means Lord of the Covenant. We have several types of Baal set before us in the Old Testament books. For

---

themselves together unto Aaron, and said, Up, make us gods which shall go before us." They demanded a visible form, and the form selected was the one with which they had become familiar in Egypt—the ox-worship of Egypt, whose rites at Heliopolis and at Memphis they knew. Jeroboam reverted to this type of idolatry when he set up his golden calves in Bethel and in Dan (1 Kings xii. 28-30).   [1] Judg viii. 33.
[2] 1 Cor. ii 5.   [3] 1 Cor. iii. 22, 23.   [4] Judg viii. 33.

Moab and Midian, there is Peor—"the opening"—to whose sacrifices Israel joined himself in the wilderness.[1] The Philistines of Ekron had their Zebub, "the fly," a divinity to which an Israelite king sent to inquire.[2] The Baal-worship was the worship of Power; and different modifications or aspects of Power were incorporated into it. Is there not a parody of the true worship in the form which the men of Shechem adopted?[3] The children of Israel turned from Jehovah of the Covenant, from the "I am" of Abraham, Isaac, and Jacob, who had manifested Himself as their Shepherd, to the vain imagination which the mind of man had projected. So it is. Covenant is a side of Power. Constituted as men are, and circumstanced as men are, union, or covenant—which means union on a defined plan—is the form and condition of strength. Those who know that the "yea and amen" in which covenant stands is the Eternal, Unseen Truth, realize that the basis of society is the Living God. Those whose foolish heart is darkened, who see not the God in the heavens, rest their society on Force—on the right of the strongest. The alternative is—the God whose name is Jah, declared in the Son, who is one with the Father; or the Baal, whose exponent is an Abimelech trampling on others and writing his covenant in characters of blood. As Mr. Maurice has so strikingly brought out, the contrast through all the ages is between the God-man and the man-god—the Covenant God whose name is Love, and the covenant deity whose name is Baal. "Consider both images well," so he urges. "Both are presented to us; we must admire and copy one of them. And whichever we take, we must resolutely discard the other. If we have ever mixed them together in our minds, a time is at hand

---

[1] Numb. xxv. 1-9. "Peor is supposed to have been the original name of the mountain, and Baal-peor to be the designation of the God worshipped there ("Cyclopædia of Biblical Literature").

[2] 2 Kings i. 2-16. Josephus ("Antiquities" ix. 2) says: "Ahaziah sent to the god *Fly* for that in the name of the God."

[3] Various meanings have been given to the word Baal-berith. (1) Baal, the god of the covenants, corresponding to the Ζεὺς Ὅρκιος of the Greeks. (2) Baal, with whom they had entered into the covenant. (3) The god of the covenant into which the Israelites entered with the Canaanites. (4) Bochart conjectures that the name means God of Berytus. (5) Stanley supposes that "a religious league had been formed between Shechem and the neighbouring towns, and that the temple was at Shechem under the name of Baal of the League." See Smith's "Dictionary of the Bible."

that will separate them for ever. One was marked on your foreheads in childhood, when you were signed with the sign of the cross, and the prayer was prayed for you that you might not be ashamed to confess the faith of Christ crucified against sin, the world, and the devil. The other, the Babylonian mark and image, your own evil nature, a corrupt society, the evil spirit, have been striving to stamp you with ever since. Each hour you are tempted to think a man less precious than the gold of Ophir. The current maxims of the world take for granted that he is: you, in a thousand ways, are acting on these maxims. Oh, remember that in them and the habits which they beget, lies the certain presage of slavery for men and nations, the foretaste of decay and ruin which no human contrivances can avert, which the gifts and blessings of God's providence only accelerate. And think this also. When once the disease has penetrated into the vitals of a people, it may be very decorous and very religious, but it cannot believe in the Son of Man."[1]

The Israelite, of the era of the Judges, no longer thought of the Sacred Bull of Egypt. Egyptian symbolism had vanished from his consciousnesss. But the disease which is shown in the preference of power after the fashion of a ruler of earth, to Power according to the pattern of the God of Abraham, had "penetrated into the vitals of the people." And it was "the certain presage of slavery." The tale of Abimelech and his kingdom is the evidence of this.

[1] "Prophets and Kings of the Old Testament," Sermon xvi.

CHAPTER XIX.

The character and effect of his rule—Apparently, there was no striking disturbance of harmony for some years after his decease: but the tendency to idolatry operated in apostacy to the worship of Baal-berith—How Gideon had prepared for this—The craving for a visible god—The warning sounded for all times—St. Paul's expression of the teaching conveyed—Baal, and the types of Baal-worship indicated in the historical books—The parody of the true worship in the form adopted by the men of Shechem—Covenant, in what is it rooted?—The contrast between the man-god and the God-man—Mr Maurice's entreaty—The lapse of Israel "the certain presage of slavery."

GIDEON had done a great work. He had reformed the nation. He had proclaimed Jehovah the God and King of Israel. He had restored the consciousness of the unity of the tribes. His rule had been generally acknowledged. The pride of Ephraim had been held in check. It had been obliged, though perhaps with sullen temper, to acknowledge the ascendancy of Manasseh and its hero; to recognize in Ophrah, the hitherto obscure village of the Abiezrite, the seat of government and even the centre of worship. For forty years the land had enjoyed its Sabbath. No hostile attack menaced it from without; no internal feud and foray reddened its fields with the blood of its people. Universal, and apparently profound, was the tranquillity when the sepulchre was closed in which had reverently been laid the remains of one of the noblest of national heroes—the illustrious Jerubbaal.[1]

[1] The name Jerubbaal becomes the prominent name in the later part of the narrative concerning Gideon and his house. It is the only name given to the hero in the ninth chapter. The overthrow of the altar of Baal was the event which appealed to the national imagination It has been con-

GIDEON: THE FATE OF HIS HOUSE. 189

intimately associated with Gideon, intensified this alienation. "What can be looked for from idolaters? If a man have cast off his God, he will easily cast off his friends. When religion is once gone, humanity will not stay long after."[1]

The episode of Abimelech's reign must not be omitted from our survey of the time of Gideon and the Judges. It completes the annals of "the house of Jerubbaal," and, in so doing, it supplies one out of many proofs of the vanity of the desire to found a family. Titles may be hereditary; not character, not force. It introduces us to the first official sovereignty in Israel—to a king before the days of monarchy. It records the destruction of the most primitive and sacred city of Palestine. As a picture of morals and manners, it sheds a lurid light on the period. It forms a striking paragraph in the book of Retributive Providence.

Our attention is directed to ancient Shechem, the city of Hamor the Canaanite, from one of whose line Jacob bought "a parcel of a field, where he had spread his tent," and on which he erected the altar called El-elohe-Israel.[2] It was on "the border of Jehovah's sanctuary;" it was itself the most venerable of sanctuaries. The twin heights of Gerizim and Ebal, the one rising behind, the other rising in front of it, were designated by the Lawgiver before the entrance into the Promised Land, the one as the pulpit for the sounding of the blessings, and the other as the pulpit for the sounding of the curses, of the Law.[3] Shechem stood near the opening of a valley renowned for its beauty[4]—"the only very beautiful spot in central Palestine." Travellers dwell on its many charms, contrasting with the barren hills in Judea, differing from Carmel, from Lebanon, from "the awful gorge of the Leontes." "Here," exclaims one traveller, "there is no wilderness, here there are no wild thickets, yet there is always verdure; always shade, not of the oak, the terebinth, and the

[1] Bishop Hall's "Contemplations," Cont. viii. Book ix.
[2] Gen xxxiii 18–20.   [3] Deut. xi. 29; Josh. viii. 33–35.
[4] The site of the modern city of Nâblus is not identical with that of the ancient Shechem. Nâblus "is one of the few instances in which the Roman, or rather the Greek, name has superseded in popular language the ancient Semitic appellation—Nâblus being the corruption of Neapolis, the new town founded by Vespasian after the ruin of the older Shechem, which probably lay farther eastward, and therefore nearer to the opening of the valley" ("Sinai and Palestine," chap. v.).

carob tree, but of the olive grove—so soft in colour, so picturesque in form, that for its sake we can willingly dispense with all other wood. Here there are no impetuous mountain-torrents, yet there is water: water, too, in more copious supplies than anywhere else in the land; and it is just to its many fountains, rills, and watercourses, that the valley owes its beauty."[1]

At Shechem, the first king in Israel was crowned; but his was an irregular and a "base" kingdom. The coronation, such as it was, marked the end of low intrigues, and it was preceded by a terrible act of blood-guiltiness.

Two causes promoted the ambitious designs of Abimelech. The one was the arrogance of the tribe of Ephraim, which had for long chafed under the ascendancy of the half-tribe of Manasseh. A government whose centre was Shechem would restore the superiority, almost claimed as a right, by the Ephraimites. And the other was the sense of kindness between the men of Shechem and the sons of the Shechemite slave. Although we cannot be certain, the probability is that she was a Hivite; and that there was a considerable Canaanite population in the old city is evident from the call addressed by the treacherous Gaal to serve the men of Hamor.[2] To this population the usurper dexterously appealed. He pointed to the seventy sons. "Whether is better for you, either that all the sons of Jerubbaal, who are threescore and ten persons, reign over you, or that one reign over you; remember also that I am your bone and your flesh."[3] Then he "communed with his mother's

---

[1] Van de Welde—quoted in "Sinai and Palestine," chap. v. This traveller also notices "the peculiar colouring which objects assumed in the vale of Shechem." Therein it contrasts with the scenery of Palestine in general. In the vale, "the exhalations remain hovering among the branches and leaves of the olive-trees, and hence that lovely bluish haze. The valley is far from broad, not exceeding in some places a few hundred feet. This you find generally enclosed on all sides; there likewise the vapours are condensed. And so you advance under the shade of the foliage along the living waters, and charmed by the melody of a host of singing birds—for they, too, know where to find their best quarters—while the perspective fades away and is lost in the damp vapoury atmosphere."

[2] Judg. ix 28 The "men" might be read the "lords" or "masters." See also Josh. xxiv. 16; 1 Sam. xxiv. 12. The "masters" are supposed by many to have been Israelites. "Just as, for a long period in our own history, the barons were almost exclusively of Norman descent" ("Cambridge Bible"—Judges). [3] Judg. ix. 2.

GIDEON: THE FATE OF HIS HOUSE. 191

brethren, and all the family of the house of his mother's father," bidding them press his claims on the community. And their representations were successful. The hearts of the citizens "inclined to follow Abimelech, for they said, He is our brother."[1]

And, in proof of their adherence, the rulers of the city vote him money wherewith to advance his claim. The temples of antiquity were repositories of wealth. The spoils of war were often presented to the Deities to whom the temples were dedicated, and, both for religious purposes and as places of safety, money and valuables were laid up within their precincts. Before the capture of Jericho, Joshua commanded that all the silver and gold, and vessels of brass and iron, were to be conveyed to the treasury of Jehovah.[2] And in the Chronicles of the kings we read that the wrath of foreign potentates was averted, or the favour of allies was purchased, by the exhaustion of the money found in the coffers of the sanctuary.[3] Heathen temples were sometimes very rich. From the temple of Delphi two and a half millions sterling were taken at one time.[4] Out of the store accumulated in the house of Baal-berith, the men of Shechem give seventy shekels to their favourite—not certainly a large sum, equivalent indeed only to about £7, but it was sufficient to secure the service of some mercenaries, ready for any enterprise which opened prospects of booty. With the money thus given, Abimlech "hired vain and light persons, who followed him."[5]

Their first action was one in consonance with the practice of Oriental despotisms. It was a precedent repeated at particular epochs in the future history of Israel. The whole family of Jeroboam was put to death by Baasha;[6] the whole family of Baasha was put to death by Zimri;[7] the seventy sons of Ahab were slain by Jehu.[8] And the annals of many Eastern mon-

---

[1] Judg. ix. 3. [2] Josh. vi. 19.
[3] 1 Kings xv. 18; 2 Kings xviii. 15, 16.
[4] The wealth of the temple at Delphi induced Xerxes, 480 B.C., to send an army for the purpose of plunder, but peals of thunder and the fall of two crags crushing many soldiers, struck the army with terror, and it fled (Smith's "Classical Dictionary").
[5] "Vain," *i.e.* empty, the same word as "Raca," Matt. v. 22. "Light," *i.e.*, boiling over, or furious.
[6] 1 Kings xv. 29. [7] 1 Kings xvi. 11, 12. [8] 2 Kings x. 7.

archies are full of similar cruelties. Even in recent times, it was the custom in Turkey either to slay or put out the eyes of the children of the deceased king, other than the heir to the throne. It is a consequence of polygamy that family union and affection are destroyed, and that claimants for power are so multiplied as to menace the welfare both of the dynasty and of the state.

A bloody and hateful massacre took place at Ophrah. The weak, unsuspecting sons of Gideon were seized, and borne one after another to the same rock—possibly the rock on which their father had offered his sacrifice, and whence had arisen the fire of the Lord; and on that rock, on one block of stone, all were put to death.[1] All, with a single exception, the youngest son, who hid himself, and of whom we hear more again.

Having thus disposed of those who might dispute his claim, Abimelech put himself at the head of the men of Shechem. We do not read of any assembly of the elders of Israel, at which the resolution to offer the crown to this son of Jerubbaal was taken. The historian makes it plain that the coronation was not the act of the tribes, or even of some of the tribes, but that it was the act of the Shechemites alone. With them were associated the men of "the house of Millo"[2]—apparently a walled and fortified place not far apart from the city. It is they, the citizens or chiefs of the city and the occupants of this keep, who make Abimelech king. We can imagine the assembly under the shadow of the famous terebinth, beneath which Jacob buried the strange gods which his household had carried away from their Syrian home,[3] and where, towards the close of his life, Joshua erected the great stone of witness.[4] At this stone or pillar, beneath the oak, the supporters of Abimelech proclaimed their brother king and lord.[5] "It marks a sad declension in the condition of Israel at this time, as compared with the days of Joshua, that

[1] Judg. ix. 5.
[2] Judg. ix. 6, "All the men of Shechem gathered together, and all the house of Millo, and went and made Abimelech king, by the plain of the pillar that was in Shechem." Millo, a strong wall, or rampart, or fortified place, near Shechem. There was a Millo at Jerusalem (2 Sam. v. 9). King Joash (2 Kings xii. 20) is said to have been murdered by conspirators in "the house of Millo, which goeth down to Silla."
[3] Gen. xxxv. 4.   [4] Josh. xxiv. 26.
[5] The words translated "the plain of the pillar," should be rendered the oak or terebinth of the pillar or the monument—probably the great stone erected by Joshua.

the Shechemite Abimelech should be made king with a view to the restoration of Baal-worship, on the very spot where their fathers had made a solemn covenant to serve the Lord "[1]

The jubilations and festivities in connection with this event have not concluded when the people are startled by a voice, clear and distinct though borne from afar.

On a lofty, outstanding bluff of Gerizim a figure is discerned, and, by some, it is recognized as the figure of Gideon's youngest son—the one who had escaped from the massacre on the stone at Ophrah. Gerizim rises to a height of nearly three thousand feet above the level of the Mediterranean. It may be objected that, from such an altitude, a voice could not so carry as to be distinctly heard by persons in the valley below. But climatic and topographical peculiarities must be taken into account. In the rare, pure air of Eastern lands, sound is conveyed through great spaces.[2] And the conformation of that part of Palestine in which Shechem was situated is remarkable. Palestine has a dividing range of mountains: and near the primitive city, this range is " cleft in twain, and a deep valley, in places scarcely more than five hundred yards wide, is sunk eight hundred feet below the enclosing mountains of Ebal to the north, and Gerizim to the south."[3] One speaking from Gerizim can be distinctly heard by another on Ebal. There is no difficulty, therefore, in conceiving that Jotham, articulating slowly and with clear voice, would be audible to the multitude assembled below.[4] Dr. Thomson reminds us that "the people in these mountainous countries are able, from long practice, so to pitch

[1] " Pulpit Commentary "—Judges, p. 98.

[2] "The deep stillness and consequent reverberation of the human voice can never be omitted in any enumeration of the characteristics of Mount Sinai.... It was the belief of the Arabs who conducted Niebuhr, that they could make themselves heard across the Gulf of Akaba, a belief doubtless exaggerated, yet probably originated or fostered by the great distance to which in those regions the voice can actually be carried " (" Sinai and Palestine," chap. i.).

[3] Canon Tristram, " Bible Places," p. 181.

[4] Lord Arthur Hervey writes: " I have myself heard the human voice utter an articulate word at a measured distance of one mile, one furlong, and seventeen yards, but it was in a peculiar state of the atmosphere. The experiment has been made in recent years, and it has been proved that a man's voice can be distinctly heard in Nâblus, and also upon Ebal, from Gerizim " (" Pulpit Commentary ").

their voices as to be heard distinctly at distances almost incredible."[1]

This son of Gideon possesses his father's courage, and possesses also the wit and readiness which Joash, his grandfather, illustrated on a memorable occasion. He delivers his charge in the form, not of a parable, but rather of a fable. His is one of only two fables found in the Old Testament.[2] Parable is the favourite clothing of truth, especially in the Gospels. For it differs from the fable in this, that its standpoint is heavenly, not earthly; it is so arranged that, through natural objects, it conveys spiritual instruction to the mind, it invites thought to the eternal side of things, to the deeper and higher verities of the moral universe. The fable is earthly in its point, in its aim. It is intended to teach lessons of prudence, of wise conduct, of foresight in action. The parable never reverses the order of nature; the fable does. Animals speak, laugh, reason, instruct.[3] In the two Old Testament fables, it is not animals but trees: in the fable before us, trees discourse to excellent purpose.

A bright, pithy, sarcastic address is that of Jotham. Its material was presented to him in the beautiful landscape which, from his craggy precipice, he contemplated. For there in luxuriance were—there, to this day, are—the olive, the fig tree, the vine, and, clinging to rock and scar, the thorny bramble. The trees are represented as bent on having a king, though the reason of the determination is not obvious. They turn to the Olive—beautiful in form and abundant in the neighbourhood of Shechem. No: to reign over others is not its mission. It will not leave its right use—that by means of which men honour God and man—that it may clutch the dignity of a crown. They apply to the Fig-tree. No: it has no mind to forsake its faculty of service; far more to it are the sweetness and the good fruit than the regal dis-

---

[1] "Land and Book"—Central Palestine, p. 141.
[2] The other fable is in 2 Kings xiv. 9.
[3] For the difference between the parable and the fable, cf. Trench on "Parables," pp. 2 and 3. In a note to p. 2, the Archbishop, referring to the two Old Testament fables, says: "In neither case is it God that is speaking, nor yet messengers of His, delivering His counsel; but men, and from an earthly standing-point, not a Divine. Jotham seeks only to teach the men of Shechem their folly, not their sin, in making Abimelech king over them; the fable never lifting itself to the rebuke of sin as it is sin: this is beyond its region; but only in so far as it is folly."

tinction. They hasten to the Vine. No : to leave the production of the cheering wine and be promoted over [1] its fellows—Never ! Thus rejected by trees of repute, the electors repair to the Bramble. And now there is no hesitation. It has no special use. It sucks the sap secreted in some rock; it bristles over with thorns; it makes none better, apparently, for its living. It is ready for any promotion. It consents. Only, in its mean vaunting, it demands, as the price of the anointing, that those over whom it is set shall place themselves under its shadow, shall surrender wholly to it : if not, there shall be destruction by a fire which will consume even the cedars of Lebanon. This was the sting of the address. Gideon had been offered the crown, and had declined it. He preferred to be the judge, to do the work, to fulfil the ministry which God had appointed to him ; he would not abandon his sweetness and nobleness and the good fruit of his office. To a man who sees into the heart of things what are mere titles ? He will not part with the substance of a God-glorifying life to grasp at shadows of promotion. He does not seek himself; he does not seek honour from man ; if honours are pressed on him he will consider them with reference to his ministry. Will he be more useful ? Is the honour in the line of world-kingships, or in the line of the man whom God chooses ? The mean, bramble-like natures have no scruples. They have nothing to lose. Their aim is to suck the moisture of others ; to be fed, or to feed themselves. And their success means the destruction of what is best and loftiest—of all the interests that are of good report, even "the cedars of Lebanon." Now, therefore, concludes the homilist, "if you are satisfied with your conduct to the family of him who fought for you and adventured his life far, and delivered you out of the hand of Midian; you who have slain his sons, threescore and ten persons upon one stone ; if this is the act which approves itself to you: if you have been honest and sincere in your choice of Abimelech, the son of my father's slave: I wish you joy—you of him and he of you. You are fit for each other. He is the sort of king whom you should have : you are the sort of subjects whom he should have. But, if

---

[1] The verb translated "to be promoted" means literally to wave over, which, in a tree, suggests rule. A moral significance has been attached to the phrase. "Here it refers to the instability of worldly greatness, or perhaps, as some suppose, to the distractions and cares of royalty" ("Cambridge Bible").

you have been duped and cajoled, you, having sown the wind will reap the whirlwind; you will be destroyed by your king, and he will be destroyed by you. And so will end the lesson."[1]

Having thus spoken, he ran away; swift on foot as he had proved himself swift in purpose, he escaped to some safe hiding-place,[2] outside the inheritance of Ephraim.[3] And we hear no more of Jotham.

But the prediction implied in his fable was fulfilled to the letter. The reign of Abimelech proved the ruin of Shechem; and in its ruin the tyrant was ruined also. The stages and the completeness of the catastrophe are graphically related in the history.

Three years pass. There has been no outbreak, but, reading between the lines of the Scripture, we can infer that an uneasy feeling, boding future trouble, prevails. For some reason not fully explained, the king does not, it would seem, reside within the walls of his capital. His lieutenant is one Zebul, named "the ruler of the city."[4] Brigandage increases:[5] and brigandage is always the sign of either a tyrannous or a feeble executive. The words of the historian show that, in this case, the government was hateful to its subjects. They are represented as dealing treacherously with their chief. His support was found in the Hivite population, and, after this population had called him to rule, it became faint-hearted and finally disloyal. The banditti who lurked in the mountain ridges not only robbed "all who came along that way," but waited for opportunities to insult and maraud the agents of Abimelech, even to take himself captive.[6] The king was informed of their designs, but, apparently, was either unwilling or unable to take vengeance on the

[1] Judg. ix. 7-20.

[2] "He spoke, like the Bard of the English ode, and before the startled assembly below could reach the rocky pinnacle where he stood, he was gone" ("Lectures on the Jewish Church," Lect. xv.).

[3] The hiding-place is called Beer, *i.e.* Wild. The place has been supposed to be Beeroth, among the heights of Benjamin (Josh. ix. 17). Ewald thinks it is the Beer beyond Jordan (Numb. xxi. 16).

[4] Zebul sends messengers, urging Abimelech to lie in wait overnight in the field, and in the morning set on the city (Judg. ix. 31-33).

[5] Judg. ix. 25.

[6] It is said, ver. 25, that "the men of Shechem set liers in wait for him in the top of the mountain." They may have intended to seize Abimelech if he should take the route by the mountains to Shechem.

rebellious robbers. And thus the storm kept brewing. It burst on the occasion of a festival of the people of the League.

Then, a blustering Hivite, heading a party from some adjacent village, gained the ear of the Shechemites. He appealed to the sentiment which prevailed amongst them. They were discontented; "an evil spirit," as it is expressed in the narrative, separated ruler from ruled. He had won their favour because of his relationship to the Canaanites of Shechem on the mother's side. "He is our brother," they had cried. "Your brother?" exclaimed this Hivite—Gaal, the son of Ebed. "Only your half-brother. He is an Israelite after all: he is the son of Jerubbaal, the antagonist of your Baal. He is not really one of us, though he boasted, for his own purposes, of being 'our bone and our flesh.' Why should we, Canaanites, serve him? Let us serve the lords who represent the Father of our city, the dynasty founded by Hamor of Shechem."[1] And the fickle hundreds to whom he spoke gave the rebel their allegiance; and, shouting his praises, and proclaiming him their head, "they went out into the fields, and gathered their vineyards, and trode the grapes, and made merry, and went into the house of their god, and did eat and drink, and cursed Abimelech."[2]

The position had become critical, and the governor of Shechem informed his master that, for him and his cause, it was now or never. Not a moment was to be lost. "Up by night, thou and the people with thee. As soon as the sun is up, thou shalt rise early, and set upon the city; and behold, when he and the people that is with him come out against thee, then mayest thou do unto them as thou shalt find occasion." Abimelech, thoroughly aroused, showed that he had inherited his father's courage and rapidity of movement. As his father, by judicious division of his small company, had realized a great effect, so now he distributed the men attached to him into four bands, whose simultaneous march from different positions might give the impression of a larger force than he had at his command, and might threaten the city on four sides. And before the sun had risen, Shechem was besieged.[3]

How Zebul trapped the foolhardy and half-intoxicated Gaal: how he contrived to delude him when he declared that he saw

[1] The words of Gaal, vers. 24, 29, have a parallel in the words of Nabul (1 Sam. xxv. 10), and of the ten tribes (1 Kings xii. 16).
[2] Judg. ix. 27.
[3] Judg. ix. 31-34.

people coming down from the top of the mountains, and other people coming by the "middle of the land,[1] and other people still coming by the oak of the sorcerers,[2] until the forces of the king were actually at the gates of the city, is briefly, but picturesquely told in the chronicle. A battle ensued, and the result was the complete discomfiture of the Hivites. And, as Gideon had chased the Midianite chiefs, so Abimelech chased Gaal, who, with his band, was driven from the city.[3] His expulsion left the work only half-done, though the people, lulled by a foolish sense of security, returned to their labours in the fields. They did not reckon that the king, who had retired to Arumah [4] after the rout of Gaal, was determined on a terrible revenge. They were seized and slain when engaged in their husbandry.[5] At the city gates Abimelech stationed his soldiers. For a whole day he and his companies fought against Shechem; he battered down its gates; he overthrew temple and houses; the ancient town was sacked, destroyed, and, in token that it was to be henceforth abandoned and desolate, it was sown with salt.[6]

The tower of Shechem [7] still held out against the besiegers. Those who occupied it crowded into an upper portion of it, sacred to the god Berith. Apparently, the tower was impregnable. But what the sword could not accomplish, fire could. Abimelech was equal to the emergency. Not far from Shechem, a little south of Gerizim was a mountain, whose snow-capped height was a familiar feature to the Ephraimites.[8] This mountain was densely wooded. Axe in hand, the king bade his soldiers follow. They cut down boughs, and, each man carrying one on his shoulder, they returned to the tower. The boughs were so arranged that, when lighted, the tower was caught in the conflagration, "so that all the men of the tower of Shechem died also, about a thousand men and women."[9]

---

[1] The margin has the word "navel." Gesenius renders "elevated portion."

[2] "The plain of Meonenim" (ver. 27) should be rendered "the oak of the sorcerers," or soothsayers. Stanley identifies it with "the well-known terebinth" ("Lectures on the Jewish Church," Lect. xv.).

[3] Vers. 39, 40.

[4] A place near Shechem; possibly the Rumah mentioned 2 Kings xxiii. 36.   [5] Ver. 42.   [6] Vers. 44, 45.

[7] Apparently the same as the house of Millo.

[8] Mount Zalmon, or "the shady." Cf. Psa. lxviii, 14.

[9] Vers. 46–49.

GIDEON: THE FATE OF HIS HOUSE.

Abimelech resolved to stamp out the rebellion. A city thirteen miles northward—perhaps the city from which Gaal had come—was implicated in the revolt. And thither Abimelech directed his forces. The story of Shechem was repeated. Like Shechem, Thebez had a tower or fortified place. When the city surrendered, the wretched inhabitants fled to the tower and crowded on its roof.[1] Abimelech had provided himself with wood for fuel, and he ordered its disposal against the door of the keep, himself pressing towards the door to indicate what was required. A very short time will suffice to complete his task. Ah, but—from the roof there is hurled downwards—and this by a woman's hand—the upper part of a mill-stone, a solid piece of heavy masonry;[2] and this missile falls on the king's head with a violence which fractures the skull.[3] In the very moment of complete triumph, he is a dead man. Even in death, the instinct of the soldier is strong. It seemed to him a reproach on his memory that it should be said that a woman slew him. His last thought was about his reputation, not his soul. Turning to his armour-bearer, he besought him to "draw his sword and slay him. And his young man thrust him through, and he died."[4]

Thus Jotham's curse was accomplished. He who had devoured the men of Shechem and the house of Millo is himself devoured in consequence of the fire—the insurrection—which had come out from the men of Shechem and the house of Millo. And his death ended his petty and abortive kingship. It had been nothing better than a house of cards, and by one blow it was swept away. In the words of Dean Stanley, "the true king of Israel is still far in the distance."[5]

The Hebrew historian sees in this tragedy the Nemesis that overtakes the wicked. It was God, he reminds us, who "sent an evil spirit between Abimelech and the men of Shechem." In

---

[1] Thebez is identified with a village "large and beautiful" called Tubâs, about thirteen miles from Shechem, between Nâblus and Beisan (Major Conder, whose Handbook accepts this, the view of Eusebius and Ritter).

[2] Literally, a *millstone rider*, the upper part of the stone "which rides, as it were, or moves over the fixed nether stone."

[3] The phrase in the Authorized Version ver. 53, is an obsolete one—"all to brake his skull." "It is mere ignorance of old English which in many copies of the Bible changed "alto brake," that is "altogether brake," into "all to break" (Principal Douglas's "Handbook").

[4] Vers. 54, 55.   [5] "Lectures on the Jewish Church," Lect. xv.

the ruin both of Shechem and its tyrant, he bids us recognize the hand of the Supreme. It was God who "rendered the wickedness of Abimelech which he did unto his father, in slaying his seventy brethren: and all the evil of the men of Shechem did God render upon their heads."[1] The conviction that the government of the Eternal is not a dream, that He is ever and in many ways fulfilling Himself, is the centre of the genuine Hebrew faith. It feels, indeed, that we can trace only a small portion of His way. But that a Purpose to realize the supremacy of the Good and True is being wrought out through all the ages, and that all kinds of things are subservient to it, is the assurance which pervades the Prophecy, Poetry, and History of Israel. "Conduct," it has been said, "is the word of common life, morality is the word of philosophical disquisition, Righteousness is the word of religion."[2] And righteousness is the grand word of the Old Testament scriptures. Their pages are often records of bloodshed and strife; the biographies to which they introduce us are marred and stained by many errors and negligences; the standards of life presented in the centuries through whose struggles we are led are imperfect, sometimes are low and confused; but there is always an Israel within the Israel, a consciousness never wholly obscured, forcing itself through cloud and darkness, that "God is good to such as are of a clean heart,"[3] and that "His face is against them that do evil."[4] It is this which makes Holy Scripture from Genesis to Revelation a teacher of mankind. There is a hand which is ever pointing upward; there is a voice ever sounding, that "the Lord is not slack concerning His promise as some men count slackness,"[5] and that the blessing of the heaven above and of the earth beneath is the portion of the righteous. The marrow of all its instruction is contained in the argument of the ancient psalm, when the mind reflects on a tale such as that of Abimelech, "I have seen the wicked in great power, and spreading himself like a green tree in its native soil. But one passed by, and lo, he was not: yea, I sought him, but he could not be found. Mark the perfect man, and behold the upright: for the latter end of that man is peace."[6]

[1] Judg. ix. 56, 57.
[2] "Literature and Dogma," p. 21.
[3] Psa. lxxiii. 1.
[4] Psa. xxxiv. 16.
[5] 2 Peter iii. 9.
[6] Psa. xxxvii. 35–37.

Gideon's house had its day—a short day—and it ceased to be. Israel itself is scattered among the nations. Its people are the "tribes of the wandering foot and weary breast."[1] The ages come and go. There is only one Permanence. The period we have rapidly surveyed reminds us, in its flux and reflux, in its unrest and change, of the word in which the man of God interprets the lesson of History, "Lord, thou hast been our dwelling place in all generations."[2]

[1] Byron's "Hebrew Melodies."   [2] Psa. xc. 1.

THE END.

www.ingramcontent.com/pod-product-compliance
Lightning Source LLC
Chambersburg PA
CBHW051052160426
43193CB00010B/1150